# JOSSEY-BASS TEACHER

*Jossey-Bass Teacher* provides K–12 teachers with essential knowledge and tools to create a positive and lifelong impact on student learning. Trusted and experienced educational mentors offer practical classroom-tested and theory-based teaching resources for improving teaching practice in a broad range of grade levels and subject areas. From one educator to another, we want to be your first source to make every day your best day in teaching. *Jossey-Bass Teacher* resources serve two types of informational needs—essential knowledge and essential tools.

Essential knowledge resources provide the foundation, strategies, and methods from which teachers may design curriculum and instruction to challenge and excite their students. Connecting theory to practice, essential knowledge books rely on a solid research base and time-tested methods, offering the best ideas and guidance from many of the most experienced and well-respected experts in the field.

Essential tools save teachers time and effort by offering proven, ready-to-use materials for in-class use. Our publications include activities, assessments, exercises, instruments, games, ready reference, and more. They enhance an entire course of study, a weekly lesson, or a daily plan. These essential tools provide insightful, practical, and comprehensive materials on topics that matter most to K–12 teachers.

# WRITING WORKSHOP
## SURVIVAL KIT

SECOND EDITION

## Gary Robert Muschla

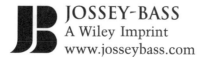

**JOSSEY-BASS**
A Wiley Imprint
www.josseybass.com

Published by Jossey-Bass
A Wiley Imprint
989 Market Street, San Francisco, CA 94103-1741   www.josseybass.com

*Library of Congress Cataloging-in-Publication Data*

Muschla, Gary Robert.
  Writing workshop survival kit / Gary Robert Muschla. — 2nd ed.
    p. cm.
  ISBN-13: 978-0-7879-7619-4 (alk. paper)
  ISBN-10: 0-7879-7619-9 (alk. paper)
  1. English language—Composition and exercises—Handbooks, manuals, etc. 2. Report writing—Study and teaching (Elementary) —Handbooks, manuals, etc. 3. Activity programs in education. 4. Teaching—Aids and devices.   I. Title.
  LB1576.M886 2005
  372.62'3044—dc22
                                                    2005013834

Printed in the United States of America
SECOND EDITION
*PB Printing*      10 9 8 7 6 5 4 3 2 1

# ABOUT THIS BOOK

Appropriate for grades 5 through 12, the *Writing Workshop Survival Kit,* Second Edition, consists of three parts. Part One offers an overview of the writing workshop and management of a writing workshop in the classroom. Part Two explains the stages of the writing process. Part Three contains 100 mini-lessons that concentrate on types of writing, writing techniques, and the mechanics of writing.

This new edition retains all of the strengths of the first edition while broadening the original book's scope and relevance. The material has been updated, and several new topics have been added, including "Enlisting Support for Your Writing Workshop," "Using Search Engines to Find Information on the Internet," "The Use of Computers in Revision," and "How to Establish a Web Site to Display Student Writing."

Like the original book, the new edition of the *Writing Workshop Survival Kit* is designed for easy use. The materials and mini-lessons may be used with students of various grades and abilities, and each activity and mini-lesson can stand alone, enabling the teacher to use the material in the manner that best benefits his or her students.

The book can serve as the foundation of a teacher's writing program. The materials and mini-lessons will help teachers provide their students with effective instruction and support students in learning and mastering the skills of competent writing.

# HOW TO USE THIS BOOK

The *Writing Workshop Survival Kit,* Second Edition, is divided into three parts. Part One, "The Dynamics of the Writing Workshop," contains two sections that offer background information for teachers. Part Two, "The Stages of the Writing Process," contains five sections that explain the stages of the writing process. Part Three, "Using Mini-Lessons in the Writing Workshop," contains three sections and provides specific mini-lessons to use in the classroom.

I suggest you read through Part One first. Section One, "An Overview of the Writing Workshop," explains the components of a successful writing workshop, and Section Two, "Managing Your Writing Workshop," offers strategies for establishing and maintaining an effective writing workshop in your classroom.

Part Two, consisting of Sections Three through Seven, focuses on the stages of the writing process: Section Three, "Prewriting," Section Four, "Drafting," Section Five, "Revision," Section Six, "Editing," and Section Seven, "Publishing." Each section contains a variety of informative handouts and activities for students. All of the handouts are reproducible. As an alternative to photocopying, you may prefer to make transparencies and display the information with overhead projectors, or use the materials with an interactive whiteboard.

Part Three consists of three sections. Section Eight, "Mini-Lessons for Types of Writing," offers lessons on the different kinds of writing your students are likely to do in class. Section Nine, "Mini-Lessons for the Art of Writing," offers lessons on author's methods, devices, and techniques. Section Ten, "Mini-Lessons for the Mechanics of Writing," provides lessons on grammar, punctuation, and word use.

Each mini-lesson stands alone and is set up in a clear, easy-to-follow format, making implementation simple. Many teachers will decide to use all of the mini-lessons through the course of the year; others, based on the abilities and needs of their students, may use only some. Many of the mini-lessons are accompanied by extensions, which reinforce the focus of the mini-lesson or offer additional information. Many of the extensions can be turned into mini-lessons of their own.

The activities, reproducibles, mini-lessons, and extensions of the three parts of the book provide more than 180 separate activities and lessons to share with your students. They will provide your students with a variety of interesting writing experiences and make your teaching in the writing workshop easier and more effective.

The writing workshop is an exciting class to teach, for it enables you and your students to become partners in the writing experience. My best wishes to you as you begin sharing with your students the skills and techniques vital to good writing.

Gary Robert Muschla

# ABOUT THE AUTHOR

Gary Robert Muschla received his B.A. and M.A.T. from Trenton State College and taught at Appleby School in Spotswood, New Jersey, for more than twenty-five years. He spent many of his years in the classroom specializing in reading and language arts. In addition, Gary has been a writer, editor, and ghostwriter. He is a member of the Authors Guild.

Gary has authored several other resources for teachers, including *English Teacher's Great Books Activities Kit* (1994), *Reading Workshop Survival Kit* (1997), *Ready-to-Use Reading Proficiency Lessons and Activities, 4th-Grade Level* (2002), *Ready-to-Use Reading Proficiency Lessons and Activities, 8th-Grade Level* (2002), *Ready-to-Use Reading Proficiency Lessons and Activities, 10th-Grade Level* (2003), and *The Writing Teacher's Book of Lists,* 2nd edition (2004), all published by Jossey-Bass.

With his wife, Judy Muschla, he has coauthored *Hands-on Math Projects with Real-Life Applications* (1996), *Math Starters! 5- to 10-Minute Activities to Make Kids Think* (1999), *The Geometry Teacher's Activities Kit* (2000), *Math Smart: Ready-to-Use Activities to Motivate and Challenge Students, Grades 6–12* (2002), *The Algebra Teacher's Activities Kit* (2003), *Math Games: 180 Reproducible Activities to Motivate, Excite, and Challenge Students* (2004), and *The Math Teacher's Book of Lists,* 2nd edition (2005), all published by Jossey-Bass.

Gary currently writes and works as a consultant in education.

*For Judy and Erin*

# ACKNOWLEDGMENTS

I thank my editor Steve D. Thompson, for giving me the opportunity to update the original edition of this book. His support through this project, and all the others on which I have had the pleasure of working with him, is most appreciated.

I also thank my many colleagues for their support and encouragement of both my teaching and writing.

Special appreciation goes to my wife, Judy, for her support of me in all my writing efforts.

Special thanks go to my daughter, Erin, who, as the first reader of this manuscript, brings a young teacher's eye to my work. She certainly caught many of my oversights and offered suggestions that helped me to strengthen this second edition.

I also thank Michele Quiroga, my production editor, for managing the production of this book, and Diane Turso for proofreading my work.

Finally, I thank my students, who over the years have given me far more than I have ever managed to give to them.

# CONTENTS

*About This Book*   *v*

*How to Use This Book*   *vi*

*About the Author*   *vii*

*Acknowledgments*   *viii*

**Part One: The Dynamics of the Writing Workshop**

*Section 1: An Overview of the Writing Workshop*   *3*

The Writing Process   4

Your New Role   5

The Teacher's Role in the Writing Workshop   6

A Model of a Typical Writing Workshop   7

Scheduling Your Writing Workshop   8

Promoting Your Writing Workshop   8

Enlisting Support for Your Writing Workshop   10

*Reproducible:* Things Parents Can Do to Foster Good
    Writing Habits in Their Children

*Section 2: Managing Your Writing Workshop*   *13*

*Reproducible:* Student Responsibilities in the Writing Workshop

Creating and Maintaining a Writing Environment   15

The Writing Environment   17

*Reproducible:* Student Writers' Tools of the Trade

*Reproducible:* Rules for Working in Groups

Planning Your Workshop Lessons 20

Managing Time in the Writing Workshop 21

Keeping Students Motivated 22

Time-Savers 23

When Discipline Is Necessary 24

Evaluation 28

Monitoring the Progress of Your Students 29

*Reproducible:* Daily Log

Writing Across the Curriculum 32

*Reproducible:* Skills Analysis Sheet

*Reproducible:* Checklist for Types of Writing

## Part Two: The Stages of the Writing Process

### *Section 3: Prewriting* 37

Prewriting Strategies 37

Freewriting 37

    **Activity 1:** A Freewriting Exercise

    *Reproducible:* Freewriting Sample

Clustering 38

    **Activity 2:** Creating Clusters

    *Reproducible:* A Sample Cluster

Idea Listing 41

    **Activity 3:** Making an Idea List

    *Reproducible:* Sample Idea List

Brainstorming 41

    **Activity 4:** Brainstorming for Ideas

    *Reproducible:* Brainstorming Guide

Rehearsing 45

    **Activity 5:** Rehearsing for Ideas

    *Reproducible:* A Prewriting Warm-Up

Role Playing 45

    **Activity 6:** Role Playing to Find Ideas

    *Reproducible:* Choose a Role

Researching 46

    **Activity 7:** Using the Internet for Research

    *Reproducible:* Using Search Engines to Find Information
        on the Internet

Organizing Writing 50

    *Reproducible:* A Structure Form

Drawing and Diagramming                                             52

Journals                                                            52

   *Reproducible:* Writing Journal Guidelines for Students

Idea Folders                                                        54

Personal Experience                                                 54

   **Activity 8:** Personal Experience and Ideas

   *Reproducible:* Inventory of Personal Experience

Observation                                                         56

   **Activity 9:** Observation and Ideas

   *Reproducible:* What Do You See?

Angles and Viewpoints                                               56

   **Activity 10:** Viewing from All Points and Angles

   *Reproducible:* Seeing All Sides

Using Questions to Explore Topics                                   58

   **Activity 11:** Focusing Topics

   *Reproducible:* Exploring a Writing Topic


*Section 4: Drafting*                                               63

Writing the Draft                                                   63

   **Activity 12:** Questions to Ask During Drafting

The Foundations of Good Writing                                     64

   **Activity 13:** The Elements of Good Writing

Strategies to Aid Drafting                                          65


*Section 5: Revision*                                               69

Revision Mechanics                                                  69

Teaching Revision                                                   69

Revising for Unity                                                  70

Revising for Order                                                  70

Revising for Conciseness                                            70

   **Activity 14:** Revision Strategies

The Use of Computers in Revision                                    72

   *Reproducible:* Computers and Writers

Revision Pitfalls to Avoid                                          74

   **Activity 15:** A Revision Plan

Writing Conferences                                                 75

   **Activity 16:** A Role-Played Writing Conference

   *Reproducible:* A Writing Conference Started by the Teacher

   *Reproducible:* A Writing Conference Started by a Student

Some Conference Strategies                                               79
Peer Conferences                                                         80
    *Reproducible:* Peer Conference Questions
    **Activity 17:** Strategies for Effective Peer Conferences
    *Reproducible:* Peer Group Guidelines
    *Reproducible:* Revision Checklist

### *Section 6: Editing*                                                 **85**

Strategies for Teaching Editing Skills                                   85
    **Activity 18:** Using a Dictionary
    *Reproducible:* Editing Reminders
    **Activity 19:** Using a Thesaurus
    **Activity 20:** Using an Author's Stylebook
Editing Partners                                                         89
Editing Groups                                                           89
    *Reproducible:* Editor's Checklist
    **Activity 21:** Using Editor's Marks
Proofreading                                                             92

### *Section 7: Publishing*                                              **93**

The Author's Chair                                                       93
Peer Group Sharing                                                       94
Computers and Publishing in the Writing Workshop                         94
A Word on Copiers                                                        95
E-Mail as a Means of Sharing and Publishing                             95
    *Reproducible:* A Model Release Form
    *Reproducible:* E-Mail Etiquette for Writers
Producing Class Magazines                                                98
Tips for Producing Class Magazines                                      100
Producing Books Written by Students                                     101
Web Sites for Sharing Writing                                           101
Web Sites That Publish the Writing of Students                          102
How to Establish a Web Site to Display Student Writing                  103
Still More Ways to Share                                                 104
Submitting Student Writing to Magazines                                 104
    **Activity 22:** Submitting Writing to Magazines
    *Reproducible:* Tips for Submitting to Magazines
    **Activity 23:** Writing a Query Letter
    *Reproducible:* Sample Query Letter
    *Reproducible:* Print Markets for Student Writers

## Part Three: Using Mini-Lessons in the Writing Workshop

*Section 8: Mini-Lessons for Types of Writing*     *113*

1. Writing Personal Narratives     114
   *Reproducible:* A Big Splash
2. Writing Essays     116
   *Reproducible:* Slowing Global Warming by Saving Energy
3. Strategies for Answering Essay Test Questions     118
   *Reproducible:* Essay Test-Taking Tips
4. Writing How-to Articles     120
   *Reproducible:* How to Make a Budget
5. Writing Straight News Articles     122
   *Reproducible:* Bat Attacks Alarm Town
   *Reproducible:* Taking Apart a Newspaper Article
6. Persuasive Writing     125
   *Reproducible:* Save Trees and the Environment by Recycling
      Newspapers
   *Reproducible:* Analyzing a Persuasive Essay
7. Writing Friendly Letters     128
   *Reproducible:* Sample Friendly Letter
8. Writing Business Letters     130
   *Reproducible:* Sample Business Letters
9. Writing Book Reviews     132
   *Reproducible:* A Sample Book Review: *A Wrinkle in Time*
      by Madeleine L'Engle
10. Writing Movie Reviews     134
    *Reproducible:* A Sample Movie Review: *The Babe*
11. Writing Fiction     136
    *Reproducible:* The Valentine's Day Dance
12. Writing Advertising     138
    *Reproducible:* Advertising Fundamentals
    *Reproducible:* Advertisement Review
13. Writing Nonrhyming Poems     141
    *Reproducible:* Nonrhyming Poems
14. Writing Rhyming Poems     143
    *Reproducible:* "Eldorado" by Edgar Allan Poe
15. Writing Plays     145
    *Reproducible:* The Parts of a Play
    *Reproducible:* Ghost Hunt
16. Writing Screenplays     148
    *Reproducible:* The Test
    *Reproducible:* Screenplay Vocabulary

### Section 9: Mini-Lessons for the Art of Writing     *151*

17. Writing Effective Leads     152
    *Reproducible*: Leads
    *Reproducible*: Sample Leads
18. Organization for Nonfiction Writing     155
    *Reproducible*: Vanishing Rain Forests
19. Writing Conclusions for Nonfiction Pieces     157
20. Conciseness     158
    *Reproducible*: Cutting Clutter
21. Avoiding Intensifiers and Qualifiers     160
22. Active and Passive Constructions     161
23. Choosing Strong Verbs for Writing     162
24. Writing Effective Transitions     163
    *Reproducible*: Nonverbal Communication
25. Developing Imagery     165
    *Reproducible*: Returning to the Beach
    *Reproducible*: Sense and Image
26. Tone     168
    *Reproducible*: How You Say It
27. Comparing and Contrasting     170
    *Reproducible*: Comparing and Contrasting—Nonfiction
    *Reproducible*: Comparing and Contrasting—Fiction
28. Avoiding Clichés     173
    *Reproducible*: Clichés
29. Conducting Interviews     175
    *Reproducible*: Guide to Great Interviews
30. Using Figures of Speech: Similes, Metaphors, and Personification     177
    *Reproducible*: Figures of Speech
31. Using Onomatopoeia     179
    *Reproducible*: Onomatopoeic Words
32. Using Alliteration     181
    *Reproducible*: A Sample of Alliteration
33. Conflict     183
    *Reproducible*: The Runaway
34. Characterization     185
    *Reproducible*: Revealing Character
    *Reproducible*: Character Chart
35. Writing Dialogue     189
    *Reproducible*: Dialogue Samples
36. Developing Settings     191
    *Reproducible*: Setting Samples

37.  Using Flashbacks                                                   193
       *Reproducible:* The Party
38.  Foreshadowing                                                      195
       *Reproducible:* The Ranch
39.  Constructing Effective Climaxes                                    197
40.  The First-Person Point of View                                    198
       *Reproducible:* First-Person Point of View Fact Sheet
41.  The Third-Person Point of View                                    200
       *Reproducible:* Third-Person Point of View Fact Sheet
42.  The Limited Point of View                                         202
       *Reproducible:* Example of Limited Point of View: Final Batter
43.  Multiple Point of View                                            204
       *Reproducible:* Example of Multiple Points of View: Final Batter
44.  Avoiding Plagiarism                                               206
       *Reproducible:* Citing Sources
45.  Choosing Titles                                                   208
       *Reproducible:* Titles

**Section 10: Mini-Lessons for the Mechanics of Writing**          **211**

46.  Types of Sentences                                                212
       *Reproducible:* Sentences
47.  Sentence Patterns                                                 214
       *Reproducible:* Examples of Sentence Patterns
48.  Subject and Verb Agreement                                        216
49.  Compound Subject and Verb Agreement                               217
50.  Subject and Verb Agreement with Intervening Phrases               218
51.  Subject and Verb Agreement: *Doesn't* or *Don't*                  219
52.  Subject and Verb Agreement: *There's, Here's,* and *Where's*      220
53.  Subject and Verb Agreement: Indefinite Pronouns                   221
54.  Subject (Pronoun) and Verb Agreement                              222
55.  Agreement of Pronouns and Antecedents                             223
56.  Possessive Nouns                                                  224
57.  Paragraphing                                                      225
       *Reproducible:* Developing Paragraphs, Sample 1
       *Reproducible:* Developing Paragraphs, Sample 2
58.  Varying Sentences to Make Writing Interesting                     228
59.  Combining Sentences for Variation                                 229
       *Reproducible:* Example of Combining Sentences
60.  Sentence Fragments                                                231
       *Reproducible:* Find the Fragments
61.  Run-On Sentences                                                  233
       *Reproducible:* Finding and Fixing Run-Ons

| | | |
|---|---|---|
| 62. | Avoiding Misplaced Modifiers | 235 |
| 63. | Tenses: Choosing the Present or the Past | 236 |
| 64. | The Past Perfect Tense: Showing Previous Past Action | 237 |
| 65. | Using *Did* or *Done* Correctly | 238 |
| 66. | Writing with Sounds That Are Not Words | 239 |
| 67. | Avoiding Double Negatives | 240 |
| 68. | Using Italics for Titles and Names | 241 |
| 69. | Using Italics for Emphasis | 242 |
| 70. | Using Quotation Marks for Titles | 243 |
| 71. | Using Quotation Marks for Emphasis | 244 |
| 72. | Using Parentheses | 245 |
| 73. | Using the Dash | 246 |
| 74. | Using Hyphens with Compound Words and Numbers | 247 |
| 75. | Writing Lists with Colons and Commas | 248 |
| 76. | Spelling Strategy 1: Dictionaries and Spell Checkers | 249 |
| 77. | Spelling Strategy 2: Proper Pronunciation | 250 |
| 78. | Spelling Strategy 3: Spelling Confusions | 251 |
| | *Reproducible:* Spelling Confusions | |
| 79. | Spelling Strategy 4: Personal Spelling Lists | 253 |
| 80. | Overusing *So* and *Then* | 254 |
| 81. | Using *Affect* and *Effect* Correctly | 255 |
| 82. | Using *All Right* and (Not) *Alright* | 256 |
| 83. | Using *Among* and *Between* Correctly | 257 |
| 84. | Using *Bad* and *Badly* Correctly | 258 |
| 85. | Avoiding *Could Of* and Similar Constructions | 259 |
| 86. | Using *Farther* and *Further* Correctly | 260 |
| 87. | Using *Fewer* and *Less* Correctly | 261 |
| 88. | Using *Good* and *Well* Correctly | 262 |
| 89. | Using *In* and *Into* Correctly | 263 |
| 90. | Using *It's* and *Its* Correctly | 264 |
| 91. | Using *There, Their,* and *They're* Correctly | 265 |
| 92. | Using *Who's* and *Whose* Correctly | 266 |
| 93. | Using *Your* and *You're* Correctly | 267 |
| 94. | Using *Lay* and *Lie* Correctly | 268 |
| 95. | Using *Lose* and *Loose* Correctly | 269 |
| 96. | Using *Off* Rather Than *Off Of* | 270 |
| 97. | Using *Sit* and *Set* Correctly | 271 |
| 98. | Using *Than* and *Then* Correctly | 272 |
| 99. | Using *To, Too,* and *Two* Correctly | 273 |
| 100. | Using *Who* and *Whom* Correctly | 274 |

*Resources*                                                                 *275*

# PART ONE

# THE DYNAMICS OF THE WRITING WORKSHOP

# SECTION 1

# AN OVERVIEW OF THE WRITING WORKSHOP

**When I began teaching** the writing workshop several years ago, I did not know what to expect. I was an experienced teacher of writing and a writer myself, and I understood and embraced the writing process. But although I had read extensively about the writing workshop, had experienced various workshops, and had gone through in-service training, I was still uncertain. I was concerned that I was stepping into yet another one of those new ideas in education that promises great success but comes up short. I felt I already had an effective writing program and worried that my students would not do as well in a new one. However, I was also drawn to the concept of the writing workshop, which provides a forum where teacher and students become partners in the experience of learning. I started that school year a hopeful skeptic and soon became a believer.

The writing workshop is much more than a program designed to help children acquire the skills necessary for written language. It is a classroom in which you and your students form bonds that become the foundation of learning. In the writing workshop, your teaching becomes individualized as students focus on topics that matter to them and you respond to their efforts. Because students write about their interests, worries, and dreams, the material of the writing workshop arises from the fabric of their lives.

The model of the writing workshop offered in this book (there are a number of variations) starts with a five- to ten-minute mini-lesson, after which your students work on their own pieces. During writing time, the classroom buzzes with a murmur of productive noise. You circulate to check writing progress, confer with individual students or groups, provide guidance, and answer questions. Your students may be engaged in various activities: prewriting, drafting, reading, revising, editing, or conferring with you, a partner, or a peer group. The entire classroom is used, with activities taking place at the students' desks, at tables, or at your desk.

Writing is a powerful tool for learning. It enables us to analyze and synthesize our thoughts, and thereby discover new ideas. When we write, we become conscious of ourselves. We define ourselves and come to understand our lives better. Through the writing workshop, you will help your students master the skills that will enable them to express themselves with clarity and competence.

## The Writing Process

Traditional writing instruction focuses on teaching students the features of different types of writing through examples. The theory assumes that once students understand the different models—for example, narratives, editorials, essays, and various kinds of fiction—they will be able to write them.

Writing instruction that focuses on the writing process, in contrast, concentrates on the way real writers work. Writing is a process composed of at least five stages: *prewriting, drafting, revising, editing,* and *publishing.* Although the stages are distinct, the process is recursive. Authors often move back and forth through these stages as they work.

*Prewriting* is the starting point. It is the period during which an author discovers his or her topic, decides on his or her audience and purpose, generates or researches ideas, and considers a form for his or her writing.

*Drafting* begins when the author starts writing. During this stage, the author switches between writing and reading. She may rewrite some of her work or reformulate her original ideas and return to the prewriting stage.

Next is *revising*: adding, deleting, rewriting, and polishing. Authors may move back and forth through drafting and prewriting several times as they rethink their work and revise.

The *editing* stage is the final preparation for publishing. This is when remaining corrections of mechanics are made and the piece is put into its finished form. Even here, though, writers may decide that more revision is necessary and shift back to some of the previous stages.

*Publishing* refers to the sharing of writing with someone else. For students, this most often is teachers, peers, parents, or the public. It may also include submitting material to traditional and online magazines, newspapers, or newsletters.

# Your New Role

You will become a nurturer, facilitator, and promoter in your writing workshop rather than a mere giver of information. Aside from mini-lessons, you will spend your time working with individual students and small groups. Since modeling can be a powerful motivator and teacher, you may write along with your students from time to time.

You will perform many tasks in your writing workshop. During the class, you might help one student narrow his topic, suggest ways in which another can improve her opening, or listen to yet another as she explains how she intends to develop her narrative about moving into a new home. From there you might meet with a group that is sharing drafts and seeking peer reactions. You will guide, encourage, and applaud students in their writing efforts and help them discover new insights, make connections among ideas, analyze information, and communicate their thoughts and feelings. You will give them personal feedback that reinforces their learning. The accompanying list, "The Teacher's Role in the Writing Workshop," suggests some of the many possible activities in which you will be engaged.

Teachers who are starting writing workshops often express three major concerns. The first is that as they circulate around the room helping individuals and small groups, other students will stop working and become disruptive. The second is that the writing workshop may run fine with small classes but not with large ones. The third is ensuring that all students will have an opportunity to learn the skills necessary for competent writing.

A well-run workshop overcomes these fears because the students become involved with their writing. Given the chance and encouragement to express themselves—to share of themselves—students become more willing to write. When students are involved with the class, disruption is reduced, even large classes can be managed efficiently, and students more easily acquire the skills they need for effective composition.

You ensure the dissemination of information and skills through mini-lessons. The material shared at the beginning of each class eventually builds a foundation of knowledge that can be referred to during individual and group conferences. Thus, the material introduced is reinforced throughout the year.

Of course, as in any class, rules must be made and expectations set and expressed. These basics are up to each teacher, and you should establish the rules for your classroom in a way you feel comfortable. At the least, you should insist that talking is to be done in quiet voices, that students conduct themselves in an appropriate manner, and that only writing-related activities may be done in the writing workshop. (For more information on discipline, see "When Discipline Is Necessary" in Section Two.)

# The Teacher's Role in the Writing Workshop

At the beginning of the writing workshop, the teacher may present a mini-lesson and then spend the rest of the period engaged in any or all of the following:

- Helping students find topics

- Helping students focus topics

- Answering student questions about writing

- Guiding students in their research efforts

- Listening to a student read a passage from his or her writing

- Offering suggestions for revision

- Working with a group brainstorming ideas

- Showing a student how to reduce clutter in his writing

- Helping a student organize her ideas

- Writing along with students

- Offering encouragement

- Applauding a student's efforts

- Conferring with students over finished pieces

- Helping a student sort through his thoughts

- Explaining the use of a thesaurus

- Helping students with technology; for example, when using word processing soft-ware, moving a block of text during revision

- Directing traffic flow around the room

- Reminding students of classroom rules

- Keeping students on task

- Assisting students in creating a class magazine

- Viewing Web sites for writers with students

# A Model of a Typical Writing Workshop

Every writing workshop reflects the personality and attitudes of its teacher. You will no doubt develop your workshop in a way that best meets the needs of your students and teaching environment. There are, in fact, many variations of the writing workshop; they differ slightly in structure but not in content. The model presented here is one of the more common ones.

The writing workshop starts with a five- to ten-minute mini-lesson that focuses on one skill or concept. The students may use the information of the mini-lesson right away or maybe not for several days or even weeks.

After the mini-lesson, students work on their writing for approximately twenty to twenty-five minutes. They may be writing in journals, searching through idea folders, or writing a story or article. It is unlikely that all students will be doing the same thing. During this time, the teacher circulates around the room and works with individual students and small groups. Along with providing help and encouragement, she also reminds students of the rules of the classroom and keeps them on task.

The last ten to fifteen minutes of the class are reserved for sharing. This may be done using the author's chair, editing partners, or peer groups. For the author's chair, students take center stage and read their work to the class. Students may first describe what they have been working on and then read from their work in progress. The rest of the class listens and may ask questions or offer suggestions. For partners or peer groups, students read their work to their partner or members of their groups, who may then comment on the student's work and offer advice or reactions. (For more information about peer groups, see "Peer Conferences" in Section Five.)

Here is a breakdown for a forty-five-minute period:

1. Mini-lesson: five to ten minutes
2. Writing time: twenty to twenty-five minutes
3. Sharing: ten to fifteen minutes

There is much flexibility within the general framework. Instead of providing a mini-lesson each day, some teachers offer mini-lessons every other day; some prefer to include a ten-minute silent writing time after the mini-lesson and reduce the general writing and sharing time; some schedule sharing only two or three days per week. You should organize your workshop in a way that is most effective for you and your students.

I like to have all students share after each class because sharing provides closure and keeps the students moving forward. Some students, if they find that there is no sharing that day, will ease off in their work. I encourage students to share even if they merely tell their editing partner or members of their peer group how they searched for a topic. Working together like this promotes an atmosphere of friendship and support as well as helps to spread understanding of the writing process. In time you are likely to see a company of writers emerge in your classroom.

## Scheduling Your Writing Workshop

Writing workshops that buzz with the activity of students working on a variety of tasks may appear to the uninitiated to be disorganized and chaotic. In fact, most of these classrooms are built on a firm foundation of efficient management and a practical schedule.

A consistent schedule is the starting point of a successful workshop. While the ideal is to set up your writing workshop for a full period, five days per week, many teachers do not have that amount of time. You can run a successful workshop meeting three or four times a week, but at fewer than three, you will have trouble maintaining continuity and keeping students interested. Some teachers incorporate the writing workshop into their English classes. Assuming they meet five days per week, they may use three classes for the workshop and spend the other two on literature or spelling and other language skills. Here, too, at fewer than three meetings per week, it may be difficult to sustain the thought and emotion necessary for an effective writing workshop.

When students know that they have writing workshop each day or every Monday, Tuesday, and Thursday, for example, they come to the workshop ready to write. When students meet regularly for writing workshop, their minds become engaged with the writing process.

In schools where it is impossible to meet regularly for the writing workshop throughout the year, the workshop may be scheduled for fixed meetings during part of the year. The writing workshop may rotate with courses like computer literacy, music, art, home economics, or industrial arts for sessions that span several weeks. Regular meetings during an eight- to ten-week period are preferable to irregular or limited meetings throughout the year.

## Promoting Your Writing Workshop

Unless your district has made a commitment to implement writing workshops in place of traditional English classes, you will probably need to promote and explain what you are doing to administrators, colleagues, and parents. You may find some resistance at first, because the writing workshop is quite different from classes in which the teacher stands before the students, offers information through lectures, and then assigns homework that reinforces the skills taught during the lesson. The writing workshop instead fosters a learning environment in which self-discovery and cooperation become paramount.

The best way to explain the writing workshop to administrators, supervisors, and colleagues is to invite them into your class. First, however, refer them to articles about the writing workshop, or provide them with a written description of your own. When they come to your class, describe what is going on and let them see how the workshop functions. Invite them back for additional visits so that they can gain an understanding of the many activities that are a part of your workshop. Sharing samples of your students' writing—either individual papers or class magazines or on class or school Web sites—is a way to show the results of your workshop.

You should inform parents about the writing workshop early in the school year. At back-to-school nights, I tell the parents of my students that I will be teaching a writing workshop instead of the traditional English class. I explain what the writing workshop is and mention that it is being used successfully throughout the country. I emphasize that their children will continue to learn the skills for effective language, including grammar, punctuation, and spelling. The single greatest concern parents have is that their children may be writing but they are not learning grammar. To many parents, writing and grammar are separate disciplines. I explain that they are inseparable. No one can write effectively without understanding grammar, but knowing grammar without being able to apply it to written language is a useless skill. Sending home copies of student magazines, making sure that the writing of your students appears on school Web sites and in school and parent-teacher organization newsletters, and liberally exhibiting the work of your students on hallway bulletin boards can quicken the acceptance of your workshop.

I always encourage parents to become involved with their children's writing experiences. Their support at home can be a significant factor in their children's progress and overall achievement. The accompanying "Things Parents Can Do to Foster Good Writing Habits in Their Children" on page 11 is an excellent handout at back-to-school night and parent-teacher conferences.

In many cases, your students will become the best advocates of your writing workshop. Their enthusiasm for the workshop will be clear, and they will speak well of it to others. That, coupled with samples of their writing, will be your strongest promotion.

When students write about topics that interest them in an environment that supports the risk taking that is vital to conceiving and developing fresh ideas, their minds and imaginations become involved with their material. When they know that their work will be shared, that others will read what they have written, and that their writing matters, students strive for precision and clarity. Of all the advantages the writing workshop offers, perhaps these are most important.

# Enlisting Support for Your Writing Workshop

The following tips can help you build support for your writing workshop:

- Obtain information about the writing workshop to share with administrators, supervisors, and colleagues. Education journals, resource books such as this one, and the Internet are good sources of information.

- Invite administrators, supervisors, and colleagues into your class so that they can observe how a writing workshop functions.

- Write a description of your writing workshop, and make it available to interested colleagues and parents.

- Publish and display the writing of your students as often as possible. Class or school magazines, parent-teacher organization publications, school Web sites, class and hallway displays, and publication in local newspapers provide your workshop with positive exposure.

- If your school has a day when parents may visit the school and observe classes, be sure to invite parents to your writing workshop.

- Write a monthly newsletter keeping parents updated about the happenings in your writing workshop. The newsletter need be no more than a page or two. Having students help write it will result in excellent public relations. Send copies of the newsletter home with students, or, if possible, e-mail copies to parents. If your school district maintains a Web site, post the newsletter there.

- Explain your writing workshop at back-to-school night. Be sure to have several examples of student writing available.

- At parent-teacher conferences, explain the benefits of the writing workshop, and note how it is different from other methods of writing instruction. Show parents examples of their children's work.

- Conduct workshops for parents with the objective of explaining how they can help their children become better writers. This is a fine time to explain your writing workshop and the benefits it provides to students.

- Organize a group of teachers who are interested in learning about the writing workshop and implementing it in their own classrooms. Shared success is effective promotion.

# Things Parents Can Do to Foster Good Writing Habits in Their Children

As a parent, there is much you can do to support the writing efforts of your children both in and out of school.

- Discuss good books and their authors. Also discuss stories, articles, and poems.

- Tell your children about your own favorite authors and what makes these authors (in your opinion) different from others.

- Share your own writing with your children. For example, let your children see you working on business reports, letters, and thank-you notes.

- Show interest in your children's writing. Be willing to read and discuss your children's stories, articles, and poems.

- Help your children understand that writing is a process of several stages: prewriting, drafting, revising, editing, and publishing (sharing).

- Realize that all writers, and especially children, progress at their own pace.

- Encourage your children to complete all writing assignments.

- Encourage your children to keep a journal and write every day.

- When you are at your child's school, make a point to read displays of student writing.

- Attend back-to-school night and parent-teacher conferences. Ask your children's teachers how you can support the school's writing program.

- Encourage your children to always do their best writing.

# SECTION 2

# MANAGING YOUR WRITING WORKSHOP

**Successful writing workshops,** in large part, are the result of effective management. Although the structure of the writing workshop is different from that of the traditional English class, you are still responsible for sustaining a learning atmosphere, monitoring and evaluating student progress, maintaining discipline, teaching new skills, imparting information, and communicating with administrators, colleagues, and parents. You have the obligations of a traditional classroom teacher, with the added task of running a program in which students are working on a variety of topics.

At the beginning of the school year, students will have countless questions, especially if they have never participated in the writing workshop before. With the press of questions for the teacher and the new type of class for the students, it is easy for everyone to feel overwhelmed.

On the first day, you should offer an overview of the writing process and the writing workshop. Describe your expectations and how the workshop will be run. You might distribute copies of the accompanying "Student Responsibilities in the Writing Workshop," and discuss the responsibilities with your students. Show them where writing materials and reference books are. If you have time, you might get students started right away by brainstorming topics with the class and encouraging students to choose their own ideas for writing. Getting everyone involved that first day is a fine start. It underscores that writing is the purpose of the class.

You will find that much of what you tell your students on this first day will need to be repeated. However, as students become more familiar with the classroom routines, they will have fewer questions on procedures, and you will have more time to work with them on their writing.

# Student Responsibilities in the Writing Workshop

This year you will be taking part in a writing workshop. As in any other class, you will assume various responsibilities. To ensure a successful experience in the writing workshop you should:

- Come to class each day ready to write.

- Maintain a writing folder in which you will keep your writing.

- Bring your writing folder to class each day.

- Find and develop topics for your writing.

- Be willing to try new kinds of writing.

- Do your best to learn the rules of written English.

- Accept the responsibility of completing pieces.

- Be willing to try new techniques, methods, and strategies to improve your writing.

- Be willing to work with your peers in the learning of writing skills and strategies.

- Behave properly. This means following directions and not disturbing others.

- Take pride in your work and produce the best work you can.

- Grow as a writer.

# Creating and Maintaining a Writing Environment

The environment you set up for your students tells much about your attitude toward writing. A classroom that is bright and cheerful, where fresh ideas, openness, and sharing are energetically promoted, and where encouragement and support are offered, elevates the importance of writing in the eyes of students.

You should do as much as possible to create and maintain a classroom that is conducive to writing. You should require students to maintain their writing in folders, which they should bring to class each day. If you have your own classroom, you might store students' writing folders in boxes or milk crates. Covering the boxes with colorful paper or fabric, filing the folders alphabetically for easy retrieval, and encouraging students to keep their folders neat and orderly sends a subtle message that writing is to be a respected activity. You might assign a different student each week to monitor the folder box and make sure that the folders are put back the right way.

Instruct students to put their names, dates, and sections on their papers, staple pages, and label individual pieces "Draft" or "Final Copy." When your actions communicate to students that you expect quality work, they are more likely to comply.

Encourage your students to treat resources and writing materials with the same respect. Set up a writer's library at one corner of the classroom and stock it with dictionaries, thesauri, rhyming dictionaries, author's stylebooks, and other references. Making references available supports students in their efforts to find their own answers to questions. Also, make available such items as paper, pencils, pens, correction fluid, paper clips, glue, and scissors. Allow students to use these materials as necessary, but instruct them to put each item back when they are done. As with their folders, you might assign different students each week to make sure that the materials are returned at the end of each period. To ensure that everyone understands how to handle the materials, you may discuss the rules during one of your class meetings.

If you have computers in your classroom for writing, establish procedures for using them. Computers should be used in an efficient manner. For example, students who are thinking of an idea to write about should not be at a computer while other students who are ready to begin their drafts are waiting. In some classes, a sign-up sheet to use the computers is necessary; in others, computer use becomes a natural routine of the class once students learn the procedures of the writing workshop.

Students need to be instructed how to move through the class. Ideally, the writing workshop has desks as well as tables for both individual and group work. If your classroom is typical, however, the ideal is seldom the reality. It is likely that students will need to move their chairs to tables and slide desks together when working in groups. To reduce the disruption, encourage students to move chairs and materials quietly and carefully. If you have a large class, you might have students move into their groups by section. Letting the left side of the room go first, then the right, eliminates a mass of jumbled bodies moving in different directions at once. When students must consult a dictionary, get paper, or work with a peer group, remind them not to stop along the way and visit with their friends. Writing is the priority in the writing workshop. You may find that you will need to remind students of these basics often, but it is necessary. Much time can be lost and many disruptions can occur as students move around the room.

There *will* be some noise in the writing workshop. Students will need to get more materials, share a draft with an editing partner, confer with you about the lead of a story, or check references. You must decide how much of the activity is purposeful and how much is mere chatter. There will be times when you will have to refocus your students. Often the reminder "Let's remember to use soft voices" is enough. Sometimes you may have to speak with students individually. You should also have students keep their desks clear of everything except writing materials. Since there will be movement throughout the class, nonessential books on desks invariably get knocked down, causing noise and confusion.

There is much group work during most writing workshops. Students regularly confer with partners and peers about their writing. This can be a management challenge. At the beginning of the year, I explain my rules for working in groups during a mini-lesson.

Discuss with your students that the purpose of meeting in groups is to share ideas and gain feedback on writing. Adhering to commonsense procedures when working together helps ensure that important ideas are discussed. Distribute copies of the accompanying "Rules for Working in Groups" on page 19 and discuss the rules with your students. (For additional information on group work, see the reproducible "Peer Group Guidelines" in Section Five.)

Modeling a group working together in front of the class is an effective way to show students how a group should function. You may take part in the group or act as a director, guiding students in their roles. During group activities, especially at the beginning of the year, you should circulate from group to group offering guidance.

To help groups work effectively, you can assign specific roles: the leader (who keeps the group on task), the recorder (who writes down any necessary notes), a noise-level monitor (who reminds group members not to get too loud), and the timekeeper (who makes sure that every group member has a chance to share). The roles should change with each group activity. Assigning roles gives each student a share in the group and responsibility for its effectiveness.

You may find that you have to remind students of the rules for effective group work often in the early part of the year. Once they realize what behavior you expect and demand, your groups will function more smoothly.

Organize your classroom so that students find it easy to write and confer within the patterns of a predictable routine. In an environment that promotes consistency and positive support, creativity and industry will flourish.

# The Writing Environment

Following are some elements of a classroom designed for writing:

- The classroom is bright and cheerful.

- Fresh ideas, openness, and sharing are promoted.

- The classroom is designed to facilitate the writing effort. Reference books and materials for writing are readily available.

- Students are encouraged to do their best work.

- Papers are headed and labeled.

- Students move through the classroom showing consideration for others.

- Noise is purposeful.

- Available technology such as computers is used efficiently.

- Students are involved with a variety of tasks: writing, revising, sharing a draft with an editing partner, conferring with a teacher, brainstorming for ideas.

- Writing is a priority.

- Writing is treated as a process including these stages: prewriting, drafting, revising, editing, and publishing.

# Student Writers' Tools of the Trade

The proper materials make the task of writing easier. Following are the materials and equipment most writers (particularly student writers) need:

- A place to write with a desk large enough on which to spread books, papers, pens, pencils, and anything else student writers need.

- Supplies such as paper, computer disks, paper clips, correction fluid, stapler, note paper, pads, pens, pencils, scissors, envelopes for mailing manuscripts, and folders for stories, articles, poems, and ideas.

- Books, including dictionaries, thesauri, grammar and usage books, author's stylebooks, and general references.

- Computer. Word processing software that contains clip art is a plus.

- Printer.

- Internet access.

- Access to a copy machine.

- Books about writing and writers.

- Magazines (such as *Writer's Digest*) containing articles for writers.

- A desire to write.

# Rules for Working in Groups

To help make sure that your group works productively in writing workshop, follow these points:

- Every student should participate in the sharing of ideas.

- Speakers should think about the points they wish to make before speaking.

- After stating their points, speakers should give the floor to someone else.

- Group members should listen politely to others.

- The discussion should be about writing.

- Questions should be appropriate and on the topic.

- Listeners should not interrupt speakers. If they have questions, they should ask after the speaker is done.

- If a listener disagrees with a speaker, he or she should explain why in a calm, clear manner.

- Comments should always be constructive.

# Planning Your Workshop Lessons

Mini-lessons are the most efficient way of imparting information to the whole class in the writing workshop. The typical mini-lesson runs between five and ten minutes and focuses on one topic or skill. That amount of time is usually sufficient to cover the material. Longer lessons take too much time away from writing.

A common question is how to write plans for a writing workshop in a plan book. Here is an example:

**Monday**

| | |
|---|---|
| Mini-lesson: | Writing personal narratives. |
| Procedure: | Students work individually or in groups. |
| Closing: | Editing partners or peer groups engage in sharing. |

**Tuesday**

| | |
|---|---|
| Mini-lesson: | Effective leads. |
| Procedure: | Students work individually or in groups. |
| Closing: | Two or three students share their work from the author's chair. |

**Wednesday**

| | |
|---|---|
| Mini-lesson: | Sentence constructions. |
| Procedure: | Students work individually or in groups. |
| Closing: | Editing partners or peer groups engage in sharing. |

**Thursday**

| | |
|---|---|
| Mini-lesson: | Sentence fragments. |
| Procedure: | Students work individually or in groups. |
| Closing: | Two or three students share their work from the author's chair. |

**Friday**

| | |
|---|---|
| Mini-lesson: | Using descriptive words. |
| Procedure: | Students work individually or in groups. |
| Closing: | Editing partners or peer groups engage in sharing. |

A mini-lesson is not the kind of lesson in which a skill or concept is taught and then every student does an assignment that reinforces the material. Rather, mini-lessons should be used to introduce new material, share techniques for improving writing, or teach the skills students need to use grammar and punctuation correctly. The information you offer through mini-lessons should always be simple and digestible. The content of the mini-lessons will be reinforced during individual and group conferences throughout the remainder of the year.

You should select mini-lessons based on the needs of your students. While most of the mini-lessons you teach will be addressed to the whole class, in some cases you will find it useful to teach a mini-lesson to a small group that is having trouble with a specific skill. The mini-lessons in Part Three of this book cover many of the skills necessary for written English. However, only you will know which skills your students need, and you may want to create your own mini-lessons by using the mini-lessons in this book as a guide.

## Managing Time in the Writing Workshop

The writing workshop can present you with a heavy workload. This is particularly true for teachers who team-teach or are departmentalized. By managing the class and your time effectively, you will be able to handle the work.

When you set up your classroom, think in terms of efficiency. If you have more than one writing workshop and your students are to leave their writing folders in the classroom, maintain a separate box or milk crate for each class. Differently colored boxes make it easy for students to go directly to their folders. Have the folders arranged alphabetically, and instruct your students to pick them up as they enter the room. If you are self-contained or if you team-teach and have students for a longer period of time, you may have a student pass out the folders instead of having each student take his or her own. Providing separate trays for drafts and final copies (you can even do this by class) reduces work by keeping papers in distinct piles. You can reduce work further by making writing materials accessible to students. Encouraging students to use materials as necessary cuts down on countless questions such as, "Where is the paper?" "Where are the paper clips?" and "May I borrow a pen?" which will intrude on the time you could be helping students with their writing.

Along with arranging your classroom for efficiency, establish procedures that foster independence and cooperation. Set up peer groups and editing partners so that students can share their writing and help each other. (See "Peer Conferences" in Section Five.) Much learning occurs through sharing. To avoid long lines at your desk, move around the classroom and work with students at their desks or tables.

Grading papers can be the biggest part of your workload. Avoid grading every paper, which is unrealistic because each student's pieces vary in quality just as the works of professional writers do. Moreover, when students feel that they will not be immediately graded on a paper, they are more likely to take risks with their writing and experiment with new forms. Sometimes this is where the greatest learning occurs.

Never take all students' papers home at one time. Distribute the grading activity over several nights or a few nights per week. When you take home too much, you will overwhelm yourself and probably not read very many of them. The papers will pile up even higher.

Students can help you in your efforts to make the workshop efficient. Appoint students to check materials, and make sure that items are put back in their proper places. You might label the number of items that belong in a box to make it easier to keep track of inventory. For example, if you have twelve scissors and eight glue sticks (for cutting and pasting), mark 12 on the box of scissors and 8 on the box of glue sticks so that the materials monitor knows how many of each should be in the box at the end of class. This eliminates the need for the monitor to ask you how many items should be there. At the conclusion of the period if all items are not returned, remind the class that some things are missing and ask them to find these materials. Monitoring materials closely discourages their disappearance. (Of course, even if you do not designate student monitors, you should still check your inventory of materials at the end of each period to make sure that you do not lose supplies.) If you use skills analysis sheets (see "Evaluation" in this section) for record keeping, allow students to contribute as much information as possible. They can at least put their names, section numbers, and topics on the sheets. Having plenty of sheets photocopied in advance and available allows students to fill out the sheets as needed.

A writing workshop that has a clear, simple structure with organized routines will function more smoothly than one in which organization is lacking. A smooth-running workshop will allow you to spend more time with students and work on their writing skills.

## Keeping Students Motivated

I have never met a teacher of writing who has not heard students complain about writing:

> "It's boring."
>
> "Do we have to write?"
>
> "I can't think of anything to write about."
>
> "Why do we have to do this?"

You will be hearing these kinds of complaints much less often in the writing workshop than you would in a traditional writing class, but you will still hear them from some students. Usually these students have a reason for not wanting to write. The complaint may be a disguise for the real reason. Perhaps they believe that they have nothing to write about, they may feel that their classmates will not accept what they write, or their reluctance may have roots in a lack of self-worth, trouble at home, learning disabilities, or problems at school.

When trying to motivate students to write, provide plenty of encouragement, praise, and support. Try to boost the self-image of these students. It is especially important to help them find topics and build ideas. Everyone has hundreds of stories to tell. These students need to be shown that others are interested in what they have to say.

Reluctant writers also benefit from the support of their peers. Whenever possible, put them in groups where they will receive support. Build a classroom environment where they feel safe enough to share their ideas. For these students, a classroom that has a firm structure and steady routines is vital. Such a classroom offers a safe haven in which they are more likely to write and experiment with ideas.

# Time-Savers

The following tips can help you use your time most efficiently:

- Color-code and alphabetize boxes that contain writing folders for easy access.

- Appoint student monitors to keep supplies and materials organized.

- Have separate baskets or trays for drafts and finished copies.

- Organize your writing workshop around clear and simple routines.

- Make sure your students understand classroom routines; repeat the rules for procedures as necessary.

- Set up editing partners and peer groups so that students can share their work and help each other.

- Avoid long lines at your desk by circulating around the room.

- Encourage students not to call out, as this only leads to noise and confusion.

- Grade only what students consider to be their best papers.

- Avoid taking large piles of papers home at night. You will likely feel overwhelmed and will not read them. Instead, take home small, manageable batches.

- Have students fill out as many record-keeping forms as possible.

For every student who does not want to write, there will be several who will embrace your workshop with vigor and passion. However, even the most motivated students vary in the quality of the work they produce. All authors experience highs and lows. You will likely see growth come in spurts, with some backsliding in between. This is normal, even for top students.

You can also expect to see a wide diversity in the abilities and skills of your students. Young authors develop at different rates. They are individuals, and their skills grow individually. You can guide learning, but you cannot rush it.

# When Discipline Is Necessary

No matter how smoothly your writing workshop functions, there will be times that you will need to discipline students. Never ignore discipline in the hopes that the workshop setting will miraculously solve problems. Although your role changes with the writing workshop, you are still the teacher, and you must not hesitate to correct students for inappropriate behavior.

They may not understand why they misbehave, but most students have a reason for disrupting class. They may be seeking attention or power, lacking self-esteem, or acting out anger. You should learn to identify these students and address any disruption immediately and calmly. Not only will you be able to manage disruptions more effectively by remaining calm, but you will make a stronger impression on the rest of the class. For severe behavior problems, you should not hesitate to use the typical disciplinary procedures of your school, which may include detention, intervention by the principal, and parent conferences.

When forced to discipline, try to separate the disruption from writing. Isolate the behavior that needs correction, and address that. Once the incident has been addressed, refocus the student on his or her work. This reinforces the importance of writing.

Following are several common discipline problems you are likely to face in the writing workshop and suggestions on how to solve them.

## Does Not Complete Writing

Speak to the student individually about the importance of starting and finishing pieces. Monitor his daily work closely. If necessary, set reasonable deadlines that the first draft must be done by, say, Tuesday, with the final finished by Friday. If the student fails to make the deadline, he must stay after school or give up a free period. Treat him just as you would any other student who does not finish assignments.

## Is Easily Distracted

Speak to this student about keeping her attention on task. Place her desk at a front corner of the classroom and surround her with quiet students, preferably those who will do little to distract her. For group work, place this student with those who are likely to remain on task. Providing her with good models will help foster appropriate behavior.

## Writes on Inappropriate Topics or with Inappropriate Language

Speak to this student privately, and explain your standards for the classroom. Ask why he is writing the way he is. If you can uncover the reason, you will be better able to address the issue and change the behavior. Often students write on inappropriate topics or use offensive language out of anger or frustration or merely as a test to see how much you will tolerate. If the student continues to write like that after you have spoken to him, you should consider contacting his parent or guardian. Confronting this problem quickly, calmly, and firmly usually leads to a solution. (Sometimes writing or talking inappropriately about sexuality is a sign of sexual abuse. If you suspect abuse, you should report it to your supervisor.)

## Criticizes or Mocks Others Orally or in Writing

If the student does this openly in class, you should address the problem before the class. Immediately intercede and explain that negative criticism or mockery is not acceptable behavior. No one has the right to hurt another's feelings. Ask students to imagine themselves in the place of those mocked. How would they feel? A quick answer from a student might be "I wouldn't care," but counter that by saying you know that she would. You might also mention that the purpose of the writing workshop is to help people learn the skills for effective communication. Everyone's efforts in the class should be directed to that purpose.

If the student criticizes or mocks others in her writing, speak to her privately. Stress the importance of providing support and encouragement to others rather than denigrating someone or his work.

## Writes About Other Students or Teachers

At the beginning of the year, I tell my students that one of the rules of the writing workshop is that students do not write about other students or teachers without the other person's permission. Sometimes students write narratives in which friends are involved; however, the rule makes it clear that writing about others without first asking is not acceptable. When a student ignores the rule, speak to him individually, reminding him that no one has the right to make someone uncomfortable by using her in a story she does not want to be a part of.

## Refuses to Share Writing

Sometimes a student may refuse to share her work because she feels that it is not good enough or it may be private. If it is private, do not insist that she share it. However, if she feels that the work is not good enough, you might have her read her writing to you first. Work with the student to improve the piece; then provide plenty of support for her to share. Placing this student in a peer group composed of students with similar abilities will make her feel less threatened than being in a group of the class's best writers. If the student is still reluctant to share, suggest that she read only the opening or merely talk about her writing. If she still hesitates, ask her if you can share her work with the class for her. Once her work is shared, the second presentation will be easier to arrange.

## Dominates Sharing During Peer Groups

To rein in a student who tries to dominate sharing, you might place him in a group with equally forceful personalities. Avoid putting the domineering student with a group that will accommodate him. If necessary, sit in on the group, model the appropriate behavior, and act as the monitor. You may have to do this a few times so that students understand the procedures and goals of a peer group. (See the reproducible "Peer Group Guidelines" in Section Five.)

## Confers Much But Accomplishes Little

Separate this student from group work unless the group work is essential. When organizing groups, put this student with others who are likely to stay on task. You might also impose deadlines to keep this student working.

## Demands Constant Attention

When a student demands your attention constantly, you must remind him, calmly but strongly, that you are working with someone else and will help him as soon as possible. Direct him back to his task by suggesting that he work with a peer or consult reference materials while he is waiting for you. Permitting this student to stand beside you as you help another will only encourage his demands.

## Lacks Patience

When a student is impatient (for example, cannot wait for her turn to use a computer), speak to her individually and explain that everyone must have a turn. If necessary, address the class on the issue using a mini-lesson about procedure. It is important to maintain strict rules on patience and sharing. If you ignore the rules for one student, you will be expected to ignore the rules for all.

## Has Trouble Sharing Materials

Speak to this student about the need for sharing. If several students have this same problem, you may want to talk about it with the entire class by way of a procedural mini-lesson.

## Plagiarizes

Plagiarism is a serious issue. Speak to the student individually and explain that plagiarism is the taking of another's writing and using it as one's own. Mention that by plagiarizing, the student is not being fair to herself. She is not allowing herself the opportunity to learn to express herself with her own words. (Mini-Lesson 44 in Section Nine focuses on plagiarism.)

## Keeps Writing the Same Type of Pieces and Refuses to Move On to Other Kinds of Writing

This student needs support and encouragement. Often the reason for not moving on to other types of writing is safety. Moving on may mean taking risks, which some students are reluctant to do. To help overcome this obstacle, try brainstorming ideas for different types of writing. A good time to do this is after explaining new types of writing during mini-lessons. (See Mini-Lessons 1 to 16 in Section Eight.) You can follow the mini-lesson with brainstorming for topics. This may provide the boost the student needs to launch into new writing forms.

## Has Indecipherable Handwriting

If the student has a severe motor coordination problem and you have computers in your classroom, let this student write using a computer. If handwriting is difficult because of a disability, the student may be able to dictate a story that you or a volunteer can write down. Some schools use community volunteers to help in such situations. (This is also a helpful strategy with English as a Second Language students who can communicate through interpreters.)

Of course, sometimes the poor handwriting of students is a result of carelessness or simply not caring. In such cases, speak to the student about being neater. Suggest that he slow down and form his letters more carefully. Explain that illegible handwriting detracts from his work. Ask him why someone would want to spend the time trying to read writing that is unreadable.

Some students need tangible incentives to write neatly. I recall one boy whose handwriting was so sloppy that he often had trouble reading his own words. When given the chance to put his work in a class magazine, however, his handwriting quickly and dramatically improved.

## Is Being Helped by a Parent or Older Sibling

Encouraging your students to write in school helps eliminate this potential problem. For students who continue to write at home and who you believe are not turning in their own work, confront them and ask. Few students will admit that someone else did their work, but many will concede that they had help. At this admission, you should explain that only by doing their own work can they expect to learn good writing skills.

In some cases, you may have to contact the student's parents or guardians. Be tactful. Do not call and bluntly accuse them of doing their child's work. Rather, mention that you notice a difference in the quality of the student's work done in class compared to the quality of work finished at home. You can then bring up the subject of help. Explain that while help is important and you appreciate the parent's concern for the child's achievement, emphasize that it is also important that the student does her own work. Not only will she learn more writing skills, but she will feel ownership of the work and will likely take more pride in it.

### Is Disruptive

Address the disruptive behavior. Speak to the student and explain why the behavior will not be tolerated. You might also mention the consequences if it happens again. If the behavior continues, use the disciplinary procedures of your school, which might include time after school, detention, or calling parents. I speak to such students in private and ask them for suggestions of how we can work together to improve their behavior. Some students will tell you why they are misbehaving, which will help you to modify their classroom interaction and thereby improve their behavior. Frequently, just talking and drawing the student out makes a difference, because the student sees that you care about him.

### Is Not Working Because of an Undiagnosed Learning Problem

You should contact the school's child study team or administrator in charge of learning disabilities and recommend that the student be tested to discover if any learning problems exist. Delay will only cause frustration to the student who is having trouble working successfully in your writing workshop because of a learning problem.

Students should never be permitted to disrupt the writing workshop. Misbehavior affects not only the individual but those around him. In most cases, common sense and being consistent in discipline will serve you well.

## Evaluation

Evaluating the writing of students is always difficult because it is a subjective process. No matter how hard a teacher may try to read a paper objectively, he invariably evaluates a student's work from the standpoint of his own biases and preconceptions. Just as readers may disagree over the merits of the same book, teachers often disagree over the strengths and weaknesses of a student's writing.

Evaluating according to specific criteria helps the cause of objectivity. When you determine grades by looking for consistent elements in papers, you are likely to be more objective. When grading, I concentrate on five major areas: focus, content, organization, style, and mechanics. A well-written paper is strong in all areas.

Some teachers choose, or are required, to give grades in numerical values. While it is certainly more difficult to do that for writing than for other subjects, referring to the following percentage breakdown of a piece's major elements can be helpful:

- *Focus:* The topic is clearly defined, and all ideas relate to the topic. (20 percent)
- *Content:* The student uses fresh, insightful, or original ideas. The topic is developed and supported with details. (25 percent)
- *Organization:* The piece progresses logically from beginning to end. For nonfiction, an interesting introduction, body, and satisfying conclusion can be easily identified. For fiction, an interesting lead, development, and climax are apparent. (25 percent)

- *Style:* The writing is appropriate for the topic and audience. There is a distinct voice and effective imagery. (15 percent)
- *Mechanics:* The writer uses correct punctuation, grammar, and spelling. (15 percent)

I like to base each student's grades on at least five papers per marking period and allow them to select the ones they want me to grade. My only requirement is that each piece is a different type of writing. For example, I will not accept five personal narratives for grading from a student. (Although most students complete more than five papers each marking period, some teachers are required to record several grades per quarter. In this case, you can grade work on the various stages of the process or perhaps other aspects of the class.)

I believe that requiring a minimum number of pieces for grading takes into account that students, like adults, vary in the quality of their work. Some topics fire their imagination, while others (which may have seemed like good ideas) fail to sustain the interest necessary to complete successfully. Counting every paper in their final grade inhibits some students from taking risks with their writing. Rather than trying something new, which may result in a low grade, these students keep writing the same things to get their A. I grade only final copies but encourage students to finish all the pieces they begin. Before they do their final drafts, I confer with students individually, offering any last suggestions for revision. When grading a final, I read through it to get a sense of its overall scope; then I reread it for content and mechanics. I base the grade on the overall paper. Since I have been working with students throughout the development of their pieces, I am familiar with their work, and grading is fairly easy.

Evaluation should not be just a form of criticism, but rather should aim to boost students in their growth as writers. It should always be based on what has been taught, and it must be consistent. I explain to my students on the first or second day of school how their grades will be determined, and I explain that to their parents on back-to-school night. Students deserve to know ahead of time how their grades will be determined.

Although my school has interim reports, I contact parents by phone, e-mail, or handwritten notes when their children fall behind in their work. Some parents hear from me by the end of the first week of school, and every year a few acquire a quasi-pen-pal status. When parents are kept informed of their children's progress, they are more likely to support your efforts. While not all parents are helpful, by keeping them informed you will at least reduce the chance they will be surprised by their child's grade.

## Monitoring the Progress of Your Students

Since your students will be working at their own rates, you must monitor their progress closely to ensure that they complete pieces in a timely manner. You must also be aware of the skills they have acquired and the ones that remain to be learned.

You can use any of several methods for recording the progress of your students. One option is to maintain a daily log. Set up on a weekly basis, you can record each student's topic and what he or she has accomplished.

Unless a piece is complicated or goes through several hard revisions, or the student has been absent, I expect a finished piece about every five class periods. I tell my students that this is a time frame to aim for and that it will result in their completing a variety of pieces for grading. For students who have trouble finishing pieces, I require that they complete at least one piece about every two weeks.

The daily log is also useful for encouraging students to come to class with a plan for writing. If they know that you recorded what they did yesterday, they know you will be expecting them to move ahead today. Keeping the log handy as you circulate around the room makes record keeping easy. Following is a sample portion of a log. (A reproducible blank log sheet is also provided.)

**Daily Log**

| | Student | Topic | 10/14 | 10/15 | 10/16 | 10/17 | 10/18 |
|---|---|---|---|---|---|---|---|
| 1. | A. Buetell | Fishing Trip | $D^1$ | TC/R | $D^2$ | EP | F |
| 2. | J. Callahan | Limericks | P | P | D | PC | TC/R |
| 3. | R. Cortland | The Grind/Parents | F | P | D | TC/R | F |
| 4. | S. Dove | The Lost Puppy | TC/P | D | PC | R | E/F |

**Codes:**

| | | | | | |
|---|---|---|---|---|---|
| P | – | Prewriting | EP | – | Editing (Partners) |
| D | – | Draft | R | – | Revision |
| PC | – | Peer Conference | F | – | Final Copy |
| TC | – | Teacher Conference | NC | – | Work Not Completed |
| E | – | Editing (Self) | | | |

# Daily Log

| | Student | Topic | Dates | | | | |
|---|---|---|---|---|---|---|---|
| 1. | | | | | | | |
| 2. | | | | | | | |
| 3. | | | | | | | |
| 4. | | | | | | | |
| 5. | | | | | | | |
| 6. | | | | | | | |
| 7. | | | | | | | |
| 8. | | | | | | | |
| 9. | | | | | | | |
| 10. | | | | | | | |
| 11. | | | | | | | |
| 12. | | | | | | | |
| 13. | | | | | | | |
| 14. | | | | | | | |
| 15. | | | | | | | |
| 16. | | | | | | | |
| 17. | | | | | | | |
| 18. | | | | | | | |
| 19. | | | | | | | |
| 20. | | | | | | | |
| 21. | | | | | | | |
| 22. | | | | | | | |
| 23. | | | | | | | |
| 24. | | | | | | | |
| 25. | | | | | | | |
| 26. | | | | | | | |

**Codes:**

| P | – | Prewriting | EP | – | Editing (Partners) |
|---|---|---|---|---|---|
| D | – | Draft | R | – | Revision |
| PC | – | Peer Conference | F | – | Final Copy |
| TC | – | Teacher Conference | NC | – | Work Not Completed |
| E | – | Editing (Self) | | | |

Another method for charting the progress of students is the use of the accompanying "Skills Analysis Sheet." These charts can be used to record the skills demonstrated on specific pieces, or they can be used as general records after every two or three pieces. The sheets are divided into categories for which you log strengths and weaknesses as well as suggestions for improvement. Skills analysis sheets enable you to follow closely the growth of a student's writing.

Along with recording the skills your students acquire, it is important that you encourage them to try different types of writing. Without a gentle nudge from their teachers, some students will write only poems, others will write only personal narratives, and still others will write only essays. I once had a boy who only wanted to write reviews of video games.

The "Checklist for Types of Writing" provides a way to ensure that students try a variety of different kinds of writing. The checklist is designed for students to keep in their writing folders. When they finish one of the forms of writing, you initial the piece and mark the date it was completed. Allowing the students to keep the checklist in their folders enables them to see what forms they need to try. Once a student's checklist is completed, you may collect it and save it for your records.

To encourage students to try various forms of writing, use mini-lessons to introduce new types of writing (see Section Eight). Encourage students to try the most recently discussed writing form for their next piece, although you need not demand that they do. Within the next few weeks, however, speak to students who still have not tried new forms, and urge them to do so. While many students will try all the forms you introduce, others will not. You must decide how many forms of writing you will teach and how many of the forms students will be required to try. Some teachers believe that advanced forms of writing (screenplays, for example) are too difficult for students of low ability. However, I have found that when shown the form and given encouragement, even these students try advanced forms.

Thoughtful monitoring of their progress will enable you to see the strengths and weaknesses of your students' writing. This in turn will help you guide their continued progress effectively.

## Writing Across the Curriculum

Writing should not be limited to the writing workshop. The writing skills your students learn with you should be carried over to their other classes.

If you have the opportunity to work with teachers of other subjects, coordinate your efforts. For example, when your students' social studies teacher assigns a report on Central America, you could cover the skills necessary for report writing in mini-lessons. You can work with the science teacher on the writing of lab reports or papers of inquiry. For their math classes, students might write review word problems for each other.

Seeing the importance of writing in various classes helps students realize the value of the writing workshop. That makes your management of the workshop easier.

# Skills Analysis Sheet

Name _____ Date _____ Section _____

Title of Piece(s) _____

| Components | Strengths | Weaknesses | Suggestions |
|---|---|---|---|
| Focus | | | |
| Content | | | |
| Structure | | | |
| Style | | | |
| Mechanics | | | |

Notes:

_____

_____

_____

_____

_____

# Checklist for Types of Writing

|                      | Title                                  | Date Completed |
| -------------------- | -------------------------------------- | -------------- |
| Narrative            | _____  | _____   |
| Essay                | _____  | _____   |
| How-to Article       | _____  | _____   |
| Newspaper Article    | _____  | _____   |
| Persuasive Article   | _____  | _____   |
| Friendly Letter      | _____  | _____   |
| Business Letter      | _____  | _____   |
| Book Review          | _____  | _____   |
| Movie Review         | _____  | _____   |
| Fiction Piece        | _____  | _____   |
| Advertising          | _____  | _____   |
| Nonrhyming Poem      | _____  | _____   |
| Rhyming Poem         | _____  | _____   |
| Play                 | _____  | _____   |
| Screenplay           | _____  | _____   |

Additional Types:

_____      _____      _____

_____      _____      _____

# PART TWO

# THE STAGES OF THE WRITING PROCESS

# SECTION 3

# PREWRITING

**Prewriting encompasses** all the activities and strategies that prepare an author to write. The prewriting stage of the writing process is the time when authors find and focus topics, generate and develop ideas, and decide on the best method to express their ideas to readers. Prewriting is an essential part of the writing process.

Prewriting can take many forms. Although no writer uses all of them, students should recognize the options so that they can select the ones they feel are most helpful to them. The value of prewriting is not in adherence to a specific plan, but in the concentrating of the writer's attention on the piece. Prewriting engages the writer's mind with the topic, fires up imagination and creativity, and provides the foundation for the writing that is to come.

## Prewriting Strategies

In the broadest sense, anything that helps a writer get ready to write is a prewriting activity. A long walk in the woods in which ideas for writing are examined might be a prewriting strategy for some authors. I know of a few authors who claim that they dream of the scenes they will write the next day. Some writers leave a topic alone for a time, hoping to develop it subconsciously while they attend to other projects. This is a prewriting strategy for them. Explain to your students that most authors rely on a number of prewriting activities. Following are some of the more common ones.

### Freewriting

Freewriting is a prewriting activity in which the author writes freely to discover and explore ideas. For many writers, topics become apparent only after they have started writing. The surprises in their writing become ideas for them. These ideas can then be organized and expanded into full-length pieces.

The goal of freewriting is to find as many ideas as possible. Thus, freewriting is fast, with the writer getting down thoughts as they come. Time should not be spent on editing or revising during freewriting. That can be done later. Fragments and even single words are acceptable. Because the focus is on ideas and not form, many students who may be reluctant to write are encouraged during freewriting.

For the first few sessions, you should keep freewriting to periods of about five minutes. As students learn the technique, you can gradually increase the writing time.

A variation of the typical freewriting is *looping*. In this method of freewriting, students freewrite, then circle an idea they discover in their freewriting, freewrite on this idea, circle a new (often narrower) idea, and continue the process until they have found a topic they wish to pursue.

The best way to demonstrate freewriting is to model it for your students. You can freewrite on an overhead projector or read examples of your own freewriting to the class. If you wish, project on an overhead the accompanying "Freewriting Sample." Discuss the example with your students and point out how the writer went from having no ideas to uncovering an experience that would make a fine personal narrative. When students freewrite, you might wish to freewrite too. There are few better ways of modeling.

Freewriting eliminates excuses not to write. It provides a no-risk atmosphere for the most reluctant of your writers.

## *Activity 1: A Freewriting Exercise*

Explain to your students what freewriting is, and tell them that they are going to participate in a freewriting session. Model freewriting or distribute copies of the "Freewriting Sample" so that students understand what they are to do. Encourage your students to think of a topic. For those who have trouble thinking of ideas, tell them to write "I can't think of anything" or a similar sentence until the ideas begin to flow. Assure them that keeping their pen or pencil point to the paper (or fingers on the keyboard) and writing will eventually generate ideas. Permit the session to run about five minutes. After the session is done, instruct your students to reread what they wrote and look for ideas that could become topics. You might have them freewrite on one of these ideas to generate details they can use in writing a draft.

### Clustering

Clustering, also known as *mapping* or *webbing,* is a form of word association that is an effective way to generate or elaborate ideas. Some people liken it to individual brainstorming.

To use this method, students select a topic in which they are interested, write it at the center of a sheet of paper, and then branch off from it, writing down words or phrases that they associate with the topic. When clustering, students should write rapidly. The purpose is to generate as many ideas as possible.

Sometimes students uncover new topics from their initial idea and cluster. Some topics naturally lead to new topics. The accompanying "A Sample Cluster" shows

---

**Freewriting Sample**

Right now I'm having trouble. I
can't think of anything to write.
I don't have ideas. I never have
ideas. When I look around the
room I see everybody writing and I
feel bad. Everybody has ideas. Not
me. Maybe I'll have an idea later.
Maybe I won't. Maybe. Maybe.
Maybe. . . . This is so hard.
Like the time I went to bat in
the pee-wee league for the first time.
I remember how scared I was.
I was seven and the kid pitching
was 9. He was good. And I was okay.

---

new major ideas being generated. Instruct your students to circle any ideas that they could use as a topic and continue clustering. Caution your students that it is important that they narrow down their topics and focus them. Encourage them to do a second or even third cluster if necessary.

## *Activity 2: Creating Clusters*

Explain clustering to your students. Hand out copies of "A Sample Cluster" as an example. To show your students how a cluster is generated, ask them to suggest a topic and, with their help, do a cluster for it on the board or an overhead projector. Using a topic suggested by students provides a good model because they know that you did not plan the cluster in advance. Also, it becomes a much more spontaneous

# A Sample Cluster

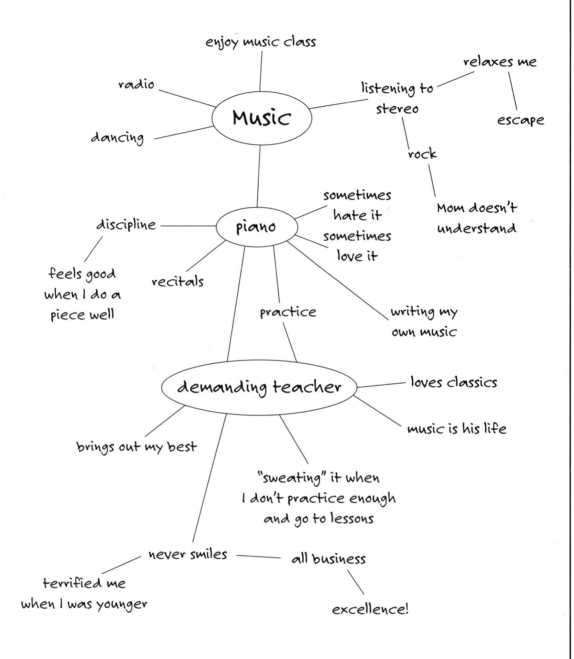

enjoy music class

radio

dancing

**Music**

listening to stereo

relaxes me

escape

rock

Mom doesn't understand

discipline

**piano**

sometimes hate it

sometimes love it

feels good when I do a piece well

recitals

practice

writing my own music

**demanding teacher**

loves classics

music is his life

brings out my best

"sweating" it when I don't practice enough and go to lessons

never smiles

all business

terrified me when I was younger

excellence!

exercise. While developing the cluster, be sure to circle any ideas that may be used as separate topics.

After you have completed the example cluster, ask your students to select a topic (you can suggest they pick an idea from their freewriting) and do a cluster for it. Once they have completed their clusters, ask them to write about their topics.

## Idea Listing

Idea listing is similar to clustering. Rather than writing the topic at the center of the paper, students write it at the top of a blank sheet. Then they list as many ideas as they can about the topic. It is not uncommon for idea lists to resemble clusters when they are finished.

When listing ideas, students should not worry about order or relationships but should simply try to write as many ideas as possible. The purpose of listing is to generate ideas. When they finish, the students review the ideas and select the ones they wish to develop, perhaps by clustering or freewriting. While not all the ideas of the list will appear in the finished piece, many will.

## *Activity 3: Making an Idea List*

Distribute copies of the accompanying "Sample Idea List," and discuss the list with your students. You should model the generation of an idea list for your students on the board or an overhead projector. Asking them to suggest a topic and offer ideas for it will involve them in the process. Emphasize the similarities between idea listing and clustering. Explain that by listing as many ideas as they can about their topics, they should be able to focus their topics (discarding much of what they generated at first) and develop good pieces. After completion of the activity, instruct your students to choose a topic and generate an idea list for it. They should then write about their topics.

## Brainstorming

Brainstorming is a prewriting strategy in which a group quickly lists everything it can about a topic. You can use brainstorming with your entire class or divide students into small groups. Effective brainstorming relies on three important rules:

1. Record *all* ideas.
2. Do not judge or criticize any ideas during the brainstorming session.
3. All group members should participate.

During the brainstorming, time should not be taken to analyze ideas or look for relationships. Effort should remain focused on generating ideas. After ideas are generated, instruct your students to go back over them and look for relationships and ways to expand them.

**Sample Idea List**

My Pet

Dog

Cairn Terrier

bought at
the pet store — Ozzie — small, fluffy

— brown and silver

chases ball — playful
chases stick
tug-of-war   energetic, bouncy

friend

guard dog — barks at
strangers, noises

mischievous

steals slippers,
chews on rug

hates cats — Mr. Smith hates Ozzie

If you brainstorm with your class, you should act as the recorder. As ideas are offered, write them down on the board or an overhead projector. You will have to be fast because students will be offering ideas as quickly as they can think of them. You can use brainstorming to generate topics for writing or ideas about a specific topic.

When doing small-group brainstorming, I suggest dividing students into groups of four to six. Each group should designate one student as the recorder—the person who writes down all the ideas. Other roles may also be assigned. For example, one student may be responsible for making sure that everyone contributes. Another's job may be to monitor the noise level and remind group members to quiet down when necessary. Still another may act as moderator during the group's discussion after brainstorming, and someone else may have the task of reporting the group's findings to the class.

In setting up your groups, be sure to consider the combinations. Including a shy student with three or four vocal ones might make it impossible for the shy one to offer any ideas. One way to ensure that everyone gets a chance in the group is to have a rule that everyone must contribute at least one idea. Expect some noise, but remember that too much noise inhibits work. If you did not appoint students to be in charge of the noise level of their groups, you must watch that the noise level does not become too high and rein your students in when it does. A preset signal (for example, blinking the lights, ringing a small bell, or activating a beeper) can recapture the attention of your students and allow you to remind them to soften their voices.

Group brainstorming is particularly effective when students are doing similar topics or writing about different aspects of the same subject. Some groups require only a topic to begin an enthusiastic brainstorming session. Others need more guidance. For this latter group of students you might consider distributing copies of the accompanying "Brainstorming Guide." The questions on it can help students offer ideas on a topic.

# *Activity 4: Brainstorming for Ideas*

Explain brainstorming to your students, and then brainstorm a list of topics for writing with the class. List the topics on the board or an overhead projector.

After listing several topics, divide the class into groups of four to six students. Instruct each group to select a topic and brainstorm ideas for it. Each group should choose a recorder who will write down all the ideas that are generated. (Other roles may also be assigned.) If you feel that it will be helpful, distribute copies of the "Brainstorming Guide." Your students may use the worksheet for notes. Put a time limit of ten minutes on the brainstorming. After brainstorming, while still in groups, students should review the ideas that were generated, identify relationships, and expand the ideas. Allow about ten minutes for this. When they are finished, each recorder or designated reporter should share the group's brainstormed list with the rest of the class. To conclude the activity, you may wish to have students write about their topics.

# Brainstorming Guide

**Directions:** Thinking about the following questions will help you to offer ideas during brainstorming. Write notes and ideas on this sheet.

Topic: _____

1. Describe your topic or subject.

2. What does it do, cause, or make?

3. Does it influence anything? If yes, how?

4. Who, if anyone, is involved with it?

5. Is it helpful or harmful to people?

6. Where is it found?

7. Where does it come from?

8. Does it depend on anything? If yes, what?

9. Does it occur at a certain place? Where?

10. Does it occur at a certain time? When?

11. Why is this topic important?

12. What would you like to tell others about it?

## Rehearsing

It often helps to share our ideas for writing before we write. This is called *rehearsing* or *discussing*. Since the rehearsal will help students order their thoughts and generate many more ideas and angles for writing, it can be a valuable prewriting activity. This is especially true for younger or inexperienced writers, as well as students with auditory learning styles.

Rehearsing is most effective when students work with a partner. Working together, one partner assumes the role of speaker while the other listens. The speaker then shares his or her ideas for writing. The listener's responsibility is to summarize what the speaker said, ask questions about anything that seems unclear, and answer any questions the speaker may have. Hearing his or her ideas repeated may help the speaker to clarify and refine them. After the speaker has received feedback, students reverse the roles, with the speaker becoming the listener and the listener the speaker.

# *Activity 5: Rehearsing for Ideas*

Explain to your students how rehearsing can be an effective prewriting activity. After the explanation, you might wish to give them practice in rehearsing. Divide students into pairs, and tell them to select a topic they would like to write about. (If you have an odd number in class, you may work with a student.) Encourage students to use either clustering or idea listing to generate ideas about their topics. Allow about ten minutes for this. Next, have them share their ideas for writing with their partner. One student acts as the speaker and the other as the listener. After the speaker is done and has received feedback, the students reverse the roles. You may find it helpful to hand out copies of the accompanying "A Prewriting Warm-Up." The listeners can use the sheet as a guide to ask questions of the speaker. After this activity, students should write about their topics.

## Role Playing

Role playing is especially useful for generating ideas, dialogue, or information when students are writing stories and must detail the feelings and actions of characters. It can help young writers create believable characters.

# *Activity 6: Role Playing to Find Ideas*

Explain to your students how role playing can be a valuable prewriting strategy. After the explanation, you may like to run the following activity to give your students practice in role playing. Divide the class into groups of four or five. Make sure that there is enough room between groups so that students have space in which to act out their roles.

Ask your students to think of a role they would like to play. They should consider the person they will be playing in a particular situation. A good example is two friends who are walking home from school and find a lost wallet. Students could role-play what the friends do next. Ideally, the situations and roles students choose should include other members of the group. Because of the interaction, having two or more people involved in a role play helps to uncover more ideas than if one role in a situation is acted out. Every member of the group should do at least one role play.

If you wish, hand out copies of the accompanying "Choose a Role," which offers several suggestions for role playing. After the practice role playing, suggest that students think of something important that happened to them, explain the event to the group, and then, with partners, role-play a scene. Afterward students may like to write about this event.

## Researching

Researching is yet another prewriting activity. After a writer has selected a topic and identified general ideas, frequently he or she must gather additional information. While much of the writing done in writing workshop will not require outside research, students should realize that many writing projects do need to be researched.

Explain to your students that before beginning research, they should formulate some initial ideas about a general topic. After deciding on their topic, they should read background information on it. Not only will this help them to identify questions they may have about the topic, it will also help them to focus their ideas and direct their additional research efforts.

The first place many students go for research is the encyclopedia. Explain that although references like encyclopedias can provide general information, students should consult specific books on their topics. They can find these books through the card catalogue of their school or public library. (If some of your students need help in using a traditional or electronic card catalogue, set up library time and present a separate lesson on it.)

With the development of the Internet, the World Wide Web has become an essential source of information. Students need to be aware of the vast data available on countless Web sites throughout the world, which they can easily access by using one of the major search engines. To help your students in searching for information on the Web, distribute copies of "Using Search Engines to Find Information on the Internet."

Finding information is but one aspect of conducting effective research. Identifying useful information is another. In taking notes, emphasize to your students the need to record only specific information that applies to their topic. To make that task easier, suggest that they ask themselves the same questions reporters ask when doing an article: *who, what, where, when, why,* and *how.* By asking themselves these questions as they conduct their research, they are more likely to concentrate on the most important information.

Taking effective notes is an essential research skill. I allow students to use either note cards or ordinary paper. I suggest that they use only one side of each card or sheet for notes and put only one topic on each, because this makes it easier to organize information later. I also require students to include full bibliographical data for each source on each sheet (author, title, place of publication, publisher, date, and pages). Full citation for electronic sources is also required. Not only does this make it easier to go back to the source if facts need to be rechecked, but it also makes compiling a complete bibliography simpler.

# A Prewriting Warm-Up

**Directions:** Listen to your partner as he or she tells you about ideas for writing. Use the following questions to help focus your attention during listening and take notes. When your partner is done, summarize the ideas.

1. What is your partner's purpose for writing? _____

_____

_____

_____

2. Who will the target audience be? _____

_____

_____

3. What is the main idea? _____

_____

_____

_____

4. What are some details? _____

_____

_____

_____

_____

_____

_____

_____

_____

_____

_____

# Choose a Role

**Directions:** Choose one of the following scenes, and role-play the characters with the members of your group.

- You are shopping with some of your friends. On the way home, one of your friends reveals the gold chain he or she shoplifted. With the members of your group, role-play what happens next.

- You and a friend (or friends) are home alone at night, studying upstairs for a big science test. You hear a noise at one of the downstairs back windows. Role-play what you do next.

- You and a friend (or friends) ride your bikes to a local convenience store to buy sodas. When you come out, one of the bikes is gone. With the members of your group, role-play what happens next.

- You did not do your homework. You know that your teacher will be angry and will likely call your parents, who will ground you for the big dance. With a partner playing the teacher, role-play your explanation to your teacher why you did not have your homework.

- You are applying for a summer job that you want very much. You must convince the boss that you are the person to hire. With a partner acting as the boss, role-play how you would handle this important meeting.

- Design your own. With the members of your group, brainstorm some situations for role playing. Select parts, and role-play the characters.

# Using Search Engines to Find Information on the Internet

Search engines are designed to help people find information on the World Wide Web. With millions of Web pages available, search engines have become essential for locating information. The following list includes some of the best search engines:

All the Web, www.alltheweb.com

AltaVista, www.altavista.com

Ask Jeeves, www.ask.com

Excite, www.excite.com

Google, www.google.com

Lycos, www.lycos.com

WebCrawler, www.webcrawler.com

Wise Nut, www.wisenut.com

Yahoo!, www.yahoo.com

Yahooligans, www.yahooligans.com

For more search engines go to www.allsearchengines.com.

## Searching Tips

A major problem when seeking information on the Web is finding too much information, much of which is not useful. Searching for "United States presidents," for example, will likely result in thousands of Web sites, far too many for anyone to check. The following tips can help you to focus your search:

- Enter precise search terms.

- Use single words whenever possible.

- Try to be specific. For example, "Abraham Lincoln" is more specific than "United States presidents."

- Enter multiple spellings when applicable.

- Follow the guidelines provided by the specific search engine.

Be sure to emphasize to your students the importance of taking notes in their own words. Using the words of another is plagiarism (see Mini-Lesson 44 in Section Nine). Make it clear that using the words of another without giving proper credit is literary theft. A plagiarist does a disservice to himself or herself as well as the person whose words are taken without permission. (See "Citing Sources" in Mini-Lesson 44.)

# Activity 7: Using the Internet for Research

This activity requires students to use computers with Internet access. If you do not have computers in your classroom, perhaps you can arrange time in your school's computer room or library.

To start the activity, explain to your students that the Internet is a marvelous resource that offers information on countless topics. There is so much information available on the Internet that the person researching can become overwhelmed. Sometimes separating valuable information from irrelevant facts is a bigger problem than finding information.

To demonstrate this, instruct your students to try a search for the word *dogs* using any of the major search engines. They will likely find a few million Web sites they can check. Explain that each site, called a *hit,* is a potential source of information. Emphasize that checking each site is impossible.

To avoid this problem, the researcher must narrow the search. Suggest that instead of "dogs," students search "hunting dogs." This may bring the number of hits down to a few hundred thousand, but this is still far too many. Now try "beagles." Although a few thousand Web sites are likely to be identified, by now students should realize that by focusing their topic and searching for a key word, or words, they are more likely to find sites with useful information.

## Organizing Writing

Effective organization helps authors write clearly and express exactly what they want to say. This is especially important for assigned topics such as research papers.

Organization can take many forms, from standard outlines to simple lists. The accompanying "A Structure Form" can help students organize ideas by listing main ideas and subsequent details. Be sure that methods of organization do not overwhelm students, making students worry more about the method than the writing. Organization strategies should aid and never inhibit writing.

When I write, I list my ideas, writing details and facts beneath main ideas. I then organize my main ideas in a form that I feel is the most effective structure for the type of writing I am doing.

Outlines or sequence lists enable the author to think through ideas before the actual writing. Tell your students it is a bit like a rehearsal. They can identify main ideas and details, sequence material, cut and paste, and map out the general direction they wish to take with their writing. Emphasize that they will likely make changes and adjustments during drafting and revision and that the basic outline should never be thought of as providing more than general guidance.

# A Structure Form

Main Idea: _____

   Detail: _____

   Detail: _____

   Detail: _____

Main Idea: _____

   Detail: _____

   Detail: _____

   Detail: _____

Main Idea: _____

   Detail: _____

   Detail: _____

   Detail: _____

Main Idea: _____

   Detail: _____

   Detail: _____

   Detail: _____

## Drawing and Diagramming

Although most students do not rely on drawing and diagramming as prewriting activities, a few do. Sometimes these students have artistic ability and feel at ease using drawings and diagrams as part of their efforts to explore ideas. And some students find that sketching can help them uncover ideas and insights. One particularly helpful prewriting method here is storyboarding, in which ideas are sequenced in picture form. Flowcharting is another. Often artwork can be used to enhance the final written piece.

## Journals

Writing journals contain an author's ideas, questions, visions, dreams, and anything in between. They are usually written in the first person and may explore a variety of topics. Sometimes the topics are personal; sometimes they are general. Journals permit students to experiment with new writing forms, help establish the habit of writing, and enable students to witness their growth as writers. Journals also become repositories of ideas for writing.

As the teacher, you must decide on the rules regarding journals in your classroom. Will they be private? Will you look at them? Will they be shared? And if they will be shared, with whom? Once set, these rules should not be violated. If they are, trust will be undermined, and some students may hesitate to write in their journals. You may wish to hand out the accompanying "Writing Journal Guidelines for Students" and discuss its points in a mini-lesson.

I recommend reviewing the journals of students periodically. This is an opportunity to respond to their writing and helps ensure that all students write in their journals regularly. While some teachers prefer to collect the journals of their students at set intervals (every two weeks, for example), others prefer to read a few from each class two or three times a week. I try to read everyone's journal at least once every two weeks or so, a schedule that I find makes the workload manageable and still enables me to keep up with my students.

To assure students of their privacy, you may instruct them to fold down any pages of their journals that they do not want you to read. In this way, students feel free to include personal thoughts in their journals. However, you should tell them that if you read something in a journal that leads you to believe someone is in danger, you are obligated to report your concerns.

While you should not grade or correct the writing in journals—only finished pieces should be used for grading—you should comment on your students' writing. Offer suggestions, constructive remarks, questions, and encouragement whenever possible. Sometimes students will respond to the teacher's comments, and they and the teacher will carry on a correspondence through the journals.

A potential problem with writing journals is that some students use them simply as a way to record the day's events. They slip into the routine of writing diary-like entries without reflection or real purpose. You can reduce this by encouraging students to write about a variety of topics and take what they feel are the better entries and develop them into finished pieces.

# Writing Journal Guidelines for Students

1. Use a standard spiral notebook for your journal. When you run out of space, continue your journal in another notebook. Number your journals.

2. Use your journal only for writing. Do not use it for other subjects.

3. Write in your journal outside class as well as during writing workshop. Write in it whenever you have something to record or reflect on.

4. Write about topics that interest you. They can be real or fiction. Date your entries.

5. Experiment with new writing forms and styles in your journal.

6. Be alert that I will read your journal periodically and offer comments and suggestions. Feel free to write back to me in your journal. We can carry on a dialogue.

7. If you have entries you do not want me to read, fold over the page and write across it, "Don't read." I will respect your privacy, but remember that if I read something that I feel endangers you or someone else, I must report it.

8. Develop some of your good journal entries into polished pieces.

9. Share what you feel are your best entries with the class.

10. Review your journal periodically and see how you are growing as a writer.

Copyright © 2006 by Gary Robert Muschla

---

**Some Possible Topics:**

| | | |
|---|---|---|
| My Family | Values | Worrying |
| Being the Youngest | Being the Oldest | Home |
| Changes in Me | Friendship | Hobbies |
| Time of Happiness | Time of Sadness | Why |

---

Journals offer students the opportunity to reflect on their world and expand their awareness of what is happening in their lives. For many students, journals become a rich source of ideas for writing.

## Idea Folders

Idea folders are containers for ideas. In this, they are similar to journals. You can use ordinary manila folders or big envelopes (ten by thirteen inches is a good size). Idea folders are the place to put clippings from newspapers or magazines, questions that do not get entered into journals, or anything else that can be an idea for further reflection or future writing.

If you encourage students to keep idea folders, remind them to go through their folders periodically as a type of house cleaning. Idea folders can be most valuable when students are having trouble finding a topic for writing.

I keep an idea folder too. It is an old box that once held envelopes. Anything that I feel might one day be an idea for writing gets dropped into the box. Although most of the tidbits do not amount to anything, a few do, and they justify the effort. If you decide to use idea folders in your classroom, you should discuss their benefits with your students.

## Personal Experience

One of the best places to find ideas for writing is in personal experience. Things that happen to us or things that we have learned about can often spark an idea.

Discuss the importance of personal experience to a person's writing. Explain to your students that it is likely that they have already had many experiences that could provide fine material for writing, but that they have not uncovered these ideas. Tell them that good ideas for writing are often hidden and tucked away in ordinary events. We must search for them.

# *Activity 8: Personal Experience and Ideas*

Explain to your students that taking a personal inventory of their experiences is a way to discover ideas for writing. The accompanying "Inventory of Personal Experience" can help students identify possible topics for writing. Hand out copies to your students, and encourage them to answer the questions of the inventory in their journals. They can write as much or as little about each question as they like. Not all the questions need to be answered in one period.

Some students look at the list of questions and find an idea for writing immediately. Others answer several questions before finding a topic. Any questions they do answer should go into their journals for later use. Whenever students become stumped for a topic during writing workshop, suggest that they check their journals for ideas.

# Inventory of Personal Experience

**Directions:** Answer the following questions in your journal. Write as much or as little as you wish about each question. Reviewing your answers from time to time will help you to generate ideas for writing.

- What am I interested in?

- What things do I especially like? What things do I dislike?

- What makes me different from other people?

- What do I like about myself? What do I dislike?

- What would I change about myself?

- What makes me feel good about myself?

- What do I care about most?

- What would I most like to know?

- What would I like to do?

- Where would I like to go?

- What exciting things have I done?

- Do I know any interesting people? Why are they interesting?

- What could I share with others?

- What would I like to change about the world?

- What are some things that have made me happy?

- What are some things that have made me sad?

- What are some things that have made me angry?

- What are some things that have made me afraid?

- What advice or insight can I share with others?

## Observation

The world is an interesting place, and it is full of ideas for writing. Encourage your students to become keen observers of their world. They should learn to see things not in isolation, but in relation to other things. How do things affect each other? How are they connected? Encourage your students to use all of their senses—seeing, hearing, touching, smelling, and tasting—to gain full appreciation of their world.

# Activity 9: Observation and Ideas

Explain to your students how observation is important to prewriting. Offer them this example. Most people see a tree only as a trunk, branches, and leaves. It is much more. Its roots hold the soil and draw water from the ground. It provides a home for birds, squirrels, and other animals. Its leaves are food and shelter for insects. Trees help provide the world's atmospheric oxygen. Every tree is a part of an ecosystem, and each of these relationships can be a possible topic for writing.

As a follow-up to your explanation, you may wish to assign this activity. Ask your students to choose a place; a park, backyard, or their rooms are some examples. (Emphasize that they should pick a safe place.) They are to stay at this place for fifteen minutes to a half-hour and observe the spot. What is there? What are the relationships? How is each of their senses affected? To help your students with their observations, you can hand out copies of "What Do You See?" Encourage your students to write about their observations in their journals.

## Angles and Viewpoints

Suggest that your students view things from various angles and viewpoints in their search for ideas and topics for writing. There are several sides to every issue. While light contains the colors of the rainbow, all those colors are rarely seen. Few issues come in simple black or white; most have several shades between extremes. Teach your students to look for those shades.

# Activity 10: Viewing from All Points and Angles

Explain to your students how excellent ideas for writing can be discovered by viewing things from various angles. When most people agree on an issue, tell your students to consider the positions of those who disagree. Why do these individuals disagree with the majority? What do they see that others do not? Why do they feel the way they do? Tell your students to look at things from the back, side, top, and bottom. Everybody knows what things look like from the front.

# What Do You See?

**Directions:** Choose a place to observe—for example, a park, backyard, or a shopping mall. (Be sure to choose a safe place.) Stay at this place for fifteen to thirty minutes and observe what happens. Answering the following questions will help focus your observations. Use the back of this sheet if you need more space. You may wish to write about your observations in your journal.

1. What is the place you selected to observe? _____
   _____

2. Describe this place in terms of your senses (sight, sound, taste, touch, and smell).
   _____
   _____
   _____
   _____
   _____
   _____
   _____
   _____

3. Describe any relationships you see. _____
   _____
   _____
   _____
   _____
   _____

4. Describe anything that was unexpected or surprising. _____
   _____
   _____
   _____
   _____
   _____

To help your students gain an appreciation of varying points of view, try this activity. Divide the class into groups of four to six and ask the students to consider this statement: "Parents have the right to search their children's rooms." Working in their groups, students are to discuss the statement. Each group should select a recorder to write down the major ideas the group discusses. Instruct your students to consider the issue from their point of view as well as the position of their parents. Why might parents search a child's room? What might they be worried about? Is such an act ever justified? What about the feelings of the child? Does the child have a right to absolute privacy? When might a child not have a right to absolute privacy?

To aid students with their discussion, you can distribute copies of "Seeing All Sides." Allow students ten to fifteen minutes to discuss the topic. After the discussion, have a member of each group report to the class the major ideas the group discussed. After each group has shared their discussion, point out how many different ideas have been discovered and how one idea usually leads to others. Before ending the class, be sure to note some of the ideas that can probably be developed into topics for writing.

## Using Questions to Explore Topics

Once students find topics for writing, many have trouble with development. They lack the skill to examine their subjects, and they are unable to gain a full understanding of them. Many good topics for writing are lost because of this.

First, students should consider the scope of their subjects. Some topics are broad and connect with other topics. What are the areas of overlap? Finding those areas can often help students zero in on fresh angles for writing. It is not uncommon for students to start with a topic and then find a better one to write about as they explore that topic.

Focusing on a topic that is narrow enough for writing is essential. Unfortunately, this is a step that many students resist. You must constantly remind them how important this is. Tell them to look for the most interesting aspect of a topic. What excites them about it? What would others like to know about it?

Students should also consider their target audience. For whom are they writing? Other students? Parents? The public? Knowing their target audience enables them to gear their writing for that particular group.

When considering nonfiction writing topics, the most basic questions to answer are the *five W's* and *how:*

- What is the subject?
- Who is/was involved?
- When does/did this happen?
- Where does/did it happen?
- Why does/did it happen?
- How does/did it happen?

These questions can help students to understand their topics in a general way. But there is more. Students should go beyond the five *W's* and *how.* The prewriting strategies discussed earlier are effective in helping students to elaborate on their topics.

Name _____  Date _____  Section _____

# Seeing All Sides

**Directions:** Think about this statement: "Parents have the right to search their children's rooms." First consider it from the point of view of a student; then imagine being a parent. How might a parent react to the statement? Answering the questions below will help you to see both sides of the issue. After completing the worksheet, you might like to explore this topic further and write about it in your journal.

1. Do parents ever have the right to search a child's room? If yes, when? If no, why not?

   Student Answer: _____

   _____

   Parent Answer: _____

   _____

2. What might a parent's reasons be for searching a child's room?

   Student Answer: _____

   _____

   Parent Answer: _____

   _____

3. Does the fact that a child is a minor in the parents' home give parents a right to search? Why or why not?

   Student Answer: _____

   _____

   Parent Answer: _____

   _____

## *Activity 11: Focusing Topics*

Explain to your students the importance of focusing their topics before writing. Stress the need to narrow their topic and also the value of recognizing how the topic is linked to other subjects. The points of connection can often provide unique insight to the topic. Discuss the target audience too. Knowing for whom he or she is writing enables an author to tailor the work for that particular reader. Finally, talk about the five *W*'s and *how,* but note that good writers go beyond these questions and ask even more. As an example, distribute copies of "Exploring a Writing Topic." Review the questions with your students, and encourage them to consider such questions when they develop topics for writing.

Prewriting encompasses the many methods that writers use to find and develop ideas. Introduce as many of the prewriting strategies as you can, and encourage your students to use the ones they feel are most helpful. A solid commitment to prewriting is the first step to effective writing.

Name _____    Date _____    Section _____

# Exploring a Writing Topic

**Directions:** Whenever you are thinking about a topic for writing, consider the following:

1.  Think of the big picture. How broad is your topic?

2.  Where does the topic overlap or connect with others? (Points of overlap can be good topics for writing.)

3.  Use the five W's and how to define your topic. (What? Who? When? Where? Why? How?)

4.  Once you understand the broad topic, narrow it down. What exactly do you want to write about?

5.  After focusing your topic, examine it again. What are the parts now? Can it be narrowed further?

6.  What is the history of your topic? Where did it come from?

7.  What is its purpose?

8.  What does it affect? How does it affect other things?

9.  How is it influenced by other things?

10. What will your topic be like in the future? How will it change?

11. Why is the topic important?

12. Why are you interested in the topic?

13. What is your purpose in writing about this topic?

14. Who will be your audience?

15. What do you want to tell your audience about this topic?

# SECTION 4

# DRAFTING

**Drafting is the stage** of the writing process when ideas are shaped and expressed on paper. After drafting begins, the author moves back and forth through composing, reviewing, and revising the draft until the draft is completed. For many authors, writing the draft is a time of high energy and emotion.

## Writing the Draft

The author reaches the drafting stage when he moves from prewriting to the actual writing of the piece. He may begin the draft fast, in a rush from prewriting to composing carried forward by great enthusiasm, or he may start slowly with hesitation, false starts, and rethinking. Perhaps the writer is not sure of his lead paragraph; maybe he is uncertain how best to support a main idea in the opening paragraph; or he might not know how to sequence his ideas.

Whether the author writes with pen on paper or with computer using the latest software, the typical composing part of the drafting stage is filled with periods of rapid and slow writing, interspersed with pauses. As the writer works, ideas are expanded, clarified, and reformulated. He becomes deeply involved with the piece.

Some teachers encourage their students to write their drafts rapidly in the belief that getting the ideas out and in some form on paper is most important. This clearly works for some writers, but it ignores the fact that each writer is an individual. For every author who writes the first draft in a swift burst of energy, there is the writer who frequently rereads what she has done so far; reconsiders the sequence of ideas; reflects on the lead, development, or conclusion; or decides to change details. For these writers, composing often overlaps with revision. (This type of revision should not be confused with the revision stage of the writing process, when authors revise a finished draft.)

Students work on drafts at their own rate. Some complete their drafts with only one or two stops, their imaginations entirely involved, while others work in spurts. Some splash ideas down onto the paper like painters, and others uncover ideas tentatively, as if never certain that the thought they are expressing is the right one. Still others revise heavily as they go along, agonizing over choosing just the right word.

Once the first draft has been completed, a student is ready for the next stage of the writing process: revision. This does not mean that drafting is done. Heavy revision may lead back to drafting, and students may produce one, two, three, or more drafts of the same piece.

## *Activity 12: Questions to Ask During Drafting*

Discuss the drafting stage of the writing process with your students, noting how writers often shift between composing, reviewing, and revising. Explain that writers who keep their purpose and readers in mind when writing their drafts usually find their overall task of writing to be easier. Write the following questions on the board or an overhead projector, and discuss them with your students. Emphasize that asking themselves questions like these will help them to keep their thoughts focused on their topic:

- What is my purpose for writing?
- What will my readers want to know about my topic?
- How can I best arrange my information to make my ideas clear to my readers?
- What will make a good lead?
- What are my main ideas?
- What details can I use to develop my main ideas?
- What will make a strong conclusion?

## The Foundations of Good Writing

Being aware of the elements of good writing can help students as they work on their drafts. While the types of writing and forms of expression vary, all good writing shares common foundations:

- *Good writing is interesting.* The words and ideas draw readers into what the writer is saying. The writer knows her audience and tailors her work so that her readers will feel a kinship with her. Readers will understand her even if they do not always agree with what she is saying.

- *Good writing is simple and concise.* The prose is tight, and ideas are expressed clearly. Unnecessary words, sentences, paragraphs, and pages have been eliminated.

- *Good writing reflects the clear thinking of its author.* The author has examined her material, considered its arrangement, and communicates exactly what she wants to say.
- *Good writing exhibits freshness.* Its style flows naturally out of the author's experiences and perceptions. It is free of redundancies and clichés and relies on strong imagery to paint pictures for readers. Its descriptions are precise and colorful, exciting the senses so that the reader is transported, through imagination, to the scene the author is sharing.
- *Good writing employs correct mechanics.* Mistakes in punctuation, grammar, spelling, and usage undermine writing and obscure ideas. They can ruin what otherwise might be a fine piece.

## *Activity 13: The Elements of Good Writing*

Discuss with your students the elements of good writing. Write the following statements on the board or an overhead projector and encourage your students to share their ideas on each. It is likely your students will find many areas of agreement:

- Good writing is interesting.
- Good writing is simple and concise.
- Good writing reflects the clear thinking of its author.
- Good writing is fresh.
- Good writing has correct mechanics.

## Strategies to Aid Drafting

Some students find drafting to be the hardest stage of the writing process. The ideas that have been generated during prewriting must now be written in an organized fashion. That can be an unnerving prospect.

There are several strategies you can employ to help your students with their drafts. First, remember that every student is an individual. Your students write at different paces. Avoid breaking down your writing schedule into a tight regimen in which everyone must be done with his or her draft on the same day. Some students will be done before that, and others will need more time. Although deadlines are appropriate to ensure that everyone completes drafts, they should be liberal enough to allow for individual working styles.

You undoubtedly will have students who say that they do not know how to start their drafts. When you ask them for some possible openings, they may have nothing to offer. For these students, you may have to suggest that they simply begin writing about their topics, which will engage their minds and warm them to the task of composing. Explain that many professional authors begin in the body of their pieces and write their openings last.

As your students are writing, refrain from interrupting them. Let them work. Interruptions—even a pat on the back—at this point can cause good ideas to be lost.

Circulate around the room and help students who have questions or are blocked. If a student is having trouble clarifying ideas, you might encourage him to tell you orally what he is trying to write. If he is having trouble deciding on a lead, you might ask him what kinds of leads he is considering and ask him to share with you what he feels are the strengths and weaknesses of each. If a student is having trouble with sequence, you might suggest that he list his ideas in order of importance.

Because they lack confidence, some students will ask you what they should do. Offer suggestions, but encourage them to make the decisions. Emphasize that the writing is theirs, and they must decide how it will be.

Sometimes during their drafting, you will need to help students focus ideas. You can help young writers over a rough spot by asking questions like: "Can you tell me more of how you would like to develop this?" or "Can you add some description here?"

When students get blocked, you might suggest they work with a partner or peer group and explain what they are trying to say. Sometimes talking about their writing can help students sort their ideas enough to resume work. At other times, the partner or peers can provide the support that can help the writer move forward.

Sometimes students will be working well on a draft when the class period ends. In such cases, suggest that they write a few ideas in the margins of their paper about how they will continue. Although they may change direction when they resume writing, jotting down a few notes helps to provide some direction and often makes it easier to retrieve thoughts. To help get the creative juices flowing the next day, suggest that students begin by rewriting (or simply copying over) the last paragraph of the day before. This will help them to reengage their minds with their drafts.

Since mechanics can be corrected during editing, they are not a priority during drafting. Tell your students to concentrate on writing now. The most important consideration when working on a draft is to keep fully involved with writing. For example, some students may feel that they must stop writing to consult a thesaurus to find a precise word in an expression. Suggest that they can do this during revision. Sometimes students stop writing to check a dictionary for the correct spelling of a word. I remember one boy, whose well-meaning mother had told him to look up words he did not know how to spell. This boy stopped repeatedly while writing his drafts to check if he was spelling words correctly. He was so concerned about spelling that he had trouble writing. To help him maintain a flow of thoughts, I suggested that he simply sound out the words he was unsure of and keep writing. He could check the spelling later. The same advice is valid for questions regarding punctuation and grammar. All can be checked and corrected during editing. Such advice does not minimize the importance of mechanics, but rather places mechanics in its proper stage of the writing process.

When students worry about mechanics while writing their drafts, they may become so anxious about making mistakes that they are distracted from communicating their ideas. Their writing becomes slow, and their enthusiasm and energy vanish. Instead of focusing on expression, unity, logic, and development, they worry about periods and commas. As your students become more skilled in writing, they will become more aware of mechanics. Moreover, the skills of mechanics that you teach during mini-lessons and conferences will begin to be internalized.

The purpose of the draft is to get ideas down on paper. Explain to your students that when drafting, they should focus on the actual writing. They should write with emotion, and try to express their ideas with power and clarity.

Students are often reluctant to do a draft because they must commit their ideas to paper in an organized manner. To some, filling that blank sheet can seem impossible. Sometimes you may have to suggest that students begin writing whatever comes to mind about their topics in an effort to start ideas flowing. For most students, once they begin the draft, the writing becomes easier.

Encourage your students to finish every draft they begin. Although revision, editing, and publishing remain to be done, the completion of the draft is in itself an accomplishment.

# SECTION 5

# REVISION

**Revision is the stage** of the writing process in which writers "re-see" their work. Although some revision may occur during drafting, the best time for revision is after the draft has been completed. Writers can then look at their drafts as whole pieces.

Revision includes activities such as adding to, deleting from, reshaping, and polishing the writing of the draft, as well as making sure that what has been said is clear and is precisely what the writer intended. Revision should always be selective and focused, concentrating on areas that need work and leaving the rest of the draft alone.

## Revision Mechanics

When you begin teaching revision, you may find that your students do not know the mechanics of how to revise their drafts—the simple ways to add and delete information. And you may find that some students are reluctant to make any changes, because their previous teachers corrected and revised their papers for them. After red-penciling, these students would merely recopy their drafts and hand in final copies, the only changes being the ones made by their teachers.

To revise their work efficiently, students must understand how to make changes. Carets (∧) can be used for inserting words, phrases, or sentences. Deletions can be made by crossing out material, and arrows can be used to connect different parts of writing. Cutting and pasting, stapling, and sticky notes are useful for changing order and making additions. A list of editor's marks (see "Editor's Marks" in Section Six) contains symbols students may use in revising their work.

## Teaching Revision

Since most students lack the skills to revise their writing, you must offer direction. I start by telling my students that virtually all writers revise their work; few manage to write exactly what they wish the first time. Good writing is a result of good revision.

Next, I suggest that before making any changes, students read their entire drafts to get a feeling for the scope and flow. Sometimes reading their drafts out loud is helpful because they can hear the rhythm of their words.

Finally, I tell my students to concentrate on the essential characteristics of good writing: unity, order, and conciseness. As they become more skilled at revision, I add more elements, which I draw from the mini-lessons in Part Three of this book.

# Revising for Unity

In revising for unity (or focus), students should determine if their words, phrases, and sentences build to a single purpose. Is there a common line that ties everything together? A piece about soccer, for example, should remain focused on soccer and not digress to baseball.

A unified piece has a clear opening, solid development, and a strong conclusion. Main ideas are supported with details, but the details do not overshadow the ideas they support. The style should also be consistent and appropriate for the piece. A lighthearted style would not be proper for a serious piece, and a straightforward style might not be a good choice for a horror short story. In a unified piece, everything draws together to give the author's ideas clarity and impact.

# Revising for Order

Order addresses logic and form. As students reread their pieces, tell them to examine the development. Does each sentence and idea logically follow the one before it? Does the piece progress from a beginning to a conclusion? Are the facts valid and presented consistently? Is the author's point getting across to the reader? Young authors often assume that readers know what they (the authors) are saying even when they fail to say it.

When students have trouble determining whether the order of their writing is consistent, suggest that they list the main ideas of their piece. A simple list can often help to clarify a logical sequence of ideas. It can also identify gaps in development that might otherwise not be apparent.

Writing that is logical and follows a consistent form is easy for readers to read. It is a goal for which all writers should strive.

# Revising for Conciseness

Conciseness is vital for clarity. When pieces become cluttered with unnecessary material in which several words are used where one or two are sufficient, ideas become obscure. The writing also becomes tiresome and boring because readers have to sort through too many words to decipher what the author is saying. Here are some cluttered sentences that can easily be made more concise:

CLUTTERED: The horse's nature was gentle.

CONCISE: The horse was gentle.

CLUTTERED: The fox came up to the rabbit slyly.

CONCISE: The fox crept up on the rabbit. [Note that the stronger verb *crept* eliminates the need for the adverb.]

Conciseness is also compromised by redundancy. A good example is the phrase "serious danger." A dangerous condition *is* serious. Another is the phrase "he thought to himself." Unless he is telepathic, to whom else *could* he think? Redundancies are easy to revise. The offending word or words are simply eliminated. (See Mini-Lesson 20 in Section Nine.)

# Activity 14: Revision Strategies

Explain the mechanics of revision to your students: how carets can be used for insertions, how material can be deleted by crossing out, and how arrows can be used to connect the sections of a piece. Also mention the advantages of cutting and pasting and using sticky notes. You may wish to project the accompanying "The Mechanics of Revision" to show your students a draft with examples of revision.

---

### THE MECHANICS OF REVISION
### Bringing a Puppy Home

There are few things as demanding as raising a puppy. But there are few things as rewarding either. ~~Puppies can bring a great deal of joy to your house, but a lot of work, too.~~

When you bring your puppy home, you should do all you can to reduce his stress. Remember, the puppy has just been separated from his mother and littermates.

He is probably frightened. ~~You should~~ show him kindness and attention but ~~not too much~~. Don't tire him out. That will only make his adjustment harder. You should have a place for your puppy to stay. Dogs are den animals by nature. They desire a small place of their own, like a wooden crate or a box. You should put a blanket or some carpeting in there for him. And you should keep it clean. Your puppy will come to like his home.

It is important that you feed your puppy a healthy diet. You should check with the person you bought him from to find out what he has been eating. Continuing that diet will prevent digestion problems. If you decide to change his food, do it gradually, mixing new food with his old.

One of your ~~first~~ responsibilities is to take your puppy to a veterinarian for an examination. ~~He~~ Your puppy must have his shots to protect him from diseases like rabies and distemper. Your vet can also advise you about ~~his~~ Your puppy's diet and answer any questions about his health that you may have.

*Raising a puppy is a big responsibility. But if you do a good job you will have a fine companion for many years to come.*

Discuss the article with your students and point out why the revisions were made. For example, the third sentence of the first paragraph was deleted because it was redundant: it said the same thing as the first two sentences. Note the change in the second paragraph and also that "not too much" is unnecessary to the writer's intention. In the revised third paragraph that begins "You should," "by nature" is unnecessary, the fragment is corrected, and connecting the two sentences helps the writing to flow more smoothly. In the fifth paragraph, one may wonder why a "first" responsibility would be placed at the end of the piece. Also in that paragraph, the change to "your puppy" reduces the chance that the reader might mistakenly think that the vet needs the shots or that his diet is being discussed. A conclusion is added as well.

If you want to take this activity a little further, ask your students if the piece addresses every question they would have about raising puppies. (They might suggest adding material on housebreaking or training.)

## The Use of Computers in Revision

I remember the days of writing on a typewriter. These are not fond memories. Revision back then was a painstaking, tedious process where the actual improvement of writing sometimes became overshadowed by the sheer drudgery of retyping pages of changes and corrections.

Computers and word processing software have eliminated much of that drudgery, freeing authors to focus on the real purpose of revision, which is to make their writing better. If your students have access to computers, encourage them to use the computers for writing.

Unfortunately, although most students will come to your class adept at using a computer, many will be relatively unskilled at using the features of their word processing software. Most have never been shown how to use a computer to revise writing, and they will use only a small fraction of their computer's capabilities. See the accompanying "Computers and Writers."

If you have access to computers in your classroom, discuss their use for writing with your students. If your students have a computer class in your school, speak with the instructor so that students are taught word processing skills. A computer teacher may be well versed in the capabilities of computers but may not provide the necessary emphasis on the features that writers use.

You may find that some students become comfortable revising entirely on computers. Others want to print out a hard copy and make corrections on paper, then return to their computers to make the changes on the text. Professional authors use both methods, with a variety of methods in between.

You may also find that with some students, you may be reading material on computers and offering suggestions for improvement. I have had students e-mail material as file attachments, which I have read, commented on, and e-mailed back. Without question, computers make revision (and the overall process of writing) easier.

I sometimes hear friends and colleagues say how they miss the good old days. I do not miss typewriters.

# Computers and Writers

Computers have become one of a writer's best tools. They make the mechanical task of writing and revising easier, freeing the author to focus on producing the best writing he or she can. Following are some of the tasks computers can help writers do.

- Add words, sentences, paragraphs, or entire pages.

- Delete words, sentences, paragraphs, or entire pages.

- Move text from one place to another.

- Automatically adjust pagination.

- Copy text.

- Save writing.

- Make backup copies of writing.

- Check spelling.

- Check grammar.

- Find the "right" word by way of an included thesaurus.

- Print writing.

- Insert art.

- Allow the writer to use various print sizes and types.

- Allow writers to check sources (through the Internet or electronic databases).

- Allow writers to communicate with others by e-mail.

# Revision Pitfalls to Avoid

Students often ask how they should revise their writing. While you may offer options, resist making the revisions yourself, since this relieves the student of the responsibility for reworking and polishing his ideas and slows his growth as a writer.

You should also be cautious of using labels like *awkward, vague,* or *illogical* when referring to the writing of your students. If they do not understand the meanings of such words, they will not know how to correct their mistakes. Instead of *awkward,* say "Your writing here could be smoother," and ask the student for some ways he could revise the material. Instead of *vague,* say, "You need more details here. What details could make this clearer for the reader?" Instead of *illogical,* ask, "Would this really happen?"

While you should be cautious in using negatives, you should discuss writing with your students using words authors use. For example, refer to the beginning of an article as the *lead* and its ending as the *conclusion.* In a story, the resolution occurs in the *climax.* Using correct terminology—words such as *scene, details, theme, mood,* and *unity*—promotes understanding and helps students to see themselves as authors.

# *Activity 15: A Revision Plan*

The steps in this activity provide a plan that students can follow when they approach revision. Start by explaining that virtually every author revises his or her work. As writers become more skilled in revision, they develop their own procedures because revision is as much art as it is craft. No two authors revise in the same way. Until your students become comfortable with their own methods for revision, they will likely find it helpful to follow a plan similar to the one offered here.

Discuss the following steps with your students. Depending on your students, you may want to break this activity into parts and cover the material in two or more sessions:

1. Read the piece silently and then aloud. Reading it aloud can highlight the flow and rhythm of the words.

2. Consider the whole piece first. What are its strengths? What parts do you like the best? What are its weaknesses? How can the weaknesses be improved? What can be added? What can be eliminated?

3. Focus on the paragraphs. Are they well organized? Does each have a main idea that is supported by details? Do the paragraphs follow each other logically? Are the transitions between them smooth?

4. Consider the sentences. Do they follow each other logically? Are they clear?

5. Focus on the words and phrases. Which should be changed? Which are examples of clutter?

# Writing Conferences

A writing conference occurs when a student meets with you or with another student or students about writing. Conferences need not be formal or lengthy. Some may last only a minute or two. They may take place at the student's desk, a writing table, the teacher's desk, or even on the floor.

The purpose of conferences is to help students improve their writing. You might listen to a student read her opening in an effort to make it stronger, help another student focus his topic, or suggest ways a student can improve imagery. Through conferences, you can share tips for better writing, help students learn the techniques of revision, and reinforce the skills you taught during mini-lessons. You can uncover common problems students are having in your class and address those problems with mini-lessons.

No matter where you meet, how long the conference lasts, or what it is about, successful writing conferences share the same elements. Most important, they are focused. You must address only one or two points in the conference. More than that will overwhelm students, making it hard for them to accomplish the necessary changes. Successful conferences require an atmosphere of support and cooperation, so that you and your students will feel comfortable enough in the conference setting to ask questions and discuss how their writing can be improved. Finally, successful conferences help students to read and evaluate their work critically, leading to the growth of writing skills.

I suggest that you move around the room and go to your students for conferences. I find that when I stay at my desk, students line up for help. Not only do some begin "fooling around," but valuable writing time is lost as they wait. By circulating, you avoid the lines. Moreover, when you move around the room, it is easier to monitor the behavior and progress of your students.

Many conferences begin with students asking you a question or sharing a problem. With others, you will have to initiate the conferences. You might start by asking, "How are you doing with this?" If a student simply says okay, ask him to read some of his writing to you. You may then respond to the writing. If a student does not need help, let him work and move on to another.

# *Activity 16: A Role-Played Writing Conference*

When most students in class do not know what to expect in a writing conference, I role-play a conference for them. (If your students have experience with the writing workshop, this activity may not be necessary.) I try to do this early in the school year. Select a student to play the part of the student. You will be the teacher. Set up a desk or a table in a section of the room.

The role playing begins with the student working on a piece. You approach, and then the two of you act out the script that is provided in this section. You might wish to make copies so that you and the student can read from it. (Note that there are two scripts: one in which you begin the conference, "A Writing Conference Started by the Teacher," and the other in which the student initiates the meeting, "A Writing Conference Started by a Student.") At the end of the role playing, point out to your students that you will offer guidance during conferences, but that they must retain the ownership of their pieces; that is, the writing must be theirs, not yours.

You will encounter various situations and problems during conferences with your students. Most require guidance or a gentle nudge to help the student around an obstacle that is blocking her. Frequently, the key is in asking questions that can get the student thinking about solutions to the problem, such as:

- Who's your audience?
- What are you trying to get across here?
- What do you want the reader to think about this?
- What are the possibilities from this point?
- What's your favorite part?
- What's the most troublesome part?

These and similar questions can help young authors around problems that can block their way to finishing a satisfying piece.

When a student asks a question about her writing, you may offer suggestions or alternatives but leave the decision of what she will do to her. Letting her find her own answer is the best way of learning. It is vital that you do not tell your students what to do or how to revise. Once you begin making decisions, you take ownership of the piece. It no longer belongs fully to the writer, and once that happens, motivation is undermined. Why should a student work as hard on a piece that is not hers anymore?

When you ask questions, make them open-ended—for example:

- What's your main point?
- What do you want to tell us about the house?
- How would you describe the storm?

# A Writing Conference Started by the Teacher

TEACHER: How are you doing?

STUDENT: Okay.

TEACHER (SITS DOWN BY STUDENT): Where are you on this?

STUDENT (FROWNS): After the opening.

TEACHER: How can I help?

STUDENT (HESITATES): I'm stuck.

TEACHER: You mean you don't know where to go next?

STUDENT (NODS): Yeah.

TEACHER: Can you read it to me?

STUDENT: All right. (BEGINS READING) "I moved from New York City last year to this town. I didn't want to move. I didn't like our new home." (LOOKS AT TEACHER)

TEACHER: I think you started out fine, but now I'd like to know more. Could you tell me why you didn't want to move? And why didn't you like your new home?

# A Writing Conference Started by a Student

(Student is seated at a desk and raises hand.)

TEACHER (APPROACHES STUDENT): How can I help, [student's name]?

STUDENT: I'm writing an essay, but I'm not sure about the sequence.

TEACHER: How did you arrange your information?

STUDENT: I just took my ideas and wrote them down.

TEACHER: What don't you like about the way it turned out?

STUDENT: Well, it just doesn't sound right.

TEACHER: Can you read what you have for me?

STUDENT (BEGINS READING FROM PAPER): "Recycling is an important way to conserve the earth's resources. When we recycle, we take materials that were used before and change them so that we can use them again. We can recycle paper, glass, plastic, steel, and aluminum. Recycling helps to save landfill space. It also helps to save energy."

TEACHER: Umm. You have a lot of good facts there, but I agree that you could arrange them better. Try thinking of ways you might reorder the sentences in that paragraph.

STUDENT (THINKS A FEW MOMENTS): What about moving the last two sentences to the beginning of the paragraph? They follow the idea of the earth's resources.

TEACHER: That's a possibility. Why don't you try that?

# Some Conference Strategies

Following are some typical writing problems and questions you might consider asking. As you pose questions to your students, they will begin to pose those same questions to themselves and each other. They will become more aware of writing and become their own evaluators. They will also eventually become more critical readers of published writing.

Conference problem:   The topic is too broad.

Teacher's questions:   What's the most important idea in your piece? What is your purpose in writing this? What's the most interesting part of this piece?

Conference problem:   The writing lacks information.

Teacher's questions:   What more can you tell me about your topic? What else might the reader want to know?

Conference problem:   There is no opening.

Teacher's questions:   How can you lead into your story? How can you hook the reader?

Conference problem:   There is no conclusion.

Teacher's questions:   How can you end your piece? Is this a satisfying ending? Does the conclusion help your reader understand your main point?

Conference problem:   The writing lacks organization.

Teacher's questions:   How can you order your ideas to make them clearer? Are some ideas more important than others? Would a sequence of some kind make sense here?

Conference problem:   The writing lacks unity.

Teacher's questions:   Do all your ideas fit your purpose? What is your main focus?

Conference problem:   The writing is bland and colorless.

Teacher's questions:   Can you tell me what it would be like if I were there? What would my senses tell me? What are some interesting details you could add to this?

Conference problem:   The writer uses too much description or lacks conciseness.

Teacher's questions:   How can you make your writing tighter? What details might you delete without taking away from the scene you have created? Are you worried about length? [Some students will admit to padding.]

| | |
|---|---|
| Conference problem: | The writer relies on passive rather than active voice. |
| Teacher's questions: | What stronger action verbs can you use? Do you know the difference between active and passive constructions? [You may have to give a quick lesson.] |

## Peer Conferences

Peer conferences are one way students can work together and help each other. These conferences can take place with partners or small groups.

During a peer conference, the writer reads her work (or an excerpt) out loud to her partner or group. The listeners respond by asking questions or offering suggestions. If necessary, the writer may clarify. The purpose of the peer conference is to help the author see how her work is being understood by readers (listeners) and decide how to improve her writing.

I often use peer conferences at the end of the class. Students meet and share their work with group members. The group members respond and help the writer plan his next steps. If a student does not have a finished draft to share, he may read a portion of what he has written. If he has spent the period developing an idea for writing, perhaps by clustering, he can explain what he has done. It is important that everyone comes to the conference with something to share. Sharing experiences and problems about writing helps to disseminate information and build a feeling of community. Even reluctant writers begin to share through gentle encouragement and cooperation. Peer conferences at the end of class provide a meaningful closure to the day's work.

Before students can be expected to carry out successful peer conferences, they need to know how conferences between students function. One of the ways you can help them is to sit in on their conferences and model the appropriate behavior. You may listen to a student read his piece and ask a question about it or react to something you liked. Make suggestions cautiously, however, since teacher-initiated suggestions can be interpreted as directives.

The following procedure is also helpful in guiding students in peer conferences. Organize the students into groups of three to five. Group members decide who reads his piece first. This student author reads his piece twice. During the first reading, the others merely listen for the overall scope. During the second reading, the listeners focus on specific areas. These areas are highlighted on the accompanying "Peer Conference Questions." During the early part of the year, you might write separate questions on note cards and assign each listener a different question to answer. This makes the conference easier for students to manage. Every time a new author reads, the cards are passed to the person to the left. This ensures that each student will have a chance to listen for a different part of writing. As students become more familiar with the process, they will be able to listen to more parts and ask their own questions.

# Peer Conference Questions

**Directions:** As you listen to the writer's piece, ask yourself the following questions. You may write notes at the bottom of the page.

- What things do I like about this writing?

- What do I want to know more about?

- What is the writer's main point?

- What are some details?

- What suggestions can I offer?

- Is any part of this piece confusing?

- What can be eliminated (words, phrases, sentences, paragraphs) without losing the author's intention?

Notes:

_____

_____

_____

_____

_____

_____

_____

_____

_____

_____

_____

_____

# *Activity 17: Strategies for Effective Peer Conferences*

Explain that the role of students in a peer group is to help other members of the group improve their writing skills. They do this by listening to writers read their papers and then sharing what they like about the papers, as well as suggesting ways to improve them. Since every student in the group gets a chance to read his or her piece, everyone benefits. Because of the experience they gain by helping others improve their work, students become better readers of their own papers. You may choose to distribute copies of the accompanying "Peer Group Guidelines" and discuss the guidelines with your students.

I like to organize peer groups prior to the first day of school to avoid wasting class time. Not knowing the students, I form these first groups randomly, then change groups regularly throughout the year. I seek balance in each group and make adjustments as necessary. For example, I try not to place a shy student with three or four vocal ones who could easily overwhelm him. Likewise, I try to avoid chatty combinations.

One of the biggest problems of peer groups is students getting off the subject. In my class, when six groups of four or five students each are in conference at the same time, I cannot oversee every group. To help with management, I appoint a monitor for each group, rotating monitors regularly so that everyone gets a chance to play this role. The monitor's responsibility is to make sure group members stay on the subject of writing. Also, since every group member must have a chance to share, the monitor (or a separate time checker) watches the time and prevents the group from dwelling on any paper too long. I instruct the students to spend between three and five minutes on each paper. I try not to allow peer conferences to run longer than twenty minutes. More time than that takes away from writing time and also induces students to talk about the latest "news" rather than writing.

I further encourage my students to confer with a partner in an effort to solve writing problems or help in revision. In most cases, I permit students to choose their partners, although I quickly separate students who do not work well together. When students realize that you will not tolerate anything except good work during peer conferences, they are more likely to keep on task.

Partners work in much the same way as group do. The writer reads her piece, and her partner listens and responds to it. The advantage of conference partners is that students need not wait until the entire group meets to confer. Having the freedom to work with a partner also encourages students to cooperate in solving writing problems. While I permit students to confer as necessary, I insist that they do not interfere with anyone else when they are meeting. Providing a separate table or a corner of the room for students to meet reduces the chance of partners' disturbing others.

As your students become better writers and more skilled at revision, they will become better at identifying and improving weaknesses in their work. To help them in their efforts, you can distribute copies of the accompanying "Revision Checklist."

As your students become more involved in the writing workshop, they will want to improve their work. They will come to view revision as an important stage of the writing process, seek help with revision, and eventually master the skills for revision that you share with them.

# Peer Group Guidelines

The purpose of your peer group is for members to help each other improve their writing. This is done by a writer reading his or her work and having the other group members respond to it. Each member should have a chance to share something, even if it is only a description of an idea for writing. To help your group work successfully, you must follow these rules:

**1.** Be a good listener. Remain quiet when others are reading and concentrate on their words.

**2.** Be polite and kind.

**3.** Remain focused on the writing.

**4.** Always find something positive in every paper.

**5.** Always find something that can be improved.

**6.** Try to offer specific comments, for example:

- Offer what you think was the main idea.

- Tell what you think was the best part of the paper and why.

- Tell the author what details seemed particularly interesting.

- Tell what you would like to see expanded.

- Tell the author about any parts you found confusing.

- Suggest ways to solve problems in the writing, especially any the writer brings up.

# Revision Checklist

_____ **1.** Did I write what I wanted to write?

_____ **2.** Is my topic focused?

_____ **3.** Will my readers understand what I am saying?

_____ **4.** Is my writing clear?

_____ **5.** Is my opening strong? Does it capture the reader's attention?

_____ **6.** Are my main ideas supported with details? Have I used examples?

_____ **7.** Does my conclusion contain a final point or summary for my piece?

_____ **8.** Is all of my information needed? Are there any words, phrases, sentences, or paragraphs that I can cut? Have I cut all clutter?

_____ **9.** Are there places I can expand my ideas?

_____ **10.** Does my piece show unity? Do all of the parts build to a whole?

_____ **11.** Are my paragraphs unified? Does each one contain only one main idea?

_____ **12.** Is the style right for the subject? Is my style consistent throughout the piece?

_____ **13.** What part of this piece do I like the best? Why?

_____

_____

_____

_____ **14.** What part do I like the least? Why? _____

_____

_____

_____

_____ **15.** What part do I feel needs improvement? How can I improve it? _____

_____

_____

_____

# SECTION 6

# EDITING

**Editing is the stage** of the writing process in which authors evaluate whether they have expressed themselves clearly, using the conventions of standard written English. While major editing should be done after the piece has been revised, editing also occurs during drafting and revision. In editing, the author concentrates on trimming clutter, tightening the flow, selecting stronger and more vivid words, and correcting any remaining mistakes in mechanics. It is the time to polish writing.

## Strategies for Teaching Editing Skills

Before students can edit their work effectively, they must possess the skills that are essential for good writing. While the skills taught to sixth graders, for example, will be different from the skills taught to seniors in high school, even young students can learn editing skills within the scope of their curriculum.

When you teach new writing skills, explain them fully, model their use on the board or an overhead projector, and refer to the skill during individual and group conferences. Encourage students to use the skill, and monitor that it is being used correctly. Once students understand a skill, they will employ it in their writing and look for it as they edit. The development of editing skills takes time, for the skills grow out of a student's overall writing experience.

You can highlight recently taught skills by maintaining an Editing Skills Bulletin Board. Using poster paper or oak tag (an easel with a roll of paper is also good), set up a bulletin board that displays editing skills. After teaching a new skill, display it on the board. You can write the skill on a strip of construction paper and tack it to the board, as in this example:

> Colons : are used before a list of items, after the salutation of a business letter, and between the hour and minute in time.

I like to display two or three skills at a time. When I add a new skill, it takes the top position, with the other skills moving down. The bulletin board reminds students of the skills that were recently taught and encourages them to use the skills in their writing and editing. As an alternative, allowing students to select two or three new skills they have trouble with in their writing encourages their involvement in the workshop and heightens interest in editing.

Similar to bulletin board checklists are personal editing checklists. I call them "Editing Reminders." (See the accompanying reproducible.) Every week or two, depending on what suits your schedule, give each student one or two skills that he or she is to focus on during editing. Here is an example:

---

**Weeks of: 11/3 and 11/10**

  **1.** Consistency in tenses.

  **2.** Watch for spelling of *believe, receive,* and *conceive.*

  **3.** Be sure transitions are smooth.

---

Explain the purpose and use of the editing reminder sheets. The student retains the editing reminder sheet in her writing folder and refers to it during editing. Each week (or every two weeks) new skills may be added. Successive sheets are paper-clipped together so that the student builds a personal packet of skills. I draw the skills from material that has been taught in mini-lessons and conferences. If a skill is not mastered, I repeat its use on the reminder sheet or come back to it later in the year. Editing reminder sheets are valuable because they address specific skills that individual students need to work on.

Three resources that editors often rely on during editing are the dictionary, the thesaurus, and an author's stylebook. It is so important that students understand how to use these resources that I teach about them early in the school year.

# *Activity 18: Using a Dictionary*

Many students view dictionaries as little more than a place to check spelling. Dictionaries, however, offer much more information than that. If you have enough dictionaries, distribute them so that each student has a copy for this activity. If you do not have enough copies, let students work in groups and share them.

Point out the following features in your dictionaries, and show students examples:

- The words in a dictionary are listed alphabetically. The guide words at the top of the page make it easy for users to find the word for which they are looking.

- Dictionaries break words into syllables.

- Dictionaries provide accent marks and phonetic spellings to show how words are pronounced.

- Dictionaries offer the correct spellings of words, their meanings, and parts of speech.

# Editing Reminders

Week(s) of: _____

_____

_____

_____

_____

_____

_____

Week(s) of: _____

_____

_____

_____

_____

_____

_____

Week(s) of: _____

_____

_____

_____

_____

_____

_____

- Dictionaries show alternative spellings and related forms such as plurals when the form is irregular or hard to spell.
- Dictionaries offer usage tips; some even show how the word might be used incorrectly.
- Dictionaries show examples of how a word may be used in a sentence.
- Dictionaries may show synonyms of words.
- Some dictionaries provide the origin of words.
- Larger dictionaries may have geographical and biographical sections, maps, and stylebooks.

# Activity 19: Using a Thesaurus

A thesaurus is a book of synonyms (and often antonyms) and is an excellent resource for writers who seek precise words to express their ideas. A thesaurus is not a dictionary, and you should caution students not to try to use it in that way. If you have copies of thesauri, distribute them to your students. If you do not have enough copies for everyone in class, allow students to work in groups for this activity.

Review the thesaurus with your students. Point out that words are listed alphabetically. Along with a list of synonyms, many thesauri also include antonyms for the entry words. Most include related words, which authors can use if they must continue looking for the word they need. Although thesauri provide great help to writers, caution your students not to use them to find the longest synonym they can. Some writers mistakenly believe that using big words enhances their style. Tell your students that the simplest style is usually the best because it is the clearest. Thesauri should be used to find the precise words that make writing clear.

# Activity 20: Using an Author's Stylebook

An author's stylebook offers suggestions on how a writer can use words and constructions correctly and clearly. While each author develops an individual style, regularly referring to a stylebook can help an author to write in a manner that makes it easy for his readers to read.

A variety of stylebooks for authors are available. Most include rules and suggestions for using punctuation, capitalization, and spelling and guidance on the use of adjectives, adverbs, metaphors, quotations, abbreviations, titles, figures, confusing words, and compound words. Most offer examples of both good and weak constructions.

For the activity, distribute copies of stylebooks to your students. Discuss the contents, and then review the sections and examples. Be sure to emphasize how a stylebook can help them to improve their writing. Encourage the use of stylebooks in your classes.

# Editing Partners

Peer editing can be done with partners or groups. Before any peer editing takes place, instruct your students to reread their revised drafts carefully and edit them individually. Self-editing is an important skill that helps students to become more aware of their writing. Only after self-editing should students take their writing to a partner or peer group for editing.

When working with a partner, the editor reads the author's piece silently, lightly underlining any errors he believes he has found. He may also write comments in the margins or on the bottom of the sheet. I encourage editors to write some things they like about the piece, as well as things they feel need to be improved, because this gives important feedback to the author.

The "Editor's Checklist" will guide student editors in their efforts to focus on specific skills. Make the checklists readily available to students. Without guidance, many students are not sure what to look for while editing. The checklist helps focus their attention on specific skills. At the beginning of the year, it is unlikely that you will have taught all the skills on the list. Since basic skills are listed first, you may instruct your students to ignore the numbers of the skills they have not learned. Asking editors to sign their names to their work adds formality to the process and encourages students to do a good job. Authors retain the checklists after completion of editing.

Once the editing is completed, the editor and author go over the piece. An author who disagrees with any of the editor's points should first check references and then consult with you. I urge students to check their work themselves because this is when some of the greatest learning occurs.

# Editing Groups

Editing groups work much the same way as partners do, but the labor for editing is divided. Groups work best with three to five students per group. Each member of the group reads the paper but looks for specific skills. If you are using the "Editor's Checklist," student 1 may edit for the first few skills, student 2 for the next few, and so on.

To ensure that everyone gets a chance to edit for different skills, the responsibility for skills should be rotated. Student 1, for example, who edited for skills 1, 2, and 3 on the first piece, might edit for skills 4, 5, and 6 on the next. Editing groups are good to use at the beginning of the year when students may be uncertain of how to edit. To ensure that students are in fact learning editing skills, you should monitor the groups closely, sit in on them, and model the skills.

A problem with editing is that papers get marked up. After a round of editing, the original may be unrecognizable, and the author will not know where to begin making changes. You can avoid this by making photocopies of originals. Editors work with the copies, and the author retains the original. Of course, this is practical only if you have easy access to a copy machine or if the piece was written on a computer and two copies were printed, but it does simplify the editing process.

# Editor's Checklist

Author: _____ Date _____ Section _____
Editor(s): _____
Title: _____

This piece has been edited for the following:

____ **1.** Sentences begin with capital letters.

____ **2.** Sentences have correct ending punctuation.

____ **3.** Sentences are complete.

____ **4.** Paragraphs are indented.

____ **5.** Commas are used in compound sentences, and for the listing of items in a series.

____ **6.** Quotation marks (where necessary) are used correctly.

____ **7.** Apostrophes are used correctly for possessive nouns and for contractions.

____ **8.** Proper nouns and adjectives are capitalized.

____ **9.** Spelling is correct.

____ **10.** The use of common homophones (there, their, they're; to, too, two; your, you're) is correct.

____ **11.** Verb tenses are correct.

____ **12.** Subjects and predicates agree.

____ **13.** Subject and object pronouns are used correctly.

____ **14.** Pronouns agree with the nouns they replace.

____ **15.** Unnecessary words, phrases, and sentences have been eliminated.

____ **16.** Colons are used correctly.

____ **17.** Semicolons are used correctly.

____ **18.** Underlining (for italics) is used correctly.

____ **19.** Parentheses are used correctly.

____ **20.** Dashes are used correctly.

Editor's Signature: _____

If you do not have access to a copier or computers for your workshop, instruct editors to write lightly in pencil. Places where the editor finds an error in punctuation or spelling can be lightly underlined. Every effort should be taken to avoid making the original so hard to read that the author cannot decode the editor's comments.

Lightly underlining has another advantage. When students are uncertain of a skill, they may think an item is incorrect but they are not sure. If they stop editing to look the item up, they may lose their focus on the piece. By underlining suspected mistakes, they can complete the editing, discuss the piece with the author, and consult references if necessary.

Whenever students work with partners or groups, you must be sure that one student does not dominate the others. Some student editors with strong personalities can convince a writer he is wrong even when he is not. This is another reason for encouraging students to consult references when disputes over usage, punctuation, grammar, or spelling arise. In cases where there is no definitive answer, the final decision should rest with the writer.

# *Activity 21: Using Editor's Marks*

To help students with the editing process, project the accompanying "Editor's Marks." The symbols simplify making minor corrections. In discussing the editor's marks, explain that professional editors and authors use the symbols with their work. The symbols may also be used during revision and self-editing. You might find it helpful to display a large copy of the editor's marks so students can refer to it during revision and editing.

After students have completed editing and have made any needed corrections, but before they do their final copy, have them put their papers in your editing tray. Do not edit pieces during class, because there are too many other demands, and your time will probably be better spent working with students on the development of their pieces. As soon as students put their pieces in the tray, they should begin new work.

Read the edited papers first for content and then once again for mechanics, noting any weaknesses and errors. Encourage students by writing notes of praise when they have done well.

During class, confer with students individually about their papers. Try to address one or two mistakes at a time. Confronting students with an assortment of mistakes will overwhelm them; they will not know where to begin to correct all the errors. Rather than teach them how to improve weak skills, you might be teaching them to dislike writing.

Although you show students their mistakes and they make corrections, many students make the same mistakes again. That is common. It may take a few pieces for them to master a skill, but they will. Learning often occurs in small steps.

## Editor's Marks

| Symbol | Meaning | Example |
|---|---|---|
| ¶ | new paragraph | for vacation. ¶ Soon... |
| ≡ | capitalize | North america |
| / | lower case | The Politician shook hands. |
| ↶ | move | They went after skating home. |
| ∧ | insert a letter | high schol |
| ∧ | insert a word | They were late for the game. |
| ⋏ | insert a comma | pencils pens, and paper. |
| ⊙ | add a period | He arrived at work⊙ |
| ℓ | delete a letter | Are you theere? |
| ℓ | delete a word | He went the the wrong way. |
| ∿ | switch letters | The game wsa exciting. |
| ∿ | switch words | They saw all it of. |
| ∨ ∨ | quotation marks | Goodby, she said. |
| Ⓝⓒ | not clear | Ⓝⓒ Tomorrow was the race. |
| ⌗ | separate | They drove tothe shore. |
| ‿ | combine | The earth quake was awful. |

## Proofreading

Proofreading is done after the piece has been revised and edited and is in its final form. The purpose of proofreading is to find any remaining errors in mechanics that may have slipped through revision.

Because it is the last step of the writing process before publishing, proofreading is vital. You must demand that published pieces contain as few mistakes as possible. Publishing is the showcase of writing, and excellence should be the goal.

Proofreading is difficult. I tell my students to read slowly during proofing and concentrate on mechanics. I suggest that they read each sentence to see if it stands alone. Are all the words spelled and used correctly? Are proper nouns capitalized? Is the ending punctuation correct? Do subjects and verbs agree? Are pronouns used correctly? Students should imagine themselves as editors reading another author's work.

Many people view editing as a time merely for catching and correcting mistakes in writing. It can be much more. When students self-edit, they have the chance to put themselves in the shoes of their readers and see if what they have written is what they intended. Editing is the final preparation for publishing.

# SECTION 7

# PUBLISHING

**Publishing, which refers to** the sharing of one's writing with readers, is crucial to your writing workshop. Students need to share their writing with others; they need others to read and react to their words. Your students will write better if they know their writing will be shared.

Publishing in the writing workshop can take many forms. Students may share their work from the author's chair, in peer groups, through articles and stories in school newspapers and magazines, on school Web sites, over the Internet, and, of course, by handing in their writing to you. Because of its importance, publishing should be a regular event in your classroom.

## The Author's Chair

One of the simplest ways to share writing is through the author's chair. A student takes center stage (a chair at the front of the classroom, for instance) and reads her work to the class. In some cases, a student may read excerpts of her writing. The other students become the audience and may ask questions or offer comments. The feedback is immediate.

Some teachers reserve the author's chair for the end of each week, while others allow students to read their work as they finish. I like to use the author's chair two or three times a week. On the days we do the author's chair, I usually have two or three students read their pieces. If students do not volunteer, I ask individuals to read their work. I try to get everyone involved during the year but do not force anyone to read his or her work. Sometimes I will read the work of a shy student, with that student's permission, of course. As they see more and more of their friends share writing from the author's chair, most students eventually volunteer.

Similar to the author's chair is author's day. You might set aside one day each week, or a day or two each month, to honor your student authors. On author's day, students may go to other classes to give readings of their work, or you might set up a special display or bulletin board to show the work of student authors. Including photographs of your students with their work can make an impressive exhibit. (Be sure to follow the policies of your school regarding the taking and displaying of student photographs.)

## Peer Group Sharing

On days I do not have the author's chair scheduled, students meet in peer groups at the end of class and share their work. I reserve about ten minutes for this. To keep the groups moving, I appoint monitors. They watch the time, and make sure that no one dominates the meeting and that everyone shares.

As I circulate, I try to sit in on each group and model appropriate behavior. If I am unable to be a part of each group on any day, I make a mental note to start the next time with the groups I missed.

All students are encouraged to share their work. They may read their piece or a part of it, or they may simply tell others what they have been working on. The group members may comment, ask questions, or offer suggestions. I like to have students share each day with the class, with a peer group, or with a partner because of the feedback they receive. Moreover, when students share their work, the feeling of a writers' community and the desire to share their work grows.

## Computers and Publishing in the Writing Workshop

Computers greatly expand the horizons of publishing and sharing in your writing workshop. If you have access to computers in class or a computer room, students may work on computers at home and bring in disks containing their material to class, and then work on computers in school as well. In these cases, the software of the computers must be compatible, or students will not be able to access the writing on their disks. A word of caution when sharing computer files: If you permit students to bring disks with their writing from home, be sure your computers have up-to-date virus protection. Shared disks are a major source of computer viruses.

Along with making printing for sharing writing easy, many word processing programs include clip art, which students can use to illustrate articles, stories, and class magazines. In addition to the images included with word processing software, many companies supply clip art on compact disks and over the Internet. Much of this clip art is available for a nominal fee and is copyright free. However, always check the conditions for use of any clip art your students are considering to use.

While students should be made aware of the value of clip art to enhance certain types of writing such as class or school magazines or newsletters, most of the writing they will be doing in class does not require clip art. The search for clip-art images should never become more important than writing.

Whenever students wish to use illustrations with their writing, I require that they complete the writing of the draft first. I have two reasons for this. First, after having completed the draft, students will have a better idea of where clip art might be used most effectively. Second, if they know that they can use clip art in their projects, some students spend an inordinate amount of time searching for images before they write a single word. If they are unable to find what they feel are good images, they may even abandon what is in fact a fine idea for writing.

Like clip art, the pictures provided by digital cameras can be a powerful enhancement to writing, especially in the production of class or school magazines. Since most major brands of digital cameras are compatible with most major brands of software, inserting digital photos in papers is surprisingly easy. Most digital cameras come with software that provides on-screen prompts to facilitate use, and most also offer support through technical staff.

Before permitting your students to add photographs to their writing, explain that they should refrain from taking pictures of anyone who does not want his or her photograph taken. Moreover, many schools have specific policies regarding the photographing of students and staff. These guidelines should be followed. Finally, before publishing anyone's photograph in any manner, explain to your students that they should obtain a signed model release form, a sample of which follows.

## A Word on Copiers

High-speed copiers enable writers to make multiple copies of their work quickly and easily. Although many copiers offer color printing, I recommend that you use simple black and white except for special projects. Black-and-white copies save time and expense and are adequate for most pieces.

If you have access to a copier for your classroom, you must avoid spending an excessive amount of time at the copy machine. If possible, have student volunteers run copies. In some schools, parent volunteers are available to do this work. If you have the opportunity to use volunteers to run copies, try to make the job as easy as possible for them. Always provide copies in order with name and class prominently displayed. Any special instructions (for example, printing back-to-back for a class magazine) should be clear.

Copiers can be a useful tool in any writing workshop. If you are fortunate and have easy access to a copier for your writing workshop, you will quickly find the machine to be indispensable.

## E-Mail as a Means of Sharing and Publishing

The Internet is not only an enormous source of information for writers, it offers writers a means of communication as well. Along with using e-mail (electronic mail) to communicate with others, your students can share their writing using e-mail.

Stories and articles can be pasted into e-mail text, or they can be sent as e-mail attachments. Either method is simple and efficient. While students can share their finished work through e-mail, they can also share their drafts and works in progress, gaining important feedback from others. E-mail offers writers an efficient means of maintaining a dialogue about writing with other writers.

Encourage your students to use e-mail as a way of sharing their writing, but also encourage them to write e-mail text clearly and in standard language. If you have ever read typical e-mail messages written by students, you were likely exposed to writing without capital letters, minimal (or no) punctuation, symbols used in place of words, and the writer's personal shorthand. This may be fine for informal e-mail chatting, but more formal communication calls for standard English. You may wish to distribute copies of "E-Mail Etiquette for Writers," and discuss the suggestions with your students.

# A Model Release Form

Before printing or displaying a person's picture, photographers must obtain a model release form. There are many examples of these forms. Depending on where a picture might be published, some are detailed and specific, while others are general. The example that follows is a basic form.

I hereby give permission to <u>your name here</u> to use my name and photographic likeness in <u>method of publication</u>.

Print Name: _____

Signature: _____

Date: _____

If the model is under age eighteen, the signature of the parent or legal guardian is also needed.

I, <u>name of parent/legal guardian</u>, as the parent/legal guardian of <u>model's name</u>, have read the above release and approve it.

Print Name: _____

Signature: _____

Date: _____

# E-Mail Etiquette for Writers

Consider the following suggestions when using e-mail for formal correspondence:

- Use standard English.

- Although it is not necessary to use a formal heading, you should include a greeting and a closing.

- Write your name after the closing.

- Use complete sentences and paragraphs.

- Use correct punctuation.

- Include details and all necessary information.

- Strive for conciseness and clarity.

- Do not include symbols in the place of words.

- As in any other type of letter, use correct spelling. If your e-mail program includes a spelling checker, be sure to use it.

- Proofread the message before sending it.

- Double-check the address of your recipient.

- If you are including a file attachment, be sure you do in fact attach the file before you send your e-mail.

# Producing Class Magazines

Class magazines are an excellent way of sharing the writing of your students. Class magazines may be simple (stapled collections of students' work written in longhand) or more elaborate efforts that are written on computers, printed in various fonts, and illustrated with clip art and photographs. In my classes, we publish at least one short magazine each month, with a longer one at least twice a year. Publishing magazines may sound like a lot of work, but it is not as much as you may think. You are also likely to find that as the year goes on, many students begin publishing their work on their own with only supervision on your part.

You do not need much equipment or specialized materials to produce a magazine for your writing workshop:

> *Materials:* Writing paper, copy/computer paper, pens, pencils, markers, correction fluid, scissors, glue, stapler, rulers, clip art
>
> *Equipment:* Computers, printers, photocopier
>
> *Optional equipment:* Digital camera, scanner

If you have copies of magazines from previous classes, pass them around so that students see what magazines produced in the writing workshop are like. It is possible that many of your students have never before been involved in the production of a class magazine. Seeing examples helps to motivate students and spur ideas.

Be sure to discuss the requirements for both the material and format of a class magazine. Will the magazine contain only fiction, only nonfiction, or both? Will it include poetry? Will any types of stories be unacceptable? If you are accepting handwritten work, stress that it must be neat and written in black ink with no cross-outs. Set a firm deadline that will allow you enough time to edit and organize the material for the magazine. You should require students to submit all finished pieces at least two weeks in advance. Finally, emphasize that work must be of high quality: every attempt must be made to publish material with sound ideas, clear writing, and correct mechanics.

To generate enthusiasm, you can brainstorm possible titles for the magazine with your class. In this way, the class takes ownership of the magazine. Feeling that it is theirs helps to motivate them to work hard to produce a quality magazine. If you prefer, you may simply give the magazine a descriptive title, for example, *The Collected Stories of Ms. Smith's Writing Classes, Volume I.* Be sure to date your magazines. At the end of the year, students who save the magazines will have a collection that details the class's writing experiences.

Whenever I publish a student magazine, I produce enough copies for every student in the class and several extras for the principal, exhibits in the school library, and hallway displays. It is important for students to know that you think their work is worthy to share with people outside the classroom.

In addition to regular magazines, you can publish special collections. For example, after a mini-lesson on limericks, one group of students wrote limericks that we published in a magazine.

If you team-teach or are departmentalized, you may decide to publish magazines for each class or include the work of students from all your classes. In either case, you should begin collecting work for the magazine in advance. If a student writes what you feel is an excellent piece, ask her if she would like it to appear in the class magazine. Even if the magazine is not scheduled to be printed for another few weeks, I put the piece in a separate "magazine" folder. If the piece needs any final revisions, have the student do them now rather than later. Once the piece is done, it will stay in the folder until the magazine is ready for printing. By collecting work early, you reduce the problems of trying to gather material for the magazine the day before printing.

My class magazines are produced on a photocopier and are bound with staples. Most of the articles and stories are written on computers, on equipment in school or on computers students have at home. If not all of your students have access to computers on which they can write articles and stories for class publications, try building a network of parent volunteers to keyboard these students' material. You can send a letter home, explaining that you plan to produce magazines containing the writings of your students and that you need help with entering the material as computer files. There are always some parents who are willing to help.

Along with producing class publications, I encourage students to produce their own magazines. One year, two of my students created a monthly magazine they titled *Video Game Review*. Each month they summarized several popular video games and offered tips on how their readers could be successful playing the games. I have no doubt that they enjoyed doing their research. Each issue of the magazine ran three to four pages, which they produced on their own computers in a fine effort month after month. Because they took great pride in what they were doing, their writing skills improved significantly.

In addition to simple magazines, I publish two or three major ones each year. I encourage students to submit stories, articles, poems, and puzzles for our big magazines. (I have even had students submit advice columns, which, depending on the student giving the advice, sometimes prove to be quite popular.) When students see their classmates writing different kinds of pieces, they are more willing to try new forms.

The major magazines include artwork (usually clip art), drawings, or photographs that tie in with the writing. For example, a science-fiction story might be illustrated with aliens, spaceships, or exotic backgrounds. The artist reads the story and creates (or, in the case of clip art, finds) illustrations that he or she feels highlight the action. For more information about class magazines, see the accompanying "Tips for Producing Class Magazines."

While most teachers produce magazines on photocopiers, there is another option. If your high school has a print shop, you might be able to have class magazines printed there. The relationship you develop with the print shop teacher will be a reciprocal one: your students receive quality magazines, and the print shop students work on a meaningful project.

# Tips for Producing Class Magazines

Producing a class magazine is not as hard as it may seem. Remembering the following points makes it even easier.

- Start collecting material early. Have students revise pieces ahead of time and store them in folders. If you are doing magazines for more than one class, keep separate folders of work for each class.

- Set standards of what is acceptable. Will you accept stories, articles, and poems? Or will the magazine contain only fiction, only nonfiction, or only poems? Will it contain puzzles, riddles, or games? What types of material will be unacceptable (for example, gory horror stories)? Also emphasize that all material must be original, and be careful that students do not plagiarize.

- Organize the magazine in parts. Do pages 1 through 4, then 5 through 8, and so on. This breaks down the job of producing the magazine to manageable parts.

- Use computers with compatible software. This makes revising, editing, and printing easier. Having stories on disks will allow you to make final editorial corrections, if necessary, right on the file, and from there print the piece.

- Use the features of your word processing software to design and produce your magazine.

- If you intend to include artwork, use clip art or ask students to do line drawings that illustrate the writing. Caution them that elaborate drawings with much detail may not reproduce well. While clip art can usually be inserted directly into the file, line drawings will either need to be scanned in or cut and pasted onto the page before final copying. Permitting students to draw directly on pages risks mistakes that might require the page to be reprinted. This results in unnecessary work.

- Before printing, appoint student proofreaders to catch last-minute errors.

- If possible, copy the magazine on both sides of each page. This will improve the appearance.

Print enough copies of your magazine for students, your principal, and for displays throughout your school.

# Producing Books Written by Students

While much of the writing of your students will be published as individual pieces in magazines, featured in displays, and shared through peer groups, you may also publish books written by your students. Student books may be relatively short—a book of poems, for example—or a long work that runs a hundred pages or more. (Long pieces require special permission from me, which I grant only to students who come to me with an idea I feel can sustain such a project. Also, the student must be highly motivated and already possess strong writing skills. For this type of student, the project usually consumes the entire marking period, with most of the student's grade based on this work.)

Some art teachers might be willing to help you produce the books your students write. In fact, working with the art teacher to produce books in art class that your students wrote in your writing workshop can be a fine interdisciplinary project.

Some high school print shops can provide glued binding for books, as well as laminated or multicolored covers. You might be able to develop a cross-curriculum relationship with the print shop teacher.

You can also produce a book in your classroom. The simplest way is to use a photocopier for printing and staples for the binding. A heavier-weight paper, thin cardboard, or report covers make durable book covers. If you are producing only one copy per student, you may allow students to create a cover with an explosion of color. Most word processing software has graphics features that can be used to make attractive covers. The commands are usually not difficult to master, and the effort will be well rewarded with distinctive book covers.

If you wish to make more elaborate books, resources are available that describe in detail the necessary steps. *Hand-Made Books: An Introduction to Bookbinding* by Rob Shepherd (1995) and *Creative Bookbinding* (reprint edition) by Pauline Johnson (1990) explain the making of books in easy-to-understand language. There are undoubtedly many more good sources in your local library. Check under "Book-binding" or "Bookmaking" in the card catalogue. And you can check with your local bookstore or on Amazon.com.

# Web Sites for Sharing Writing

The Internet offers vast opportunities for writers of all ages. Not only does it allow writers to conduct research, it is also an electronic forum where writers can chat with other writers, learn more about writing, and even publish their work. Most Web sites designed for student writers are free and offer a variety of writing-related activities, including tips and suggestions for improving writing, grammar games, writing contests, and places where students can post their work. See the accompanying "Web Sites That Publish the Writing of Students."

You might also consider establishing your own Web site where students can show their writing. Creating and maintaining a quality Web site is not difficult. The accompanying "How to Establish a Web Site to Display Student Writing" offers suggestions. Once your Web site is set up, you may expand it to include information and articles about writing to go along with examples of your students' work.

# Web Sites That Publish the Writing of Students

At the time of this book's printing, the following Web sites published the writing of students. Always visit a Web site before submitting any material to find out its current guidelines.

- Cyberkids, www.cyberkids.com, ages 7 to 12

- Cyberteens, www.cyberteens.com, ages 13 to 17

- Jupiter Sky Magazine, www.jupitersky.com, ages 14 to college

- KidsOnline Magazine, www.kidsonlinemagazine.com, ages through 18

- The Magicoul's Nook, www.magicoul.com, ages 10 to 14

For other sites that contain material of interest to student writers, go to www.yahooligans.com and conduct a search for "writing" or similar key words.

# How to Establish a Web Site to Display Student Writing

Displaying the work of your students on the World Wide Web is a wonderful way to support their writing efforts. It is not as difficult as many people think.

1. Decide where to post your site. Most Internet service providers offer Web hosting, including the service with their subscription fee. If your school or district maintains a Web site, you may be able to establish Web pages on the site to display your students' work. Check with your school's administrator and computer technician.

2. Once you have obtained space, plan your site. What will it contain? You may decide to display stories, articles, and poems; offer grammar puzzlers; run contests; or publish an e-newsletter about writing. Most teachers, especially when they are starting out, primarily display examples of their students' writing. Such sites are relatively easy to build and maintain. A little more challenging are sites that offer animation, sound effects, and multiple pages. A good idea is to start small and gradually build up to a more complex site.

3. Organize the site. Think of each Web page as a page in a book. In this book, however, viewers will be able to go to any page with a mere click of a mouse. A good strategy is to visit established Web sites and note how they are set up. Next, decide how many pages you will need, and map out the site as a flowchart. Use index cards to get an idea of the scope of your site. Try to keep the site at a manageable size because you will have to maintain it.

4. In the past, those interested in building a Web site either had to learn HTML (HyperText Markup Language), the programming language of the Web, or enlist the services of a programmer. Now, many Web hosts offer templates for building sites that, for the most part, allow the site builder to work in English. Many offer detailed step-by-step guides and even provide technical assistance. Maybe your school's tech person can set up a site for you.

5. Once the site has been established, you will want people to know about it. The first step is to publish the site's URL (address) in school and parent-teacher organization publications. Perhaps send a flyer home to parents informing them of the site and inviting them to visit it. You might also wish to inform the major search engines. Most search engines accept new listings; many are free. Go to the home page of the search engine and look for links that will enable you to register your site. A good place to find the best search engines is www.allsearchengines.com.

6. After the Web site is up and running, you must maintain it. Regularly post the work of your students. If the site is limited in size, consider posting the work of the Writing Student of the Month or display excerpts of writing.

Do not overlook the resources in your class. Students who are savvy with Web site building and management would probably be more than happy to help you set up and maintain a site.

## Still More Ways to Share

Along with class magazines, books, and Web sites, there are many other ways to share the writing of your students. One of the easiest is to photocopy individual pieces and distribute copies to the class.

If your school district maintains an intranet, you may use the system's capacity for sharing and managing information. Writing can easily be made available to all users of the system.

District or parent-teacher organization magazines and newsletters are another option for sharing. Many of these publications are receptive to good material submitted by students. Contact the person who is in charge of the publication, and explain that the students in your writing workshop have material that they would like to publish.

Local newspapers are yet another possible outlet for publishing. If the paper does not normally carry the work of students, call the editor and ask if the paper would be willing to run a column that your students will write about your school.

Writing contests are another possibility. Be alert for information about contests your students might be able to enter. You might also sponsor your own writing contest within your school or among schools in the district. Teachers from various grade levels whose students are not participating may serve as judges.

In your sharing of the writing of your students, do not neglect the use of bulletin boards, hallway displays, and library exhibits. These are easy ways to make the work of your students available to others.

Another way of sharing is for students to give readings of their work. You might arrange for your students to visit another class and read their work to the students there. On another day, those students may visit your class and read their work to your class. A twist on this activity is to have older students read their work to younger ones.

Finally, you should not hesitate to share your own writing with students. When a teacher shares his or her writing, students see a wonderful example of an adult using a skill they are learning. It adds to the importance of writing.

## Submitting Student Writing to Magazines

One of the most exciting things that can happen to students in your writing workshop is to have their work accepted for publication by a magazine. The odds are stiff, but the reward of acceptance will justify the hard work.

Mention submitting their writing to a magazine, and students will rush for the envelopes. Of course, this is the quickest way to rejection.

Students increase their chances for acceptance of their writing by studying several past issues of the magazines they are considering. Obtain some copies for them, perhaps from the school or local library. Students might also write to publications and request guidelines and sample copies, or obtain information online. Most publishers offer free guidelines, and some provide free copies. Studying past issues will help students to see what kind of material each magazine prefers and avoid writing about a topic that has been covered in a recent issue. When students are studying the magazine, they should look not only at topics but also at how the material is developed. What kinds of leads do the articles have? How are the stories written? What is the tone, the style? Attention to such details increases the odds of acceptance.

You should also discuss rejection. Point out that many pieces (called manuscripts) are rejected because of the strong competition. Receiving a rejection does not always mean that the writing of a student is lacking. It may be that the editor at the magazine has a similar piece in stock or that the piece is not right for the magazine. Emphasize that all authors suffer rejection.

Some publications prefer query letters to manuscripts. Students should write to the editors of these magazines first, describing their proposed article to see if the editor is interested. They should enclose a SASE (self-addressed, stamped envelope) for a reply. If students are interested in submitting to an online publication, they should query by e-mail. Encourage your students to submit to only one magazine at a time unless editorial guidelines state that the magazine will consider multiple submissions.

An effective query letter is concise. It should explain the proposed article and why the magazine's readers would enjoy it. If the student has any qualifications for writing the piece, he or she should include them.

## *Activity 22: Submitting Writing to Magazines*

Explain to your students that submitting their work, which is now called a manuscript, to magazines that publish the writing of students is one of the best ways of sharing, because the author can reach thousands of readers. Tell them that because the competition is heavy, they should submit only their best work.

You might wish to distribute copies of the accompanying "Tips for Submitting to Magazines." Discussing the information on the sheet will highlight the steps students should take for sending their manuscripts to editors.

# Tips for Submitting to Magazines

Following these suggestions can increase your chances of having an article, story, or poem accepted for publication by a magazine.

- Become familiar with the magazine you intend to submit to. Study several past issues to gain an understanding of the material the editors use, recent topics, and the tone and style of the magazine. Do not write on a topic that has already been done. Strive for freshness.

- When a magazine asks for queries only, do not send the manuscript. Send a query.

- When submitting material by mail to a magazine, always include a SASE (self-addressed, stamped envelope) so that your material may be returned if the magazine cannot use it.

- Unless editors at a magazine will consider simultaneous submissions (the sending of a query or manuscript to several magazines at the same time), send to only one at a time.

- Always follow the magazine's guidelines. If the editors prefer to be contacted by e-mail, do not send a letter. If they prefer to be contacted by regular mail, do not send e-mail. If the editors want articles or stories of about 1,000 words, do not send pieces of 500 or 1,500 words.

- If you send a photocopy, be sure it is clear and has crisp lettering. (If you make it hard for editors to read your work, they will not bother.)

- Your material should be printed on standard 8½ by 11-inch white paper. Your name, postal address, and e-mail address should appear at the top left corner of the title page with the word count, rounded to the nearest hundred, at the top right. The title, with your name beneath it, should be centered on the first page, about one-third of the way down. Starting with page 2, your last name and a few key words of the title should appear at the top left of every page. This is called the *pageheading* and makes it easier for editors to find pages of your manuscript should they become separated. Numbers of the pages may be at the top right or centered. Use paper clips, not staples, to keep the manuscript together.

- Always keep a copy of everything you mail. You will not be the first author to have a manuscript get lost.

- Include a short cover letter when you send your work to a magazine, briefly introducing your work and you. Avoid trying to tell the editor everything about your manuscript in the cover letter; let your work speak for itself.

- Set up a chart recording when and where you sent your manuscript. If it is rejected, cross off that magazine and send the manuscript to another. A rejection does not mean your piece is no good. It may simply be that the magazine could not use it.

## *Activity 23: Writing a Query Letter*

Distribute copies of the accompanying "Sample Query Letter." Discuss what a query letter is, and discuss its parts with your students. Note that the first paragraph explains the focus of the article, the second offers background for the proposed article, the third asks the editor if she is interested in seeing the article, and the fourth states the author's qualifications. The letter ends with a thank-you.

There are many print markets that publish the writing of students. However, they are not well publicized, and many teachers and students are unaware of them. They are listed in "Print Markets for Student Writers."

Since markets change, the needs of editors vary, and magazines may merge or fold, I suggest you contact or check a current issue of these markets before having your students send material to them. A helpful resource is *The Young Writer's Guide to Getting Published* by Kathy Henderson (2001). This resource offers detailed information about writing, as well as markets and contests that seek manuscripts from students. *Writer's Market,* edited by Kathryn S. Brogan (updated annually), provides detailed market listings for beginning and professional authors. Older students might find this book useful. Many libraries carry up-to-date copies. You might also search the Internet for markets, using terms such as "Publishing Student Writing."

The writing workshop provides the environment for students to write the way real authors do. It allows time for prewriting, drafting, revising, editing, and publishing. With students working individually or with a partner or in a small group, the writing workshop is a classroom of activity, diversity, and ideas. It is a place of self-discovery, learning, and growth.

# Sample Query Letter

Author's Name
Address
City, State ZIP Code
Date

Editor's Name
Name of Magazine
Address
City, State ZIP Code

Dear [Editor's Name; or Dear Sir or Madam]:

Pollution is a serious problem for everyone. While many adults belong to groups that fight pollution, kids can get involved too.

At Jefferson Middle School, students have organized Young People Against Pollution. It is a club that seeks to make young people aware of the problems caused by pollution. We also organize activities that help fight pollution. This year we cleared litter from our town's parks, and wrote letters to the state assembly about reducing air pollution. We plan more activities in the coming year.

Would [magazine name] be interested in an article about how eighth graders can fight pollution? In the article I would tell your readers about our club and explain how they may organize a similar one.

I feel confident I can write this article. I am the founder of Young People Against Pollution and serve as its current president.

Thank you for your time.

Sincerely,

[Author's Name]

# Print Markets for Student Writers

Because of the constant changes that occur in publishing, contact the following markets before sending material to them.

- *Creative Kids,* P.O. Box 8813, Waco, TX 76144-8813. www.prufrock.com/prufrock_jm_createkids.cfm. Stories, articles, editorials, poems, plays. Ages 8 to 14.

- *Merlyn's Pen,* P.O. Box 910, East Greenwich, RI 02818. www.merlynspen.com. Stories, essays, poems, reviews. Ages 11 to 15.

- *New Moon: The Magazine for Girls and Their Dreams,* 34 East Superior St., Ste. 200, Duluth, MN 55802-3003. www.newmoon.org/magazine/writerGirl.htm. Stories, articles, poems. Girls, ages 8 to 14.

- *Scholastic Writing Contests,* 557 Broadway, New York, NY 10012. www.scholastic.com/artandwriting awards/enter.htm. Write or check Web site for details. Students, grades 7 to 12.

- *Skipping Stones,* P.O. Box 3939, Eugene, OR 97403-0939. www.skippingstones.org. Stories, essays, riddles. Ages 8 to 16.

- *Stone Soup,* P.O. Box 83, Santa Cruz, CA 95063. www.stonesoup.com. Stories, poems, book reviews. Ages through 13.

- *Teen Ink,* P.O. Box 30, Newton, MA 02461. www.teenink.com. Stories, articles, poems, reviews, interviews. Ages 13 to 19.

- *Young Voices Magazine,* P.O. Box 2321, Olympia, WA 98507. www.youngvoicesmagazine.com/. Stories, articles, poetry. Students, elementary through high school.

# PART THREE

# USING MINI-LESSONS IN THE WRITING WORKSHOP

**Mini-lessons are a fine way** to begin writing workshops. They provide a time when the entire class is drawn together and you may address everyone at once. Mini-lessons afford you the opportunity to introduce students to various types of writing, discuss specific writing techniques, teach basic language skills, and share information about writing.

Mini-lessons should be short, not more than five to ten minutes, and should focus on one topic. Your students may use the information they learn in mini-lessons right away or may not incorporate it into their writing for some time. Reviewing the information presented in your mini-lessons during individual and small-group conferences will provide your students with the reinforcement needed to master the more difficult skills.

This part of the book comprises three types of mini-lessons:

- Mini-lessons for types of writing
- Mini-lessons for the art of writing
- Mini-lessons for the mechanics of writing

All are arranged in a lesson plan format. Background information is provided, followed by specific procedures, and, where necessary, reproducibles. Some mini-lessons also include extensions, which are activities that provide additional practice on the topic of the lesson.

The mini-lessons offer a wide assortment of topics and skills you can present to your students. It is also likely that you will develop others, based on the needs of your class. Feel free to use the mini-lessons here as models to create your own mini-lessons.

# SECTION 8

# MINI-LESSONS FOR TYPES OF WRITING

# Mini-Lesson 1: **Writing Personal Narratives**

*Narratives* are compositions in which the writer tells about a personal experience. Most are brief accounts of something that happened to the writer. A focused main idea, strong details, and examples are the keys to effective narratives. Personal narratives provide good opportunities for students to write because the students draw on their own experiences. You will find that much of the writing that goes on in your writing workshop will be personal narratives.

**Procedure**

1. Discuss the features of a narrative with your students.

2. Read a narrative to the class. This may be a narrative written by a former student (be sure to get permission) or a narrative from a source such as a reading text. If you wish, distribute copies of (or project) the accompanying personal narrative, "A Big Splash." Either read the narrative aloud to your students or ask your students to read it silently. If you read it, be sure to read with feeling.

3. Emphasize the features of the narrative you read by pointing out specific examples.

4. Note that narratives are usually told in the first person (using the pronoun *I*).

5. Mention that while most narratives are told in chronological order, some use flashback (see Mini-Lesson 37 in Section Nine) or rearrange time order to tell the narrative in a more interesting way.

# A Big Splash

I remember not being able to sleep. By four A.M. I was up and dressed and bounding into my uncle Bob's room. That's how you are when you're ten years old and going fishing with your favorite uncle who just came back from the navy.

I had to wake him up. But by six-thirty we were at the dock on the lake.

Uncle Bob instructed me to get into the boat so that he could hand me the fishing gear. There was plenty of it—poles, tackle box, bait box, the cooler that contained our lunches, a long-handled net, and extra sweatshirts. I climbed into the boat thinking, "This is gonna be great."

He handed me my small tackle box and pole first. I put them on the back seat of the rowboat and promptly opened the box and began looking for just the right hook. After all, there was no time to waste. The biggest bass in the state was waiting for me!

So involved was I that I didn't notice my uncle piling the rest of our gear into the boat. He had one foot on the dock and one on the boat. I also didn't notice that as I fuddled about in the back, the boat began to ease away from the dock.

"Pull the boat in with the line," said my uncle. I turned. I wasn't sure what he meant. I did see him with one foot on the dock and one on the boat. They were spread precariously far apart.

"Pull the boat in!" he said more urgently.

Realizing what was happening, I jumped up to get to the front of the boat. But my movement caused the boat to slip farther from the dock.

"Pull—"

It was too late. My uncle Bob made a big splash.

# Mini-Lesson 2: **Writing Essays**

An *essay* is a short piece in which a writer discusses a specific topic. Since your students will often be required to write essays in school to answer test questions, or out of school for competency tests or for application to college, the essay is an important form of writing for students to learn.

## Procedure

1. Discuss the essay form with your students.

2. Explain that the typical essay follows the format of introduction, body, and conclusion. The author states his purpose or main point of the essay in the introduction, explains the main idea in the body, and concludes with a final point that adds more weight to his arguments.

3. Emphasize that essays should be written in a clear, concise style. All main ideas must be supported with details or examples.

4. Distribute copies of (or project) and read the accompanying sample essay, "Slowing Global Warming by Saving Energy." Point out and discuss the introduction, body, and conclusion of the essay.

## Extension

- Suggest to your students that they read other examples of essays, which can be found on the op-ed pages of many newspapers and in many magazines.

# Slowing Global Warming by Saving Energy

One of the easiest ways to slow global warming is to save energy. The burning of fossil fuels, for instance, releases carbon dioxide into the atmosphere. The carbon dioxide traps the sun's heat and is one of the causes of global warming. By reducing the amount of fossil fuels we use, we will reduce the amount of carbon dioxide in the atmosphere, and global warming will slow.

There are many ways we can reduce the amount of fossil fuels that we burn. Since most homes are heated by burning natural gas or oil, keeping the thermostats a few degrees lower in the winter can save much energy.

The electricity that most homes use is produced by burning coal, oil, or natural gas. The less electricity we use, the less fossil fuel power plants need. Even something as simple as shutting off the light in an empty room can lead to big energy savings if it is done in homes across the country.

Reducing the amount of gasoline we use is another way to save. Gasoline is refined from oil. When gasoline is burned, carbon dioxide is released to the atmosphere. We can reduce the amount of gasoline we use by car pooling and taking mass transit.

Reducing the amount of energy each of us uses can conserve the fossil fuels we use. Each of us will then be helping to slow global warming.

# Mini-Lesson 3: **Strategies for Answering Essay Test Questions**

To answer essay test questions effectively, students must know the subject matter and write with competence and clarity. Just knowing the facts is not good enough; students must be able to analyze, organize, and explain those facts. That time is at a premium makes this a particular challenge.

## Procedure

1.  Explain that the first step in answering an essay question is to understand precisely what the question is asking. Tell your students to look for key words, which can help them determine the focus of the essay. Common key words may ask essay writers to *identify, compare, contrast, discuss, explain, analyze,* or *summarize* information about a topic. Make sure that your students know what these key words mean.

2.  Distribute copies of (or project) "Essay Test-Taking Tips," which follows. Discuss the suggestions with your students, emphasizing that following the suggestions will help them to improve their scores on essay tests.

3.  Note that since time is usually a factor during essay tests, students should write as well as they can the first time.

# Essay Test-Taking Tips

The following suggestions can help you to improve your scores on essay tests.

1. Be familiar with any test topics your teacher provides. Review any relevant notes or materials on the subject or subjects. Studying helps you to prepare and builds confidence.

2. Get a full night's sleep the night before the test. Wake up on time, and eat a solid breakfast. This will help you to be alert and concentrate during the test.

3. Remain calm, and think positively during the test. People who have prepared and expect to do well on essay tests usually score higher than those who are unprepared and believe they will do poorly.

4. Listen carefully to all instructions, and follow them exactly. Ask your teacher if you are unclear about something.

5. If you are given a choice of questions, read them all to determine which one or ones you are best able to answer.

6. Read each question carefully. Be sure you know exactly what it is asking. Look for key words such as *summarize, identify, describe, explain, compare, contrast, analyze,* and *discuss.*

7. Write main ideas down on scrap paper, if possible, and organize them in a logical manner. Look for relationships between ideas.

8. As you write, support all main ideas with facts and examples. Keep your writing concise, and be sure to stay on the topic and answer the question.

9. Pace yourself. Be aware of time limits. Work quickly, and do not panic. Remember that most essay tests allow students enough time to finish.

10. If you finish your essay and time remains, reread your work, and make any final changes. Keep in mind, though, that changes at this point should be minor.

# Mini-Lesson 4: **Writing How-to Articles**

*How-to articles* are a popular form of nonfiction writing. They explain how something can be done. Countless examples of how-to books and articles can be found in libraries and bookstores.

Since how-tos can be written about special talents or skills, they are a form of writing that most students can easily attempt. I remember one student who usually had little interest in writing. He did, however, like to fish. He enjoyed the sport so much that he made his own fishing lures. After explaining how-to articles during a mini-lesson, I suggested to him that he might write a piece about how his classmates could design and make their own fishing lures. The piece turned out to be the best he wrote that year.

## Procedure

1. Explain what a how-to article is.

2. Emphasize that since a how-to tells the reader how to do something, the writing must be clear, logical, and easy to follow. The writer must be sure not to leave any steps out, or readers will become lost. Many how-to articles list steps for their readers.

3. Distribute copies of (or project) the accompanying sample how-to article, "How to Make a Budget." Read the article aloud, or have students read it silently. Point out how the writer identifies each step to making a budget by using words like *first, after,* and *next.*

4. Note how examples are included to support the main points.

5. Suggest that before writing a how-to, students list their main ideas and put them in step-by-step order. Listing their information in the prewriting stage of the writing process will enable them to see if they have inadvertently missed an important step or detail.

## Extension

- Ask your students to review magazines they receive at home or that are available in your school or local library. Instruct them to identify examples of how-to articles. If possible, students should bring the magazines to class and share them with peer groups.

# How to Make a Budget

Have you ever run out of money at the end of the month? If you have, you are like countless other people. And, like many of them, you can avoid this problem by making a budget.

To make a budget, you need to balance your income and expenses. First, you must list all of your expenses. Include everything that you regularly spend money on. For example, you should list the money you need for clothes, lunch, going out with your friends, or entertainment (like CDs or DVDs). If you intend to save some money each month by putting it in the bank, count this as an expense too. It is important not to leave anything out. After listing your expenses, add them up.

Next, list your sources of income. This includes any allowance, as well as money you earn doing chores or working.

Now subtract your expenses from your income. Money left over is called a surplus. You may spend it, or choose to save it. If you do not have enough money to pay for all of your expenses, you must either increase your income or reduce your expenses.

Although most people will agree that sticking to a budget can be harder than making one, they will also agree that a good budget is an excellent tool for keeping track of your money.

# Mini-Lesson 5: **Writing Straight News Articles**

*Straight news articles* are written in clear, concise sentences. They focus on facts and develop their material around the *five W's* and *how: What* happened? *When* did it happen? *Where* did it happen? *Who* was involved? *Why* did it happen? And *how* did it happen? Most, if not all, of these questions are usually answered in the lead (the first few paragraphs) in straight news. The rest of the article offers details, organized so that the most important information comes first. This structure, called an *inverted pyramid form,* enables busy readers to gain the essential information quickly and allows editors to drop the final paragraphs if they run out of space.

### Procedure

1. Explain that the typical newspaper article is developed around answering the *five W's* and *how.*

2. Explain the importance of the lead.

3. Distribute copies of (or project) the accompanying sample newspaper article, "Bat Attacks Alarm Town." Read the article with your class and explain how it answers the questions:

    *What?* Bats attack people.

    *When?* At dusk, this past week.

    *Where?* In the town of Darden's Mill.

    *Who?* Townspeople.

    *Why?* The reason is being investigated.

    *How?* Flying around people's heads and faces.

4. Discuss that news articles should be objective, a factual reporting of the event. The reporter should refrain from offering his or her opinions about the event. Opinions should be reserved for editorials. (See Mini-Lesson 6.)

### Extensions:

- Ask students to bring in newspapers from home. Point out that the typical newspaper contains several sections: the main news, features (which often do not follow the inverted pyramid structure), editorial page, finance, TV and movie listings, the weather, sports, fashion, the obituaries, comics, and classified ads. Discuss the sections, particularly the main news, editorials, and features.

- Ask students to bring in newspapers from home. Divide students into groups of four to six, and ask them to review different articles and identify how the articles are structured. Each student should take at least one article and look for the *five W's* and *how.* To help them, hand out copies of "Taking Apart a Newspaper Article." After reviewing their articles, students should share their findings with their groups, summarizing the articles and explaining how the articles answer the *five W's* and *how.*

- Organize and publish a class newspaper to give students experience in newspaper writing.

- With another teacher, stage an event in the classroom, and ask students to report on it in a straight news story. Discuss the variety of approaches and articles that result.

# Bat Attacks Alarm Town

DARDEN'S MILL, APRIL 17—At a public meeting last night in the municipal building, residents of Darden's Mill voiced alarm over a recent flurry of bat attacks. Mayor Paul Burke directed Police Chief Steve Harkins to contact experts on bats at the state university for help in figuring out the bats' strange behavior.

The first reported attack was April 12. Just after dusk a bat attacked Robert Williams as he was taking out his garbage. "The bat kept circling around my head, like a big mosquito buzzing in my ear," Williams said. Although shaken by the attack, Williams was unhurt.

At least four more attacks have occurred in the same area since then. Each attack came around dusk, and in each case the bats repeatedly flew around the head and face of their targets. So far, no injuries have been reported.

That is little consolation to frightened townspeople. "Those bats might be rabid," said Audrey Martin, who was attacked at her home last night. She worries about her two small children.

Although bats have been known to carry rabies, this does not seem to be the case here. "No one has been bitten, and there is no evidence that these bats are diseased," said Chief Harkins.

The mayor concurs. "There's no need to panic until we find out why the bats are behaving like this," he said. He asks people to remain cautious but calm until the researchers from the university complete their investigation.

# Taking Apart a Newspaper Article

**Directions:** Select a news article. Read it carefully, and identify how it answers the questions: What? Who? When? Where? Why? How? Share your findings with your group.

What? _____

_____

_____

_____

Who? _____

_____

_____

_____

When? _____

_____

_____

_____

Where? _____

_____

_____

_____

Why? _____

_____

_____

_____

How? _____

_____

_____

_____

# Mini-Lesson 6: **Persuasive Writing**

*Persuasive writing,* often called *editorials, opinion pieces,* or *personal essays,* expresses an author's opinion about a topic. Many newspapers contain op-ed pages or sections of "letters to the editor," where the newspaper's readers can publish their opinions about problems or controversial subjects. Some magazines also carry opinion pieces. The authors of these pieces often try to persuade readers to adopt a particular view on an issue.

## Procedure

1. Explain what persuasive writing is.

2. Distribute copies of (or project) the accompanying "Save Trees and the Environment by Recycling Newspapers." Read the piece with your students.

3. Explain that all persuasive writing pieces follow the structure of introduction, body, and conclusion. Point out the three parts on the sample.

   - Note that the introduction contains a strong opening sentence that hooks the reader. It also mentions the problem.

   - Note that the author develops her position in the body. In the typical persuasive piece, authors use facts, examples, and explanations to support main ideas. Depending on the complexity of the topic, the body may be one or several paragraphs long.

   - Explain that in the conclusion, the author offers suggestions of what should be done about the problem. Often the author will call on readers to become involved or take personal action. A strong ending sentence emphasizes the main point of the piece.

## Extension

   - Distribute copies of "Analyzing a Persuasive Essay." Instruct your students to find examples of persuasive essays in newspapers, magazines, or online sources, and then analyze them by completing the worksheet. Students should share the essays and their analyses with their peer groups.

# Save Trees and the Environment by Recycling Newspapers

Recycling newspapers is a way to save trees and our environment. Each week Americans throw out about 300 million newspapers. That equals about 750,000 trees. Although our town has had a recycling program for several years, less than half of our residents bother to recycle newspapers.

This is unfortunate, because recycling can significantly lessen the burden on our environment. Recycling newspapers reduces the need for trees to be cut down. Making paper from recycled paper uses up to 50 percent less energy than making paper from trees, and it also reduces related air pollution by 95 percent. Since trees help to filter carbon dioxide and pollutants from the air, saving trees is an important step in reducing overall air pollution.

Everybody can help in the recycling drive. All one needs to do is tie newspapers in bundles and put the bundles out at the curb on the day for recycling.

Recycling will help save trees and the environment. It is everybody's responsibility to get involved.

# Analyzing a Persuasive Essay

**Directions:** Select and analyze a persuasive essay. Answer the following questions, and share the essay and your findings with your group.

1. Title of essay: _____

   Publication or online source in which it appeared: _____

   _____

   _____

   Volume (if magazine): _____ Date: _____

2. What is the author's hook? _____

   _____

   _____

3. What is the main idea of the essay? _____

   _____

   _____

   _____

4. What facts, examples, or statistics does the author use to support his or her

   main idea? _____

   _____

   _____

   _____

   _____

5. How does the author conclude his or her essay? _____

   _____

   _____

   _____

# Mini-Lesson 7: **Writing Friendly Letters**

*Friendly letters* are personal letters written to friends or relatives. Although with the increasing use of e-mail, friendly letters for many people have become obsolete, students should still be aware of them.

## Procedure

1. Explain that the purpose of a friendly letter is to tell a friend or relative about something in the author's life. Friendly letters are informal and are often written in a conversational tone. They should include enough details so that the reader understands what the writer intends. If a writer is responding to a letter she has received, she should attempt to answer any questions the sender has asked.

2. Distribute copies of (or project) the accompanying example of a friendly letter. Read it with your students. Point out the main parts: heading, salutation, body, closing, and signature. Emphasize the punctuation, particularly the commas in the heading and those after the salutation and closing.

3. Tell your students that friendly letters are usually handwritten on letter stationery (although with the increasing use of computers, many are now printed). Handwriting should be neat, and margins of at least 1 inch should be left at the top, sides, and bottoms. If more than one sheet is used, page 2 and following pages should be numbered.

4. Note that for many people, e-mail has replaced the friendly letter. Still, to ensure that communication using e-mail is clear, the guidelines below should be followed:

   - Use a specific subject heading, which identifies the purpose of the e-mail. It is not necessary to include your return postal address unless you expect the person to send a letter back to you.

   - Use standard English with correct grammar and punctuation.

   - Write in a conversational tone. "Friendly" e-mail need not be formal.

   - Like all other writing, strive for clarity in the expression of what you wish to say.

## Sample Friendly Letter

129 Deer Run
Peterville, NJ 09423
Nov. 10, 2005

Dear Jimmy,

Thanks for your last letter. I was glad to hear from you. Everybody around here still misses you.

Did you watch the last game of the Series? I can't believe how it ended. Even though I lost a $5 bet with my Dad, I enjoyed every minute of every game. I suppose I'll always be a baseball fanatic.

Do you think you'll be able to visit during Thanksgiving break? My Mom says you can stay as long as you want. That'll be great. Let me know if you can come.

I'll be looking forward to your next letter.

Your friend,
Sean

# Mini-Lesson 8: **Writing Business Letters**

*Business letters* are used to share ideas about business projects, apply for job opportunities, request information about a company, order products or services, or register complaints. They are more formal and briefer than friendly letters. You might mention that query letters are a special kind of business letter in which an author contacts an editor and asks if the editor would be interested in the author's proposed work. (See "Submitting Student Writing to Magazines" in Section Seven.) While standard business letters are still common, e-mail has assumed great importance in the business world.

**Procedure**

1. Explain the purpose of the typical business letter.

2. Distribute copies of (or project) the accompanying "Sample Business Letters." Point out the major parts: heading, inside address, salutation, body, closing, and signature.

3. Emphasize that an inside address is included and that a colon follows the salutation.

4. Mention that the business letter may use a block or semiblock form, and note the differences on the samples.

5. Inform students that unlike friendly letters, business letters should be printed on 8½ by 11-inch white paper.

6. Suggest that if students use e-mail for the purpose of a business letter, they follow the guidelines below:

   • Use a specific subject heading.

   • Be sure to address the message to the correct individual.

   • Use standard English and correct grammar and punctuation. (Remind students that they are not chatting with friends.)

   • Write clearly and concisely. (No one wants to read long, rambling e-mails at work.)

   • Be sure to include contact information such as your name, address, and phone number if you expect a response other than via e-mail.

# Sample Business Letters

## Semiblock Form

123 Hill Street
Holly Hill, NY 17625
April 3, 2005

Ellis Poster Company
1507 Field Road
Farmingdale, IA 64389

Dear Sir or Madam:

    I would like to order your "Save the Earth" poster, catalogue #873642. Enclosed is $15.95, which includes the cost of postage and shipping.

    Thank you.

Sincerely,

Jason Smith

## Block Form

123 Hill Street
Holly Hill, NY 17625
April 3, 2005

Ellis Poster Company
1507 Field Road
Farmingdale, IA 64389

Dear Sir or Madam:

I would like to order your "Save the Earth" poster, catalogue #873642. Enclosed is $15.95, which includes the cost of postage and shipping.

Thank you.

Sincerely,

Jason Smith

# Mini-Lesson 9: **Writing Book Reviews**

A *book review* is an in-depth, insightful analysis of a book. An effective review explains what the book is about and usually offers the reviewer's opinion. Many newspapers offer reviews of books, particularly in their Sunday editions. One of the best known is the book review section of *The Sunday New York Times*.

The connection between reading and writing is a strong one. Most good writers are good readers. When students read a book to write a review, they must read critically, which will help them to become better readers of their own writing.

### Procedure

1. Explain that the typical book review includes the title of the book, the author's name, and the publisher. It may also include the date of publication, the price, and where the book can be obtained.

2. Distribute copies of (or project) the accompanying sample review of *A Wrinkle in Time* by Madeleine L'Engle. Give students a minute or so to read the review.

3. Explain that for a review of a fictional work, the reviewer should include an introduction of the plot, a description of the characters, and an outline of the characters' motivations that provides the basis of the story. Any outstanding elements such as quality of writing, fast action, exotic settings, or unusual twists might also be mentioned. The review writer should not reveal the climax, since readers may decide to read the book, but he or she can express an opinion about the ending. Point out that the sample review follows this pattern.

4. For nonfiction, note that reviewers usually explain the scope of the book. The importance of the book, and what it offers, or fails to offer, are highlighted.

### Extension

• Set up a corner of the room to display reviews written by your students. This is an excellent way to support both reading and writing in your classroom.

# A Sample Book Review: *A Wrinkle in Time* by Madeleine L'Engle (New York: Dell, 1962)

A reader's first impression of *A Wrinkle in Time* by Madeleine L'Engle will probably be that the story is science fiction. But he or she will soon realize that it is much more. It is a story of mystery, suspense, horror, and love.

Meg Murray, a teenager, cannot sleep because of a storm that rages in the night. It is not just the storm that is bothering Meg, though. She has problems fitting in at school, she is convinced that she is not pretty, and she frets that she cannot do anything right. On top of all this, her father, a scientist who works for the government, has disappeared.

She goes downstairs where she finds her five-year-old brother, Charles Wallace. Most people think he is a moron, but Charles Wallace has strange and wonderful abilities. A short while later, Meg and Charles Wallace are joined by their mother. (Twin ten-year-old brothers, Sandy and Dennys, complete the family. Unlike Meg and Charles Wallace, they are very normal and play a small part in the story.)

Meg, Charles Wallace, and their mother are interrupted by Mrs. Whatsit, an unusual, unearthly woman. Charles Wallace knows her and greets her warmly, but Meg is suspicious. She thinks Mrs. Whatsit is a tramp.

When Mrs. Whatsit casually mentions that "there is such a thing as a tesseract" (a wrinkle in time), Mrs. Murray is shocked. That was what Mr. Murray had been researching before he disappeared.

This is the beginning of an incredible journey for Meg and Charles Wallace. They soon meet Mrs. Who and Mrs. Which and Calvin O'Keefe, a teenager who, like Charles Wallace, possesses extraordinary powers. Together they journey through wrinkles in time in search of Meg's father. They learn that he is fighting great evil. To help him, the children must confront that evil, too.

Through this confrontation, Megs finds more than her father. She also finds herself.

*A Wrinkle in Time* is a fine story that is likely to hold any reader's interest.

# Mini-Lesson 10: **Writing Movie Reviews**

*Movie reviews* are similar to book reviews in basic structure; however, they usually include a discussion of the cinematography with the storyline. Many newspapers contain movie reviews in their TV and movie sections.

## Procedure

1. Explain that a review of a movie tells a reader what the movie is about.

2. Distribute copies of (or project) the accompanying sample review of *The Babe*. Ask students to read the review.

3. Explain that in the typical movie review, the reviewer summarizes the plot (without giving away the climax), describes the characters, and offers information about the film's visual impact. Some of the questions reviews answer include:

   - Who are the actors and actresses who portray the lead characters?
   - Who produced and/or directed the film? (This is usually noted if the producer or director is well known.)
   - Was the action exciting?
   - How interesting or amusing was the film?
   - How believable were the action, dialogue, and characterization?
   - How good (or bad) was the acting?
   - If special effects were used, were they believable?
   - Were the costumes and settings realistic?
   - Did the movie have an effective or moving soundtrack?

4. Note that reviewers sometimes mention the movie rating of the movie and offer their opinion of who would be suitable viewers.

## Extensions

- Include a section of movie reviews in a class magazine.

- Ask students to bring in movie reviews from newspapers. They should share and discuss the reviews with their peer groups. Caution them to keep the discussion on the way the reviews were written, and not a mere discussion of the movie.

- Suggest that students bring to class different reviews of the same movie. While working in groups, ask students to compare and contrast the reviews. Often different reviewers offer quite different reviews of the same movie. Ask your students what the reasons might be for this.

# A Sample Movie Review: *The Babe*

a Universal release, written and produced by John Fusco

Everybody knows Babe Ruth. *The Babe* is a sentimental movie that pays respect to Babe Ruth's bigger-than-life legend. John Goodman plays George Herman Ruth, showing Babe's ready smile and swagger.

The script moves quickly through the Babe's youth, at times sacrificing historical reality for dramatic appeal. Believing that the boy is incorrigible, his parents leave him at an orphanage. Suffering from guilt and rage, the Babe finds an outlet in baseball. It is not long before he winds up with the Baltimore Orioles. By the time he is traded to Boston, he has learned about cigars, liquor, and women. It is becoming clear that Babe is a complicated man. Shy, sensitive, and prone to being vulgar, all that Babe truly wants is respect.

He finds plenty of that after his sale to the New York Yankees. In the greatest years of his career, Babe becomes a baseball hero.

The movie follows his success and also his decline. It takes us through his two marriages, the loss of his skills, and his disappointment at not becoming a baseball manager.

Director Arthur Hiller moves the story smoothly through period settings that add realism to the film. In many of the stadium scenes, the viewer almost feels that he is in the stands, rooting for the Babe.

Although Goodman plays the Babe with a fine touch, revealing that through much of his life, Babe Ruth was an overgrown boy, he fails to bring to the screen the Babe's great appeal. After all, this was a man who made baseball the national pastime. But Goodman should not be faulted for this. It is unlikely that anyone can recreate the true Babe Ruth.

*The Babe* is not a home run. It will not please baseball purists, but it is surely worth a triple.

# Mini-Lesson 11: **Writing Fiction**

There are many genres of fiction—mysteries, adventures, westerns, horrors, romances, science fiction, and fantasies are just some examples—and all require a plot. This is the action plan of the story. For students to write effective stories, they must understand the elements of a good plot. (For more information on story elements and the role they play in writing fiction, see Mini-Lessons 33 through 39 in Section Nine.)

**Procedure**

1. Explain that in the most common plot, the lead character has a problem, and the story grows around his trying to solve it. The more he tries to solve the problem, unfortunately, the worse things become. These setbacks are called complications. The lead character keeps running into complications until the story reaches the climax. This is the point where he either solves the problem or he fails.

2. Distribute copies of (or project) the following sample plot for "The Valentine's Day Dance." Allow time for students to read the plot.

3. Explain the plot breakdown:

   *Problem:* Peter wants to ask Sara to the Valentine's Day Dance.

   *Complications:* His spilling water on her during the science experiment, his dropping her lunch, and his calling her and becoming so nervous that he hangs up make it seem unlikely to him that she will ever go out with him.

   *Solution:* When Sara needs help with science after school, Peter is the only one willing to help her. Because of this, they learn that they like each other, and Sara agrees to go to the dance with him.

4. Note that this is an example of a plot with a happy ending. Sometimes lead characters do not solve their problems. Tragedies often end with the lead character failing.

# The Valentine's Day Dance

Peter would like to ask Sara to the Valentine's Day Dance. His problem is that Sara hardly knows he is alive. Making the problem worse is Sara's popularity. Being one of the prettiest cheerleaders in the school, Sara is besieged by offers for dates.

To gain her attention, Peter does everything he can to impress her. In science class he tries to help her with an experiment, but it backfires and he splashes her with water. At lunch he offers to carry her tray, but he drops it. That night he calls her on the phone to apologize, but he becomes so nervous that he abruptly hangs up. The next day he tries to tell her that they were disconnected because the battery of his cell phone suddenly ran out, but she does not believe him and becomes angry with him. Peter's chances to date Sara do not look good.

The next day Peter goes to the science lab after school to finish an experiment. He finds Sara there. She is desperately working on an assignment that she needs to get a good grade on her report card. None of her friends were willing to stay and help her. At first Peter hesitates, thinking of how foolish he has been acting. But he decides to help her anyway, because it is the right thing to do. Afterward, Sara realizes that Peter is a nice boy whom she would like to get to know better. When he summons enough courage to ask her to go to the dance, she agrees.

# Mini-Lesson 12: **Writing Advertising**

Advertisements bombard us. Powerful messages to buy products and services come to us on TV; through the radio; in junk mail, newspapers, and magazines; on billboards; on the Internet; and in spam in e-mail. Almost everywhere we go, we find advertisements (or, more accurately, advertisements find us). Since you will probably focus on written advertisements in the writing workshop, you should bring in examples of junk mail, brochures, and ads that appear in newspapers and magazines. (Whenever you or your students bring in examples of junk mail, you should blacken out names and addresses to protect privacy.)

## Procedure

1. Explain that advertising is an important writing form. Every ad is the creation of a writer. Advertisements range from the slickest TV spot to the simplest classified. The purpose of every ad is to sell a product, service, cause, or person. Ask your students to volunteer an example of each.

2. Distribute copies of (or project) the accompanying "Advertising Fundamentals."

3. Discuss the fundamentals with your students.

4. Emphasize that because ad writers always have a limited amount of space or time to get their message across, they make sure that every word is purposeful. Every word must build to the whole to sell.

## Extensions

- Distribute copies of junk mail, brochures, and ads that appear in newspapers or magazines. (A few days in advance of this activity, ask students to bring in examples of advertisements from home.) Also hand out copies of "Advertisement Review." Divide the class into groups of four to six students. Each student should have one ad to review. After reviewing the ad and completing the worksheet, students are to report to their group members their overall impressions of the ad according to the categories on the worksheet. You may then have each group pick what its members feel is the most persuasive ad and have one of the members report about it to the class.

- Suggest that students write advertisements (silly or serious) that will be printed in a class magazine.

# Advertising Fundamentals

The average person in the United States sees, hears, or reads thousands of advertisements each week. Ads may be on TV or the radio, in newspapers or magazines, on the Internet, on billboards and posters; they even arrive in postal mail and e-mail. Although advertisements may vary in content and form, all have common elements.

Every advertisement:

- *Attracts attention* through headlines, photographs, or illustrations. Some ads use only one or two of these devices; others use them all. TV commercials add in music and live action. The best headline catches attention immediately. Ads may show people using or needing a product or service or dedicating themselves to a cause, or they may associate the product or service with an important person, attractive people, wealth, beauty, status, or success.

- *Arouses interest* by promising benefits to the audience of the ad. Effective ads show how purchasing the product or service, or accepting the cause of the person being advertised, can help the targeted individual.

- *Creates desire* by showing the target audience why it needs to accept what the ad is selling. This is done through solid writing that uses strong appeal words and phrases like *best, easy, free, fresh, new, improved, guaranteed, save, inexpensive, help, proven results, money back if not satisfied,* and *full warranty.* Appeals to self-esteem, personal satisfaction, and responsibility are often used by ads that are selling a cause or a person; for example, a politician running for election.

- *Calls for action* by telling the target audience to buy now, order today, or make a commitment as soon as possible. Some ads include offers of free gifts or discounts as incentives.

# Advertisement Review

**Directions:** Review your advertisement and decide how it follows the fundamentals of sound advertising. When you are done, share your findings with your group. Attach your ad to this sheet.

Attracts attention by: _____

_____

_____

_____

Arouses interest by: _____

_____

_____

_____

Creates desire by: _____

_____

_____

_____

Calls for action by: _____

_____

_____

_____

My opinion of this ad: _____

_____

_____

_____

# Mini-Lesson 13: **Writing Nonrhyming Poems**

Many poems do not rhyme. Nonrhyming poems offer students a chance to write poetry without worrying about matching words with the same sounds, thus freeing them to concentrate on ideas and imagery.

Among the many books of poems you can use in teaching poetry to your students, one of the best I have found is Kenneth Koch's *Rose, Where Did You Get That Red?* (1989).

### Procedure

1.  Explain that most poems do not rhyme. This may be a surprise to some students who have read mostly rhyming verse.

2.  Distribute copies of (or project) the accompanying "Nonrhyming Poems" to your students. Ask students to read the two poems.

3.  Note that each of the poems expresses its ideas without rhyme or meter.

4.  Point out that poets select their words carefully so that they can evoke strong images in the minds of their readers. Sometimes they use short lines or one-word lines for emphasis. Note some examples on the poems.

5.  Mention that poets often ignore the standard rules of punctuation. They may do this to provide emphasis or as a way to let their ideas stand out in contrast to prose.

### Extensions

-   Publish examples of students' poems in a class or school magazine.

-   Encourage your students to write haiku, cinquain, or other types of nonrhyming poems. You can easily devote a number of mini-lessons to various poetry formats.

# Nonrhyming Poems

**Morning Song**

A new day starts
   With the singing of birds.
Their melodies are light,
   Happy in the coming of the new sun.
The notes arise to the treetops,
   Announcing to the world that a new day has arrived.

Listening to the birds
   I realize I'd rather
Remain in bed
   Than confront the day.

**Love Dying**

How can you tell
When love's ended?
Is there a sign that says
The End?
Does love stop of a sudden?
Without warning?
Or does it slowly slip
Away and die like a
Flower at the end of its time?
First the richness of its color fades,
Then the sweetness of its nectar dries,
Until, at last,
Its petals wrinkle and fall away and
Turn to dust,
Scattered by the wind?

# Mini-Lesson 14: **Writing Rhyming Poems**

Rhyming poems are likely to be the most familiar poems to your students. They are popular and are found in many collections. *Rose, Where Did You Get That Red?* by Kenneth Koch, noted in Mini-Lesson 13, is a good source here as well. Much of the poetry of Edgar Allan Poe offers fine examples of rhyme and meter. A good source is the *Complete Stories and Poems of Edgar Allan Poe* (1991).

**Procedure**

1. Mention that most people are familiar with rhyming poems.

2. Distribute copies of (or project) "Eldorado" by Edgar Allan Poe. Ask students to read the poem.

3. Point out the rhyme and rhythm of the poem.

4. Share the legend of El Dorado, a fabled city of gold thought to exist in the northern part of South America. Explorers and adventurers attempted to find the city and its fabulous wealth, but none succeeded. You may want to mention that many people believe that Poe wrote "Eldorado" to symbolize endless searching, which characterized much of his own life.

**Extensions**

- Explain that poets use various rhyme patterns. Select examples of poems and read them to your students, noting the rhyme patterns. Common rhyme patterns include these:

  *First* and *second* lines rhyme, *third* and *fourth* lines rhyme.

  *First* and *third* lines rhyme, *second* and *fourth* lines rhyme.

  *First* and *fourth* lines rhyme, *second* and *third* lines rhyme.

- To help your students write rhyming poems, suggest that they develop rhyming word lists. A rhyming word list is generated by taking a word such as *snow* and listing other words that rhyme with it. Write *snow* on the board or an overhead projector, and have students offer words that rhyme with it:

  *Snow:* know, no, grow, glow, flow, whoa, so, go, doe, throw, blow, slow, hoe, ho, bow, crow, low

- Discuss the use of a rhyming dictionary. Point out that these books typically list sounds, after which words that rhyme with the sound are offered. If you have a rhyming dictionary available, encourage your students to use it when writing poetry.

- Publish the poems of your students in a class or school magazine.

- Hold a class poetry reading session.

- Encourage students to write limericks.

# "Eldorado" by Edgar Allan Poe

Gaily bedight,
A gallant knight,
In sunshine and in shadow,
Had journeyed long,
Singing a song,
In search of Eldorado.

But he grew old—
This knight so bold—
And o'er his heart a shadow
Fell, as he found
No spot of ground
That looked like Eldorado.

And, as his strength
Failed him at length
He met a pilgrim shadow—
"Shadow," said he,
"Where can it be—
This land of Eldorado?"

"Over the Mountains
Of the Moon,
Down the Valley of the Shadow,
Ride, boldly ride,"
The Shade replied,—
"If you seek for Eldorado!"

# Mini-Lesson 15: **Writing Plays**

*Plays* are a form of literature designed to be performed on a stage. Thus, the play-wright must consider the visual appeal of her writing along with her words. She must plan carefully what she wishes to say, as well as how it will be said.

## Procedure

1. Explain that a play is a story performed on a stage.

2. Hand out copies of (or project) the accompanying "The Parts of a Play," and review the information with your students.

3. Depending on the type of problem and number of obstacles and complications, a play can be relatively short, just a scene or two, or quite lengthy, with several acts and scenes. No matter how long or complicated, however, the basic structure of most plays is the same.

4. Hand out copies of (or project) the accompanying sample beginning of the play "Ghost Hunt." (This is not the structure that professional play-wrights use, but it works well for students.) Briefly point out the format on the sample.

   - Plays are organized in acts and scenes, which divide the play into sections.

   - The setting is described at the beginning of scenes, and AT RISE relates the action as the curtain goes up.

   - In dialogue, the names of characters are capitalized and followed by a colon.

   - Brief stage directions and descriptions may be included with dialogue and are set in parentheses, but detailed stage directions or descriptions are usually separated from dialogue and written in parentheses.

   - A line is skipped between characters.

   - The word CURTAIN is used to end a scene.

## Extensions

- Produce some of the plays your students write.
- Stage informal readings of plays your students have written. (The actors can simply read from their lines; costumes and sets are unnecessary.)

# The Parts of a Play

Most plays are created around the following parts:

*Opening:* A problem is revealed (or suggested) and background information is supplied.

*Plan:* The lead character (or characters) tries to solve the problem and reach a goal.

*Obstacles and complications:* Events, situations, and dilemmas block the characters in their attempts to solve the problem.

*Climax:* The characters solve the problem, or they fail. Based on either solving or failing to solve the problem, the goal is reached or not reached.

# Ghost Hunt

CHARACTERS:  Todd, 15 years old
                   Cindy, 15 years old
                   Billy, 14 years old

## ACT I
### Scene 1

SETTING:  A garage in which a variety of tools and lawn implements are scattered about. It is night. Outside the window, it is dark. A long workbench with three knapsacks loaded with flashlights, cameras, lanterns, and other equipment stretches against the back wall.

AT RISE:  Todd, Billy, and Cindy are at the workbench. Todd is checking one of the knapsacks. When he is satisfied with its contents, he slips in a water bottle.

TODD (turning to others): That's it. We're set.

BILLY: You may be set, but I'm not sure I am.

CINDY: You're not afraid, are you? (Skeptically) You don't really think we're going to find any ghosts in old man Fraser's house.

BILLY: People say it's been haunted for years. The place gives me the creeps.

TODD (confidently): If there are ghosts there, we're going to prove it.

(He pulls out a digital camera from his knapsack and holds it up. He is quite pleased with it.)

TODD: This little baby is fast enough to catch anything on film.

BILLY: Even ghosts?

TODD: Even ghosts.

CINDY: Well, you've photographed just about everything else. Why not add some ghosts to your albums?

TODD (grinning): You got it. Let's go.

# Mini-Lesson 16: **Writing Screenplays**

*Screenplays,* sometimes referred to as scripts, are stories written for the movies or television. There are many sources for formats for screenplays. One I refer to is *The Elements of Screenwriting* by Irwin R. Blacker (1996). With the aid of a basic video camera and VCR, your students can write, produce, and view TV shows.

### Procedure

1. Explain what a screenplay is. Note that except for live events, virtually every TV show or movie is written before it is produced. Even on live shows, background information is often scripted.

2. Hand out copies of (or project) the accompanying sample beginning of the screenplay "The Test." Instruct students to read the script, paying close attention to the format and content.

3. Point out the special format:

   • Screenplays begin with a title.

   • Acts divide the screenplay into parts.

   • Individual scenes are numbered on the right-hand side of the script. Emphasize that a scene is a segment of the story that takes place in a particular setting.

   • The names of characters are capitalized and centered on the script. Dialogue appears under the speaker's name.

   • Dialogue and any descriptions are single-spaced, with double-spacing between the words of different characters and scenes.

### Extensions

• For students who show particular interest in writing screenplays, hand out copies of "Screenplay Vocabulary."

• With the aid of a video camera, produce and record some of the scripts your students write. Set aside time to view the productions.

# The Test

## ACT I

FADE IN:

EXT., FRONT YARD OF SCHOOL                                                    1

The camera shows the front yard of a modern, suburban school. Grass on the front court is trimmed; nicely pruned shrubs dot the area. Students are arriving to begin the day. It is bright and sunny. Three teenage friends, PETER JANSON, TOM REYNOLDS, AND DEBBIE WILLIAMS, are walking together toward the school.

The camera moves in on the three teenagers.                                  2

> DEBBIE
> (sighing, worried)
>
> I don't know how I'm going to pass that history test today.

> PETER
>
> Yeah . . . old lady Skinner's tests are murder. I need a good grade
> or I'm grounded.

> TOM
> (smiling)
>
> What's passing worth to you?

> PETER
>
> What do you mean?
>
> TOM takes a crumpled sheet of paper from his pocket.

> DEBBIE
>
> What's that?

> TOM
>
> Nothing much . . . just the answers to the test.

# Screenplay Vocabulary

Writers of movies and TV programs use a special vocabulary in developing their scripts.

*Angle on*   what the camera sees, the viewpoint of the camera

*Back to*   a return to the previous scene

*Close-up*   a close shot

*Cut to*   a switch from the viewpoint of one camera to the viewpoint of another, often employed to change scenes

*Director*   the person who supervises the filming of a screenplay

*Dissolve*   the gradual disappearing of one scene to be replaced with another

*Ext.*   abbreviation for *exterior;* used when a scene takes place outside

*Fade in*   the gradual appearing of a scene

*Fade out*   the gradual disappearing of a scene

*Favoring*   a shot that focuses on one character in a group

*Insert*   a shot of something put into a scene; for example, a letter or a map

*Int.*   abbreviation for *interior;* used when a scene takes place inside

*Long shot*   a camera shot of an entire scene

*Pan*   a camera shot that moves from side to side

*POV*   a shot taken from a character's point of view, showing what the character sees

*Producer*   the person who plans, coordinates, and supervises all phases of the making of a motion picture or TV show

*Vo*   abbreviation for *voice over,* a scene in which a character's voice is heard but he or she is not seen

# SECTION 9

# MINI-LESSONS FOR THE ART OF WRITING

# Mini-Lesson 17: **Writing Effective Leads**

The *lead* is the beginning of any piece. If the lead is not interesting, it is unlikely that the rest of the piece will be read. Good writers know how important the lead is, and many spend more time on it proportionally than they do on the other parts of their work.

## Procedure

1. Explain that every lead must hook the reader immediately. An effective lead captures the reader's interest, introduces the subject or problem, and carries the reader into the following material.

2. Mention that some leads may be a few sentences in length, while others may run several paragraphs. The leads of books may last several pages or fill an entire chapter.

3. Distribute copies of (or project) the accompanying "Leads," and discuss the information with your students. Emphasize the many ways that authors write leads.

4. Suggest that students write three, four, or more leads for a piece, and then pick what they feel is the best one. Students may also read their leads to a partner or peer group, and ask their peers to help them decide on the best lead.

5. Offer these tips for students who have trouble writing a lead:

   • They should make sure that the focus of the piece is clear.

   • Sometimes the second paragraph of a piece makes a better lead than the first.

   • When ideas for leads just do not come, students should meet with a partner or peer group, tell their peers what they intend to write, and ask for suggestions for possible leads. Stress that the author must be the one to make the final decision about the lead.

   • Some authors write the lead of a piece last. After having written the piece, it is sometimes easier to determine the best way to write the lead.

## Extensions

• Distribute copies of (or project) the accompanying "Sample Leads." Instruct your students to read the four possible leads of an article about how to study effectively for tests. Point out the differences among the leads:

   Lead 1 uses an example.

   Lead 2 relies on a quote.

   Lead 3 asks the reader a question.

   Lead 4 starts with a statement of the problem.

• Note that there are many other possible leads for the article. Divide your students into peer groups, and have them brainstorm some other leads.

• Suggest that students review the leads of various articles and stories and identify the method the author used. They may refer to the handout "Leads." Students should share their findings in peer groups.

# Leads

Whatever type of lead you choose for a piece, it must:

- Capture the reader's interest.

- Introduce the subject or problem.

- Move smoothly into the body of your piece.

Here are some ways you can write leads:

**For nonfiction:**

- State a problem.

- Use an interesting quotation.

- Ask the reader a direct question.

- Offer an interesting or unusual fact.

- Offer an alarming or surprising statistic.

- Relate a compelling anecdote or a joke.

- Offer an exaggeration of a common situation.

**For fiction:**

- Show a problem or conflict the characters have.

- Show action (in which a character is performing a task) that is related to a problem.

- Start with dialogue in which characters are talking about a problem.

- Create a sense of foreboding; something important (the problem) is about to happen.

- Depict a humorous situation.

# Sample Leads

Following are four possible leads for an article about how to study effectively for tests.

### Lead 1

Jason is a typical high school sophomore. Last night he was studying for a major history test. Feeling that music relaxes him, he put on the stereo and opened his book. After two hours—during which he treated himself to some snacks and his favorite TV show—he decided that he had studied enough. After all, he had spent two hours.

The next day Jason failed the test. Why? He does not know how to study effectively.

### Lead 2

"Students fail tests because they don't know how to study," says Ed Harmon, a high school history teacher. Harmon's statement is echoed by teachers throughout the country.

### Lead 3

Do you know how to study for tests? If you answered yes, you are in the minority. Most students do not know how to study for tests effectively.

### Lead 4

Test-taking is a major activity in American schools. It is also one of the most anxiety-causing. The reason for this comes down to a simple fact—most students do not know how to study for tests.

# Mini-Lesson 18: **Organization for Nonfiction Writing**

In writing, good organization results in a smooth flow of main ideas and details that carry the reader along and build to a whole. Just as a house is constructed one brick at a time, an article or story is written by building one idea on top of another. (For additional information, see "Organizing Writing" in Section Three.)

## Procedure

1. Explain that nonfiction writing is most often organized in a *chronological* or *logical* manner.

2. In a *chronological* pattern, ideas or events are usually arranged in the sequence in which they occur. For example, what happens first in time appears first, what happens second appears second, and what happens third appears third, building to a conclusion. The chronological pattern is common for personal narratives, articles, and fiction.

3. In a *logical* pattern, ideas are arranged in some systematic way. A description of a place, for instance, might be organized from left to right, inside to outside, or up to down. Another logical pattern is arranging ideas in order from least to most important, or from most to least important.

4. Caution students that whatever way they organize their information, their ideas must be supported with facts and examples.

5. Distribute copies of (or project) the accompanying "Vanishing Rain Forests." Instruct students to read the article. Note that after the opening, ideas are presented that support the article's main purpose: to explain what a rain forest is, why rain forests are important, how they are being destroyed, and what can be done to stop the destruction.

## Extensions

- Suggest that students look for the organizational patterns in articles that they read.

- Give students a collection of facts, and have them work together in small groups to organize the facts into a report.

# Vanishing Rain Forests

The rain forests of the earth are disappearing. Once covering over 4 billion acres, rain forests now cover about half that area, with more forest land being lost each day. Most scientists agree that continued destruction of the rain forests will have far-reaching consequences and affect people the world over.

A rain forest is thickly wooded land usually found in a warm, tropical climate. The typical rain forest receives about 100 inches of rainfall per year and has an average temperature of about 80° Fahrenheit. Most rain forests are located in Latin America, Asia, and Africa, in a wide belt between the Tropic of Cancer and the Tropic of Capricorn.

Although rain forests cover only about 7 percent of the world's land, they are a precious resource. More than 50 percent of the earth's plant and animal species flourish in the abundant rainfall and warm temperatures of rain forests. Rain forests influence climate, absorb carbon dioxide from the atmosphere, and replenish oxygen in the air we breathe. Many products, including wood, dyes, foods, and medicines, come from rain forests.

The primary cause of the destruction of the rain forests is human activity. Millions of people live in rain forests, relying on the forests for their livelihood and shelter. Each year, thousands of square miles of rain forest are cleared for farming, ranching, mining, and logging.

Fortunately, governments, scientists, and many other concerned individuals recognize the importance of preserving the rain forests. These organizations and people support improved land-use practices and education to slow the rate of deforestation. They hope that appropriate legislation can bring about management of the resources of the rain forests in a manner that will benefit everyone and yet save the forests.

Because of their environmental and economic significance, rain forests are a crucial resource. Loss of the rain forests will affect the earth in ways scientists can as yet only estimate.

# Mini-Lesson 19: **Writing Conclusions for Nonfiction Pieces**

Many students (and professional writers too!) have trouble knowing when to end a piece. Some writers, not sure how to conclude, end their writing abruptly once they run out of ideas. Others continue to write after a piece is done, stretching it out and weakening the impression it would otherwise have on the reader. Some students, of course, keep writing in the hope that if they write more, they will get a better grade. In whatever manner it is done (or not done), a weak conclusion detracts from the writing that comes before it.

## Procedure

1. Explain that a good conclusion flows naturally out of the body of the piece. Tell your students that once they have gotten across all the ideas they wish to share in their writing, it is time to conclude. Continuing to write after that will only repeat ideas or include ideas that do not belong.

2. Distribute copies of (or project) "Vanishing Rain Forests" from Mini-Lesson 18. Instruct students to read the article, and focus on the conclusion.

3. Explain these two common methods for concluding a piece:

   - A conclusion may be a summary of the main ideas of a piece. While this may be acceptable for writers who are still uncertain of themselves, it is not the best conclusion.

   - A better way to conclude a piece is to leave the reader with a final thought that ties together the main ideas. This method is used in "Vanishing Rain Forests." Note how the main point is restated and the reader is left with a final idea to consider.

## Extension

- Encourage your students to read magazine articles to see how the authors concluded their articles. They should share their findings with members of their peer groups and discuss the ways authors conclude their work. In this way, students will be exposed to different kinds of conclusions.

# Mini-Lesson 20: **Conciseness**

Most of the best writing is concise. Brevity helps writing to flow smoothly and makes it easier for the reader to comprehend the author's ideas. Everything becomes clearer; less becomes more.

## Procedure

1. Explain that to write concisely requires eliminating all unnecessary words. This is difficult even for professional authors.

2. Suggest that when they finish a draft, students ask an editing partner to read the piece carefully and underline every word, phrase, and sentence that the editor feels might be eliminated. The final decision for deleting material rests with the author, but the identification of possible places to cut is the first step to reaching conciseness.

3. Distribute copies of (or project) "Cutting Clutter." Briefly go over the examples that show how clutter can be eliminated and concise writing achieved. Emphasize that these are only some examples, and that good writers are always on the lookout for ways to make their writing concise.

# Cutting Clutter

Good writing is concise. The author tries to eliminate all unnecessary words, phrases, and sentences. Following are examples of wordy phrases with concise alternatives. Look for phrases like these in your writing and revise them.

| Cluttered Phrase | Alternative |
|---|---|
| great in size | great |
| twenty in number | twenty |
| personal friend | friend |
| with regard to | about |
| that there | that |
| all of a sudden | suddenly |
| at the present time | now |
| by means of | by |
| completely filled | filled |
| during the time that | while |
| foreign imports | imports |
| basic fundamentals | fundamentals |
| for the purpose of | for |
| in relation to | about |
| doctor by profession | doctor |
| order up | order |
| referred to as | called |
| in view of the fact that | as |
| with the exception of | except |
| thought to himself or herself | thought |
| until such a time | until |
| prior to the start of | before |
| seems to be | is |
| entirely finished | finished |
| red in color | red |
| on the subject of | about |
| absolutely necessary | necessary |
| due to the fact that | because |
| past experience | experience |
| totally destroyed | destroyed |

# Mini-Lesson 21: **Avoiding Intensifiers and Qualifiers**

*Intensifiers* and *qualifiers* can fill a piece with useless words and phrases that obscure ideas. Although writers often use them in an attempt to strengthen their writing, intensifiers and qualifiers instead weaken their work.

## Procedure

1. Explain that writers may use intensifiers and qualifiers in the hope of adding emphasis to their words. Strong writing, however, does not need them.

2. Offer these examples of intensifiers and qualifiers by writing them on the board or an overhead projector:

   | **Intensifiers** | **Qualifiers** |
   |---|---|
   | really | in a sense |
   | very | sort of |
   | quite | kind of |
   | so | a bit |
   | seemingly | |
   | somewhat | |

3. Note that intensifiers like *very* and *really* are unnecessary to just about any sentence. Suppose a day is cloudy. How much cloudier must it be to be "very" cloudy? Cloudy is cloudy. *Really* in most cases is simply a wasted word. It offers no additional meaning to a word it modifies. Is there a difference between good and "really" good?

4. Explain that a thing is never "sort of" or "in a sense." It is or it is not. For example, a day may be partly cloudy, but it is not "sort of" cloudy. "Sort of" in that example is vague. It does not convey the idea clearly.

5. Explain that "a bit" or "somewhat" means a part of something. Yet we often use these qualifiers in sentences like "All it takes is a bit of luck to win a lottery." "A bit" does not add to the sentence. After all, how much is "a bit" of luck?

6. Mention that intensifiers and qualifiers can weaken writing. Offer these examples:

   "She was a very lovely woman" sounds weaker than "She was a lovely woman."

   "He was really angry" sounds weaker than "He was angry."

7. Emphasize that intensifiers and qualifiers slip into writing easily. Authors must proofread their work carefully to eliminate them.

# Mini-Lesson 22: Active and Passive Constructions

Good writers use *active* rather than *passive* constructions. Active constructions are forceful and add clarity to writing. Passive constructions are weak.

Here is a sentence using an active verb: "Jim punched Joe." It is strong and direct and paints a clear image. Compare it to its passive counterpart. "Joe was punched by Jim." This is wordy and less vivid. Writing that is filled with passive constructions plods. Too much of it makes writing flat.

**Procedure**

1. Put the following examples of active and passive constructions on the board or an overhead projector and discuss them with your students:

   The mother carried her baby. (ACTIVE)
   The baby was carried by her mother. (PASSIVE)

   Jeff smiled at Kim. (ACTIVE)
   Kim was smiled at by Jeff. (PASSIVE)

   Point out that although the main verbs are the same, the construction of the sentences is different.

2. Point out that passive constructions include uses of the verb "to be" with a past participle. Share this example:

   Ted built the model. (ACTIVE)

   The model was built by Ted. (PASSIVE)

   Explain that passive verb phrases can often be rewritten using the main verb; for example, using the verb *built* instead of *was built*.

3. Point out the wordiness and loss of energy in the passive sentences compared to the active ones. Active constructions help readers to visualize action easier.

**Extension**

- Suggest that students choose one of their pieces, read through it, and circle any passive constructions they find. They should then revise the passive constructions, making them active.

# Mini-Lesson 23: **Choosing Strong Verbs for Writing**

Along with choosing active constructions, encourage your students to select strong, precise verbs. Rather than rely on adverbs to help the reader visualize the action, good writers pick verbs that can stand alone.

### Procedure

1. Write the following examples of verbs on the board or an overhead projector.

    walked unsteadily—staggered

    walked softly—tiptoed

    yelled loudly—shouted

    punched furiously—pummeled

    held tightly—clutched

    said softly—whispered

    beat wildly—pounded

2. Explain that while the verbs combined with the adverbs on the left are acceptable, the verbs on the right are precise and forceful. They draw a clear image in the reader's mind and help to make writing more concise.

### Extension

• Suggest that students proofread one of their pieces specifically for instances where they have used adverbs to describe verbs. They should try to replace those verbs with precise, forceful counterparts.

# Mini-Lesson 24: **Writing Effective Transitions**

*Transitions* are words and phrases that link ideas. They help writing flow smoothly by forming bridges that enable the reader to move easily from one idea to another. Without effective transitions, writing becomes rough and choppy as the switch between ideas is abrupt. The reader is jarred, and the coherence of the piece is shattered.

## Procedure

1. Explain the importance of transitions.

2. Distribute copies of (or project) the accompanying "Nonverbal Communication," which is the beginning of an article. The example highlights a transition.

3. Instruct students to read the first version of the example, which is missing an important transition. Ask students to find where a transition is needed. Tell them to read the revised version that includes the missing transition. It is in the beginning of paragraph 3. In the first version, starting that paragraph with "A smile communicates happiness or pleasure" is an abrupt shift from the description of head gestures. The revision, "Like the head, the face also can be used for communication," carries the main idea of the previous paragraph into the following one, bridging the gap between them. The transition tells the reader that the article has shifted to a description of facial gestures. It helps the article to flow smoothly.

## Extensions

- Explain that along with the carryover of ideas to make transitions, writers also use special words and phrases to link ideas. Put the following words on the board or an overhead projector:

  | | | |
  |---|---|---|
  | after | but | in addition to |
  | also | during | instead of |
  | although | earlier | just as |
  | at last | finally | later |
  | before | for example | rather than |
  | beyond | however | therefore |

- Mention that these are some of the more common words used for transitions and that there are many others. Any word or phrase that links ideas can be used.

- Suggest that as they read stories or articles, students look for transitions and see how authors construct them.

# Nonverbal Communication

## Version 1

When most people think of communication, they think of talking. But people can speak nonverbally, too, through various gestures. Head, facial, hand, and body gestures can send clear messages to others.

The most common head gestures are the shake and nod. When a person shakes his head, he moves his head horizontally from side to side. The message sent is no. The head nod, however, in which the head moves up and down, means yes. Since the head nod is found in every culture of the world, some psychologists believe that it is an inborn gesture.

A smile communicates happiness or pleasure. A frown expresses sadness or anger. The eyes also are used to communicate. When a person is frustrated, he will often roll his eyes upward. A wink, on the other hand, expresses secrecy. It may affirm something that two people know that others present do not know. It may be an expression of fondness, or it may be a greeting when verbal communication is inappropriate.

## Version 2

When most people think of communication, they think of talking. But people can speak nonverbally, too, through various gestures. Head, facial, hand, and body gestures can send clear messages to others.

The most common head gestures are the shake and nod. When a person shakes his head, he moves his head horizontally from side to side. The message sent is no. The head nod, however, in which the head moves up and down, means yes. Since the head nod is found in every culture of the world, some psychologists believe that it is an inborn gesture.

Like the head, the face also can be used for communication. A smile communicates happiness or pleasure. A frown expresses sadness or anger. The eyes also are used to communicate. When a person is frustrated, he will often roll his eyes upward. A wink, on the other hand, expresses secrecy. It may affirm something that two people know that others present do not know. It may be an expression of fondness, or it may be a greeting when verbal communication is inappropriate.

# Mini-Lesson 25: **Developing Imagery**

*Imagery* refers to the pictures that readers see in their minds as they read. Specific details that appeal to the senses and make a dominant impression help to create powerful images.

## Procedure

1. Explain what imagery is.

2. Distribute copies of (or project) the accompanying sample, "Returning to the Beach." Ask students to read the description and then point out the details that build the images—for example:

   "breathed deeply of the salty air" (smell)

   "warm sand scrunching beneath my feet and pushing up between my toes." (touch)

   "The breeze . . . was cool." (touch)

   "cries of the gulls" (hearing)

3. Emphasize that strong imagery is built on an appeal to the senses (sight, touch, taste, hearing, and smell). Details should be specific and concrete. Offer these examples:

   Instead of "flower," choose "yellow tulip."

   Instead of "strong smell," choose "pungent odor of garlic."

   Instead of "rain," choose "cold, December rain."

   Instead of "sound of the horn," choose "shrill blast of the horn."

   Instead of "great-tasting cake," choose "rich chocolate cake."

## Extension

- Explain that the ability to write strong imagery comes largely from being a good observer of the world. Suggest that students train themselves to be good observers. Whenever they are at an event, they should look for the details that impress their senses. Distribute copies of the "Sense and Image" worksheet, which students can use as a guide to becoming keen observers of the world around them. After completing the sheet, they may discuss their impressions with members of a peer group.

# Returning to the Beach

I had not been to the beach in several months. The moment I stepped out of the car I realized how I had missed it.

As I breathed deeply of the salty air, I felt invigorated and renewed. Slipping off my shoes, I walked toward the surf, warm sand scrunching beneath my feet and pushing up between my toes.

The breeze coming off the ocean was cool. That was not surprising in early June, but the sun was hot and high, a sign of summer. The cries of the nearby gulls were soothing, for they reminded me of the many summers I had spent here.

# Sense and Image

**Directions:** Select a place for observation. Some places you might consider include a sporting event, the school cafeteria at lunch time, or your backyard. Observe the details of this place, and record how your senses are stimulated.

Sight: _____

_____

_____

_____

Touch: _____

_____

_____

_____

Hearing: _____

_____

_____

_____

Smell: _____

_____

_____

_____

Taste: _____

_____

_____

_____

# Mini-Lesson 26: **Tone**

The *tone* an author uses in a piece helps to communicate her ideas. For example, the sentence "That's fine." can have different meanings depending on the context in which it is used. It may be said matter-of-factly, sarcastically, or with sympathy. Tone in writing is similar to tone in speaking. Often it communicates just as much as words.

**Procedure**

1. Explain that tone is a manner of expression that helps to enhance or clarify a writer's words.

2. Explain that the best tone for a piece is one that is appropriate for the material and audience.

3. Note that tone can be formal, tragic, angry, kindly, cheerful, sarcastic, personal, or impersonal. It can reflect the entire range of human emotions. The tone of a how-to article, for example, should be simple and straightforward, while the tone of a comedy piece should be playful and light.

4. Distribute copies of (or project) "How You Say It." Instruct your students to read the examples, which display different tones. Discuss the examples, noting the differences:

   Example 1: A. understanding tone; B. cruel tone

   Example 2: A. impatient tone; B. moderate tone

   Example 3: A. impersonal tone; B. humorous tone

   Example 4: A. angry tone; B. moderate tone; C. sarcastic tone

**Extensions**

- Suggest that students try to identify the tone in articles and stories they read.

- If a student writes a piece with a distinctive tone, have that student read the piece from the author's chair. Point out how the tone fits the piece and supports the author's intention.

# How You Say It

Much meaning can be obtained from an author's tone, which is revealed in the way an author constructs a sentence to communicate an idea. Depending on the context of a sentence, tone may communicate as much meaning as words do. Although the following examples communicate the same general idea, they have different tones. Identify the different tones.

## Example 1

**A.** Sara's little sister always seems to hang out with Sara and her friends.

**B.** Sara's little sister is a nuisance; she is always bothering Sara and her friends.

## Example 2

**A.** The government must enact the appropriate legislation now.

**B.** The government should take the lead by passing the appropriate legislation.

## Example 3

**A.** He ate all of the cookies.

**B.** He gulped the entire box of cookies.

## Example 4

**A.** Move that car right now! It's blocking the driveway!

**B.** Please move the car. It's blocking the driveway.

**C.** Move the car. Can't you see it's blocking the driveway?

# Mini-Lesson 27: **Comparing and Contrasting**

Authors use the techniques of comparing and contrasting to show similarities and differences between things. Although the words *compare* and *contrast* are often used together, they have different meanings. *Comparing* examines similarities; *contrasting* looks at differences.

## Procedure

1. Explain the meanings of *comparing* and *contrasting*.

2. Explain that comparing and contrasting can be used in both fiction and non-fiction.

3. Note that comparing and contrasting are excellent methods for showing details. They help to paint clear images.

4. Distribute copies of (or project) the accompanying "Comparing and Contrasting—Nonfiction." Instruct your students to read the two examples. Briefly discuss them.

5. Note that there are two ways to compare or contrast.

   - The author describes the first idea, event, situation, or character completely. He then describes the second and compares or contrasts it with the first.

   - The author takes one point in common from each idea, event, situation, or character and compares or contrasts it directly. He then compares or contrasts a second point, then a third, and so on.

## Extension

- Distribute copies of (or project) "Comparing and Contrasting—Fiction." Have students read the two examples and then discuss their impressions. Be sure to note how the author compares and contrasts ideas.

# Comparing and Contrasting—Nonfiction

The following paragraphs are about Earth and Venus. Read the paragraphs and note how the planets are compared and contrasted.

## Comparing

Venus and Earth are often called sister planets. They have much in common. They are inner planets, Venus being the second planet from the sun and the Earth being the third. Both are about the same size and have a similar mass and density. Both are composed mostly of rock and iron and possess well-defined land masses. Recent observations indicate that the continents of Venus shift as do the continents of Earth, leading to periodic volcanic eruptions and Venusquakes.

## Contrasting

However, the similarities soon end. Just like sisters who do not get along, Earth and Venus have many distinct features. While the average surface temperature of the Earth is about 59° Fahrenheit, the average surface temperature of Venus is near 900°Fahrenheit, hot enough to melt lead. Unlike Earth's atmosphere, which is composed mostly of nitrogen and oxygen, with traces of gases like carbon dioxide, Venus's atmosphere is almost all carbon dioxide. Since carbon dioxide traps the heat of the sun, Venus is an example of a runaway greenhouse effect. Once Venus was thought to be much like Earth, but now astronomers know that it is very different from our own planet.

# Comparing and Contrasting—Fiction

## Comparing

It was obvious to Laurie that Tim was John's younger brother. They had the same blond hair, gray eyes, and quick smiles. Both were tall and had the rugged good looks of boys who enjoyed the outdoors.

[By comparing Tim to John, the author paints a clear physical description of both brothers.]

## Contrasting

Tara was unlike her sister, Jill. Jill was happy, but Tara was moody. Whereas Jill always seemed to be smiling, Tara wore a constant frown. Even their hair and eyes were different. Jill had light hair and green eyes, while Tara's dark hair and eyes were striking in their utter lack of color.

[By contrasting the two sisters, both are characterized and shown to be different.]

# Mini-Lesson 28: **Avoiding Clichés**

*Clichés* are expressions that have been used so often in writing and speaking that they are familiar to readers. That familiarity tarnishes writing. It steals freshness from an author's words, detracts from style, and ruins originality. Clichés, which slip into writing easily, should always be revised.

**Procedure**

1. Distribute copies of "Clichés," and review the list with your students. Suggest that they retain the list in their writing folders and refer to it periodically. This will help them to become aware of cliché phrases. Note that this is only a partial list and that they can add many clichés to it.

2. Explain that clichés undermine style and freshness in writing.

3. Emphasize that clichés should always be rewritten. Model how that can be done by writing the following examples on the board or an overhead projector:

   Jamil soon realized that the job *was easier said than done.*
   Jamil soon realized that the job would be difficult.

   She *sighed in relief.*
   She sighed, relieved.

   Rachel was *as busy as a bee.*
   Rachel was busy.

4. Explain that in the first two examples, the clichés are eliminated and the ideas are expressed through revision. In the third, the cliché is eliminated by simply cutting unnecessary words.

5. Note that if a phrase comes to mind easily or if it sounds familiar, it is likely to be a cliché.

6. Mention that even professional authors have trouble keeping clichés off their pages. It takes careful editing to find them.

# Clichés

Clichés are phrases that have been used so much in writing and speaking that they are familiar to readers. Because they are familiar, they make writing stale and boring. Following are some common clichés. Revise them whenever you find them in your writing.

| | |
|---|---|
| add insult to injury | grinning from ear to ear |
| green with envy | in this day and age |
| long arm of the law | few and far between |
| depths of despair | word to the wise |
| at death's door | got a tiger by the tail |
| one in a million | not a second too soon |
| writing on the wall | heart on his sleeve |
| to the bitter end | on cloud nine |
| in a jiffy | weary bones |
| bury the hatchet | it's in the bag |
| weigh a ton | cried her eyes out |
| beyond a shadow of a doubt | accidents will happen |
| white as a ghost | calm before the storm |
| break the ice | in the same boat |
| stopped dead in her tracks | once in a lifetime |
| heart skipped a beat | raining cats and dogs |
| sighed in relief | busy as a bee |
| easier said than done | to make a long story short |

# Mini-Lesson 29: **Conducting Interviews**

*Interviews* can be an important source of information. Although most people associate interviews with nonfiction writing, interviews can also be a source of excellent information for stories.

### Procedure

1. Explain that interviews can provide authors with firsthand information that they may not be able to obtain elsewhere.

2. Mention that interviews with people who are experts on a subject or have personal experience with something can provide interesting information and quotes that can highlight an author's writing.

3. Explain that effective interviews are the result of several factors. Distribute copies of the accompanying "Guide to Great Interviews" and review these factors with your students. Suggest that students retain the handout for future reference.

### Extensions

- Encourage your students to interview people who can provide information on topics the students are writing about. For example, an uncle who worked overseas, a cousin who is a police officer, or an aunt who owns a business might be interesting people to interview and write about.

- Suggest that students work with a partner and conduct interviews of each other. After gathering information, students should write biographical sketches of their partners. Collect the pieces and publish them in a class book.

# Guide to Great Interviews

Interviews can provide authors with information that might be hard or impossible to find elsewhere. Every good interview is a result of several factors:

1. Before attempting to interview anyone on a topic, you must understand the topic. Collect background information.

2. Think of people who can give you the information you need. For example, if you are writing a piece on a fitness plan a person can follow at home, a gym teacher or athletic coach might be a good choice to interview.

3. Before the interview, think of questions you would like to ask. Use questions that encourage explanations. Do not ask: "Is exercise good for a person?" The answer will be a simple yes. Instead ask: "What benefits can a person get from exercise?" Write down your questions so that you will not forget to ask them during the interview.

4. Be alert to the answers you receive. They can lead to more questions. If you are not sure about an answer, politely ask for clarification.

5. Take notes or use a recorder. If you plan to use a recorder, first ask if the person you are speaking with minds being taped. Some people do. If you use a recorder, make sure it is working properly and that you have an extra set of batteries.

   If you take notes, do not try to write everything down. You will never be able to. Write down key points. Inventing your own shorthand is helpful. For example, use *S* for *Mr. Smith, jg* for *jogging, ex* for *exercise,* and a plus sign for *and.* Such codes speed your note taking.

6. When you quote the person, be sure to use his or her exact words. In your writing, put those words in quotation marks.

7. Do not stretch out the interview longer than necessary. Once you have your information, recheck important facts and thank the person. Be genuinely appreciative. You might also write a thank-you note a few days later. Remember, no one has to give you an interview.

# Mini-Lesson 30: Using Figures of Speech: Similes, Metaphors, and Personification

*Figures of speech* can enhance writing style and make ideas distinct. *Similes* and *metaphors* make comparisons; *personification* gives nonhuman things or ideas human qualities. When used properly, figures of speech can elevate a piece from the ordinary to the outstanding.

**Procedure**

1. Explain that similes, metaphors, and personification are known as figures of speech.

2. Distribute copies of (or project) the accompanying "Figures of Speech."

3. Explain that similes make comparisons using the words *like, as,* or *than.* Instruct students to read the three examples of similes. Point out the comparisons.

4. Explain that metaphors make comparisons without using *like, as,* or *than.* Have students read the two examples. Point out the comparisons.

5. Explain that personification permits authors to give human qualities to animals, plants, things, and ideas. Have students read the three examples and point out the personifications.

6. Encourage students to use figures of speech in their writing.

**Extension**

- Suggest that students look for figures of speech in their reading. Studying how authors use similes, metaphors, and personification will help them use figures of speech in their own writing.

# Figures of Speech

Authors use figures of speech to compare ideas and create strong images. Figures of speech include similes, metaphors, and personification.

## Similes

Similes use *like, as,* or *than* to make comparisons.

Her eyes twinkled like the stars.

His brooding eyes were dark as night.

He was craftier than a fox.

## Metaphors

Metaphors make comparisons without using the signaling words *like, as,* or *than.*

The mountain range was a wall blocking them from the fertile lands to the south.

The boxer was a true warrior.

## Personification

Personification gives human qualities to nonhuman things or ideas.

The creatures of the night have their own songs.

Even the sky wept.

Two giant boulders stood guard at the entrance of the secret cave.

# Mini-Lesson 31: **Using Onomatopoeia**

*Onomatopoeia* is the use of words that sound like the things they name. Because they appeal to the sense of sound, onomatopoeic words can evoke clear, strong images.

**Procedure**

1. Explain what onomatopoeia is.

2. Ask your students to listen for the sounds as you read these following examples:

   - The bee buzzed through the garden, stopping at each flower in search of pollen.

   Note that *buzzed* sounds like a bee and helps the reader-listener to see that bee in his or her imagination.

   - The smoke detector blared at 2:00 A.M., shocking Jim awake.

   Point out that *blared* suggests the sound of a smoke detector and adds vigor to the scene.

   - The magician smiled as the green powder fizzed in the potion.

   Note that *fizzed* relates the sound it describes.

3. Encourage students to use onomatopoeic words when appropriate in their writing, but warn them not to overuse these words.

**Extension**

- Distribute copies of the accompanying "Onomatopoeic Words." Review the list with your students. Suggest that students try to add words to the list, then share the lists with partners or peer groups.

# Onomatopoeic Words

Onomatopoeic words suggest the sounds they describe. They appeal to the sense of hearing. Bees buzz, cows moo, and lions roar. Several other examples of onomatopoeic words follow. After reviewing the list, see if you can add more.

| | | |
|---|---|---|
| bang | hiss | sizzle |
| boom | honk | slurp |
| bow-wow | hoot | splash |
| clang | howl | squish |
| clink | hum | swish |
| coo | meow | tick-tock |
| crackle | moan | thud |
| cuckoo | neigh | thump |
| fizz | puff | tinkle |
| growl | rev | twang |
| grunt | ring | whistle |
| gurgle | rustle | whiz |

What others can you add?

_____

_____

_____

_____

_____

_____

_____

_____

_____

_____

_____

_____

# Mini-Lesson 32: **Using Alliteration**

*Alliteration* is the use of two or more words in a sentence that have the same beginning sounds. Effective use of alliteration can enhance writing style, add rhythm and flow to words, or emphasize ideas.

## Procedure

1. Explain what alliteration is.

2. Distribute copies of (or project) "A Sample of Alliteration," which highlights alliteration through poetry. Ask students to read the poem and then discuss the examples of alliteration:

   *Line 1,* sun, sea (note that "rises" also has an "s" sound which adds to the effect)

   *Line 2,* glow, glare

   *Line 3,* burst, brightness

   *Line 4,* sweeps, sea (note that "across" also has an "s" sound)

   *Line 9,* scattered, sunbeams; brilliant, sunbeams (although the "b" sound is on the second syllable in "sunbeams," this still produces an alliterative sound)

   *Line 10,* waits, west

   *Line 11,* another, night

   *Line 12,* dominates, day

3. Note that while these examples are of poetry, alliteration can also be used effectively in prose.

4. Caution students that while alliteration can add to their writing, too much of it can detract from their words and ideas.

## Extension

- Ask students to work with a partner. Partners should read some of each other's previous writings and note examples of alliteration. They should then discuss how the alliteration enhanced the piece. They may also identify places where alliteration could be added to improve the piece.

# A Sample of Alliteration

The following poem has several examples of alliteration. Find as many examples as you can.

### Sunburst

|  |  |
|---|---|
| 1 | The sun rises from the sea, |
| 2 | First a glow, then a glare. |
| 3 | Then a burst of brightness |
| 4 | That sweeps across the sea, |
| 5 | Making a dazzling golden road over |
| 6 | The waves to the land. |
|  |  |
| 7 | The morning star blazes, |
| 8 | But its light soon fades, |
| 9 | Scattered by brilliant sunbeams. |
|  |  |
| 10 | Only the moon waits in the west |
| 11 | For another night, its luster gone. |
| 12 | The sun dominates the new day. |

# Mini-Lesson 33: **Conflict**

*Conflict* is an essential component of every story. It is the fuel for the plot. As characters try to solve the problems they encounter in a story, they inevitably find themselves in conflict with others, their environment, or themselves. (See Mini-Lesson 11 in Section Eight for information on plots.)

**Procedure**

1. Explain that conflict is a vital part of every story. Without it, there would be no action, suspense, or urgency. Stories would be boring.

2. Explain conflict in terms of goals. Characters have goals—things that they want to achieve. As they try to reach their goals, they are blocked by others, the environment, or their own limitations. Trying to overcome these obstacles puts the characters in conflict.

3. Distribute copies of (or project) the outline for the story "The Runaway." Review the outline with your students, and discuss the conflict that arises out of the plot:

    - In the opening, the conflict arises between Sue and her mother over Eddie.

    - After Sue runs away, she is in conflict with Eddie, who tries to convince her to go home.

    - At the bus terminal, Sue is in conflict with herself as she struggles to decide what to do.

    - The resolution of the story occurs when she decides to go home and try to solve the problem.

    Note that the outline offers the basic plot and that the story would be developed with more details, action, and dialogue.

**Extensions**

- Suggest that students look for conflict in the stories they read and see how conflict arises from the plot.

- Conduct a class discussion about the conflict in a story students have read or in a movie they have seen.

# The Runaway

Determine the conflict in the following plot outline. Notice how the conflict switches between people.

I. Sue walks home from school with Eddie, her boyfriend. They stop a few blocks from her house. Sue is not supposed to be seeing Eddie because her parents disapprove of him. They say he is not good enough for her. Unknown to Sue and Eddie, her mother is driving by and sees her with Eddie.

II. Sue arrives home. Her mother is waiting for her, and they argue about Eddie. Sue believes that her parents do not understand her; her mother counters that Sue is too young to understand what is good for her. Crying, Sue runs to her room.

III. Later that night, Sue decides to run away. She packs some things and slips out. She goes to Eddie's house. When she tells him what she has done, he tries to convince her that what she is doing will not solve the problem. Sue refuses to listen to him and runs off before he can stop her.

IV. Eddie calls Sue's parents and tells them what has happened. At first her parents do not believe him, but when Sue's mother checks her room, she realizes that Eddie is telling the truth. Together, Eddie and Sue's parents begin searching for her.

V. It is late at night. Sue is waiting, alone, at a bus terminal. She is thinking about what Eddie said, that running away will not solve their problem. She also thinks about her feelings for him, and her love for her parents. She begins to realize that he was right. Finally, she decides to go home. She meets Eddie and her parents at the front door of the bus terminal.

# Mini-Lesson 34: **Characterization**

*Characterization* is the way a writer delineates characters. Effective characterization is achieved by revealing the natures of characters and making them seem like real people with whom readers can identify.

## Procedure

1. Explain that when we think of a good story, we usually think of the characters. It is hard to think of a story without recalling the characters.

2. Explain that authors invent characters and show their traits through actions, descriptions, dialogue, and thoughts. In this way they reveal the natures of characters.

3. Distribute copies of (or project) the accompanying "Revealing Character," and review the information with your students. Identify the different traits the examples show.

   ### Through Action
   Example 1: Joe is dishonest.

   Example 2: Jan is courageous.

   Example 3: Julio is confident.

   Example 4: Peter is not confident.

   Example 5: Alice is trustworthy.

   ### Through Description
   Example 6: Samantha's hair is brown and curly.

   Example 7: Mario is big and strong for a fourteen-year-old boy.

   Example 8: Bailey is mean.

   ### Through Thoughts
   Example 9: Marty gives up easily.

   Example 10: Marsha is determined.

4. Caution students not to overcharacterize. Readers do not need to know every detail about a character. They do not need to know everything a character wears or witness every thought. Only traits necessary to the story should be revealed. Minor characters may need only one or two traits.

5. Emphasize that the actions of characters must always be motivated. Characters must have logical reasons for doing the things they do.

6. Note that names should fit the personalities of characters. Names carry impressions. *Laurie,* for instance, sounds like a wholesome young woman. *Barker* sounds tough—a good name for a detective. *William* sounds bookish or maybe nerdy, but *Bill* is one of the guys.

7. Mention that character tags refer to favorite phrases, gestures, or manner-isms like snapping the fingers or clicking the tongue that a character does repeatedly. Tags are excellent ways to characterize because they reinforce an impression on readers, but they must be used with care so that they do not become tiresome.

### Extensions

- Ask students to think of a favorite character from a story, TV show, or movie. Distribute copies of the accompanying "Character Chart" and ask them to identify that character's traits. They should share their charts with a partner or a peer group.

- Distribute copies of "Character Chart" for students to use in the creation of characters for their own stories. Explain that many professional authors use character charts to help them develop characters. Mention that there are many types of charts and that this is a common example.

- Suggest that students focus their attention on characterization as they read a story or watch a movie or TV show. They should ask themselves the following:

  How are the characters developed?

  What traits are revealed?

  How are the traits revealed?

# Revealing Character

You can reveal your characters to readers in three ways.

## Through Action

- What the character does.

  *Example 1:* Joe steals a bike.

  *Example 2:* The building is on fire, and Jan rushes in and saves her little sister.

- What the character says.

  *Example 3:* "I think we can do it," Julio said, looking up at the mountain.

  *Example 4:* "We'll never make it," Peter said, looking up at the mountain.

- What other characters say or think about a character.

  *Example 5:* "Alice Foster is one person you can count on," Jake said.

## Through Description

*Example 6:* Samantha's brown hair curled down to her shoulders.

*Example 7:* Mario's muscles bulged as he helped his father move the couch. At fourteen he was big for his age and could lift as much as many men.

*Example 8:* Bailey's eyes were cold and blue and he talked like the bad guy in a typical Western—slowly, between gritted teeth, as if he might lose his patience at any moment and just shoot you.

## Through Thoughts

*Example 9:* I'll never pass that test, Marty thought, sighing. It's hopeless.

*Example 10:* Marsha thought of the upcoming swim meet. There's no way I'll let Deanna beat me.

# Character Chart

Character's Name: _____ Age: _____

Background: _____

_____

_____

Positive Traits: _____

_____

_____

Negative Traits: _____

_____

_____

Ambitions/Goals: _____

_____

_____

Clothing: _____

_____

Most Distinctive Trait: _____

Color Eyes: _____ Glasses/Contacts: _____

Color Hair: _____ Hair Style: _____

Height: _____ Weight: _____

What Others Think of the Character: _____

_____

_____

_____

# Mini-Lesson 35: **Writing Dialogue**

*Dialogue* is an important element of any story. It adds to the action and allows readers to experience what the characters say. Characters become credible through effective dialogue. Without characters who converse, most stories would be flat and uninteresting.

## Procedure

1. Explain that dialogue occurs when characters speak to each other.

2. Point out that dialogue is an important part of any story. It is a major part of action and can help to show conflicts, thoughts, motivations, and goals. It should always be a part of the plot and move the story forward.

3. Explain that characters should sound the way real people speak. For example, most people speak in short sentences and phrases. Most use contractions. The words of characters should match the setting of a story and their lifestyle. For example, people of sixteenth-century England speak differently from people today. A rich woman will not speak like someone who has known poverty all her life. However, dialogue in stories cannot be exactly the same as in real life; the "Uhs," "Ahs," and "You knows" would be too distracting. (And some real-life dialogue is inappropriate for school writing.)

4. Distribute copies of (or project) "Dialogue Samples." Review the examples on the sheet and point out the correct way to write dialogue. Especially note that in Example 2, a comma follows *said* and the "a" in *at* is lowercase. In Example 3, a period follows *Joe,* and the "T" in *Those* is capitalized. In Example 4, the question mark takes the place of a comma.

5. Suggest that students look at an example of published dialogue in a story or book when they need to refresh their memory of the rules of punctuation for dialogue.

## Extension

- Suggest that students study the dialogue of characters in stories they read and ask themselves the following questions:

  Why do the character's words sound realistic?

  How do the words show what kind of person the character is?

# Dialogue Samples

Dialogue is an important part of stories. When writing dialogue, remember the following:

- Dialogue requires the use of quotation marks.

- Commas and end marks always go inside the quotation marks.

- The words of new speakers begin new paragraphs.

- Dialogue should always be a part of the plot and move the story forward.

Study these examples:

*Example 1:* "It looks like rain today," said Joe. He pointed at the dark clouds. "I bet our baseball game will be rained out."

*Example 2:* "The rain might hold off," Mary Ellen said, "at least until the game is done."

*Example 3:* "I doubt it," said Joe. "Those clouds are going to open up any minute."

*Example 4:* "Do you really think so?" asked Mary Ellen. "It seems a little brighter toward town."

## Mini-Lesson 36: **Developing Settings**

The *setting* of a story is the background against which a story takes place. It can be an open prairie, a residential neighborhood, or the inside of a spaceship. The setting of a story helps to build and shape mood.

### Procedure

1. Explain that the setting of a story is the time and place a story happens.

2. Note that the setting helps to build and shape mood. For example, a dark, cold, rainy night in an old castle provides a good setting for a ghost story or a murder mystery. The setting should always support the action of a story.

3. Explain that the best way to describe settings is by weaving descriptions in with the action. In this way, the action keeps moving. When too much description is given in a paragraph, readers often skip over it so that they can continue with the action. By weaving description in with action, details of the setting are given and the action keeps moving.

4. Hand out copies of (or project) the accompanying "Setting Samples." Instruct your students to read the two examples in which the setting is described.

   • Point out that although the first offers good details, it slows the action.

   • In the second example, the setting is interwoven with the action, keeping the story moving forward.

### Extension

• Suggest that students choose a story they wrote earlier and look for places where they might have written too much description. They should revise the story and interweave the description of the setting with the action.

# Setting Samples

The following samples show two ways to write descriptions. In Sample 1, the setting is described in one paragraph. In Sample 2, it is woven through the action. Which one do you like better?

## Sample 1

Tom looked at Jason.

"This can't be the place," Tom said nervously.

The dark house loomed before them, brightened eerily by the glow of the full moon. A broken sign, confirming the address, hung crookedly on the front of the rusty iron fence that surrounded the weed-choked property. The place looked to be two hundred years old. A gust of wind blew one of the shutters, making it creak.

"Sam said to meet him here," Jason said.

"Are you sure you want to join this club?" asked Tom, swallowing hard.

"If we want to be paranormal investigators, I suppose this is a good place to start," said Jason. He forced a smile. "Let's go inside."

## Sample 2

Tom looked at Jason.

"This can't be the place," Tom said nervously. The dark house loomed before them, brightened eerily by the glow of the full moon.

"Sam said to meet him here," Jason said. "That's the address." He pointed at the broken sign on the rusty fence that surrounded the weed-choked property.

Tom swallowed hard. "Are you sure you want to join this club?" He looked at the house again. "That place must be two hundred years old." He shuddered as a gust of wind blew one of the shutters and made it creak.

"If we want to be paranormal investigators, I suppose this is a good place to start," said Jason. He forced a smile. "Let's go inside."

# Mini-Lesson 37: **Using Flashbacks**

*Flashbacks* are an author's device through which current action can be explained by events and action that happened in the past. The reason for a character's current fear of heights, for example, can easily be shown through a flashback.

## Procedure

1. Tell students that authors use flashbacks to explain current action that is a result of past events. Flashbacks are used when providing that past information with the current action would disrupt the story. Here is an example: a sixteen-year-old girl is afraid of dogs because she was attacked by a dog when she was five. To open the story when the girl is five just to show why she is afraid of dogs would be impractical. Instead, the author uses a flashback.

2. Distribute copies of the accompanying "The Party." Allow students a few minutes to read the story, and then ask them to point out the flashback: Monica's recalling the party at her previous town and the tragedy that resulted. Explain that the flashback is necessary for the reader to understand Monica's action of leaving the party. Note how the flashback is entered smoothly and how the last sentence of the flashback leads back into the current action.

3. Warn students to use flashbacks carefully. Unnecessary flashbacks slow the action and confuse or frustrate readers. Flashbacks should be used only when a past event affects the current action.

## Extension

- Suggest that students look for examples of flashbacks in the stories they read. They should share their findings with the class, a partner, or their peer groups, explaining how the flashback is necessary to the story.

# The Party

Monica was excited as she and Lisa hurried up the front steps to Deena's house. This was the first party she had been invited to since she moved to Glennville six months ago. At first she had had trouble making friends, but now she felt that she was a friend of one of the most popular girls in school—Deena Sanford.

"This is going to be a great party," Lisa said as she rang the doorbell. "Deena's parents aren't home."

The way she said that bothered Monica. "They're not?"

"No. Isn't that fantastic?"

Before Monica could answer, Deena opened the door and greeted them. Several kids were already there. Music blared from a stereo and kids were dancing. It was louder and wilder than Monica thought it would be.

She mingled with the other kids, who seemed glad that she had come. That made Monica feel accepted.

Just as she was starting to relax, Deena emerged from the kitchen with several cans of beer on a tray.

"Here's what everybody's been waiting for," she announced.

Monica watched as her friends crowded around Deena, all eager for a can of beer. Monica's mind flew back to this same scene in her former town. There was drinking at that party, too. She recalled how she and her best friend, Stacy, had become drunk, and then, walking home, Stacy had been hit by a car. Remembering the flashing lights, the sirens, the questions, and explanations made her shudder. That Stacy had recovered made little difference to Monica now.

When Deena handed Monica a can, Monica shook her head.

"Oh come on," said Deena. "Take one. You won't get into any trouble with just one."

"No," Monica said. "I don't want any." She headed to the closet to get her coat. Pulling her coat on, she left.

# Mini-Lesson 38: **Foreshadowing**

An author uses *foreshadowing* to hint at events to come and arouse anticipation in the reader. Foreshadowing makes action believable because the reader can see a logical progression of events. Foreshadowing is used in virtually all types of fiction.

## Procedure

1. Explain that foreshadowing is an author's device that hints of events to come in a story. For example, when an author mentions that dark clouds are gathering in the western sky and a tornado hits the town later, the event is believable because it was foreshadowed.

2. Mention that foreshadowing should be done subtly. It works best when it is interwoven with the action. Foreshadowing should always be an outgrowth of the plot and not call attention to itself.

3. Distribute copies of the accompanying "The Ranch." Allow your students time to read the excerpt of the story, then point out the examples of foreshadowing:

   Paragraph 1: the heat and humidity

   Paragraph 3: the skittish horses

   Paragraph 6: the high thunderheads looming

   Paragraph 7: the increasing wind and the dark clouds filling the sky

   All of these foreshadow the storm that comes. Without them, the storm would simply appear and the story would lose believability.

## Extension

- Ask your students to look for examples of foreshadowing in stories they read. They should share examples with partners or peer groups and discuss how the author used foreshadowing.

# The Ranch

Sweat beaded Brad's forehead and his shirt stuck to his back as he helped his father feed the horses in the corral. Even though it was early morning, the humidity was like the kind that came late in the afternoon.

After feeding the horses, Brad's father went to town to buy supplies, and Brad started repairing the rails on the corral behind the barn. He enjoyed working with his hands and, within an hour, had the broken rails replaced. Standing back, he smiled. He looked forward to the school year ending so that he could help his father on the ranch every day. During school he only worked on Saturdays.

As he stood back and admired his work, he noticed that the horses seemed skittish. Walking to the corral, Brad tried calming them by speaking with a soothing voice. He had never seen them like this.

He watched his father drive up in the pickup truck filled with supplies.

"Give me a hand unloading," his father said. "I don't like the looks of that." He nodded toward the west.

Brad turned and saw the high thunderheads looming like angry giants in the distance. "We'd better hurry," he said.

By the time they finished unloading the supplies, the wind had started blowing and dark clouds filled the sky.

"This'll be a big one," Brad said as the first raindrops began to fall.

His father's voice was sharp. "Go inside and take your mother down to the basement."

Brad turned and looked in the direction of his father's gaze. A huge funnel cloud was dropping out of the sky.

"Hurry!" his father said.

Brad ran for the back door, his heart pounding.

"Mom! Mom! Tornado!"

# Mini-Lesson 39: **Constructing Effective Climaxes**

The *climax* of a story is that moment when the lead character either solves the problem or fails. It is distinct from the end of the story, which serves to tie any loose ends together.

### Procedure

1.  Explain that the climax is the point of the story at which the lead character either succeeds or fails to solve the problem he faces.

2.  Explain that for a climax to be satisfactory, it must grow logically out of the plot. Problems cannot be solved through coincidence or luck. Good climaxes result when the lead character solves the problem himself. He cannot do something that is out of his powers.

3.  Note that the ending of a story follows the climax. The ending shows the aftermath of the climax.

4.  Share these climaxes that should be avoided because they are weak or clichéd:

    *   The lead character faces incredible hardship. When everything seems hopeless, he wakes up. It was only a dream.

    *   The lead character wakes up from the dream, only to find that the dream is coming true.

    *   When failure seems inevitable, a rich uncle, aunt, lost parent, or someone else arrives to save the day.

    *   The problem turns out to be a misunderstanding. There never was a real problem.

    *   The character performs an amazing feat of supernatural strength.

    *   The character is saved by luck or coincidence.

### Extension

*   Discuss the climaxes of some stories your students recently read or some popular movies they have seen.

# Mini-Lesson 40: **The First-Person Point of View**

Many students find it difficult to maintain a consistent *point of view* (POV) in their writing. They may start a piece in the first person, then switch to the third, or even the second, disrupting the unity of the piece. Since the first-person POV is one that almost all students use, I suggest that you begin teaching POV with it.

**Procedure**

1. Explain that POV is the way an author tells his piece, whether it is fiction or nonfiction. To gain an understanding of POV, students should imagine a camera resting on the shoulder of the lead character in a story. Whatever the camera records, the reader experiences. Things outside the camera's view are outside the POV, and the reader is not made aware of them.

2. Mention that there are many types of POVs. One of the easiest to use is the first-person POV. Personal narratives and autobiographies are examples of the first-person POV.

3. Explain that in fiction, the first-person POV is a character, usually the lead, who tells the story as he or she participates in events. The viewpoint character refers to himself or herself as "I" throughout the story.

4. Distribute copies of (or project) the accompanying "First-Person Point of View Fact Sheet" and review the information with your students.

5. Emphasize that once an author selects a POV, he or she should remain consistent with it and not switch to others.

**Extension**

• Suggest that students find examples of the first-person POV in stories, articles, and books that they read. Tell them to note how the author remained consistent with the POV.

# First-Person Point of View Fact Sheet

## Advantages of the First-Person Point of View (POV)

1. The first-person POV makes it easy for an author to use his or her own voice.

2. The first-person POV can be easier to write with power and emotion. After all, the narrator is a part, or an observer, of all the action.

3. The first-person POV is often easier for authors to handle the emotions and thoughts of the viewpoint character, because the author assumes that character's role.

## Disadvantages of the First-Person Point of View

1. The author can reveal only what the viewpoint character experiences or has learned. For example, the narrator cannot reveal the thoughts of other characters unless he or she is a mind-reader.

2. The dramatic structure of the piece is limited to what the narrator participates in or learns about and can relate.

The following is an example of the first-person POV:

I knew it was going to be a bad day when I stepped out of bed and stubbed my toe on the dresser. From there it only got worse. There was no hot water in the shower, I burned my toast for breakfast, and found that a tire on my car had gone flat during the night.

When I arrived at work an hour late, my boss was waiting for me.

"Where have you been?" he said anxiously. "Mr. Hawkins has been here for a half-hour. You have the report for him, right?"

I groaned. The report was in the ledger—the one I had left on the kitchen table.

# Mini-Lesson 41: **The Third-Person Point of View**

The third-person point of view (POV) is the most commonly used POV. It is sometimes called the "he/she" POV.

## Procedure

1.  Explain that in the third-person POV, the author takes a position outside the piece. The characters are referred to by name or as "he" or "she." The author is not a part of the action.

2.  Explain that the author chooses the character(s) whose point of view he or she will use to tell the story. Tell your students to imagine a camera resting on each viewpoint character's shoulder recording the action. The reader experiences what the viewpoint character does.

3.  Explain that as with any other POV, consistency is important. Shifting POVs unnecessarily is distracting and confusing to readers.

4.  Distribute copies of (or project) the accompanying "Third-Person Point of View Fact Sheet" and review the information with your students. (Note that the example is the same as the example for the first-person POV, but it has been rewritten in the third person.)

## Extension

*   Explain that the second-person POV is rarely used in fiction. In the second-person POV, the author uses "you," as if the reader is a part of the action. Here is an example:

    "You walk through the meadow. The wind feels cool against your face, and the grass is soft beneath your feet."

The second-person POV forces the reader to be a part of the action, but the constant use of "you" can feel artificial, especially in fiction. After all, the reader is not an actual participant in the story.

# Third-Person Point of View Fact Sheet

## Advantages of the Third-Person Point of View (POV)

1. The third-person POV enables the author to set himself or herself apart from the action, making it easier to control the events of the story.

2. The third-person POV enables the author to control the characters more easily than does the first-person POV.

3. The third-person POV allows the author to choose either a limited or omniscient POV. (See Mini-Lessons 42 and 43.)

## Disadvantage of the Third-Person Point of View

The third-person POV can be more difficult than the first-person POV for some writers to handle. These writers often need the immediacy that the first-person POV provides if they are to write with emotion and power.

The following is an example of the third-person POV:

Eddie knew it was going to be a bad day when he stepped out of bed and stubbed his toe on the dresser. From there it only got worse. There was no hot water in the shower, he burned his toast for breakfast, and found that a tire on his car had gone flat during the night.

When he arrived at work an hour late, Eddie's boss was waiting for him.

"Where have you been?" he said anxiously. "Mr. Hawkins has been here for a half-hour. You have the report for him, right?"

Eddie groaned. The report was in the ledger—the one he had left on the kitchen table.

# Mini-Lesson 42: **The Limited Point of View**

Along with the choices of either first- or third-person POVs, your students should be aware of the difference between limited and omniscient POVs. The focus of this mini-lesson is the limited POV.

**Procedure**

1. Explain that in a limited point of view (POV), the author "limits" thoughts and emotions to his or her lead viewpoint character. The "camera" is over the shoulder of the viewpoint character only.

2. Explain that limiting the POV to the lead character permits the reader to know only what the lead character knows. The reader lives through the story as the character does, resulting in a feeling of immediacy.

3. Distribute copies of the accompanying "Example of Limited Point of View: Final Batter." Ask students to read the story, and then briefly lead a class discussion about the story. Point out how the author tells the story through Jessie's eyes, sharing her thoughts and feelings with the reader.

**Extension**

- Suggest that students look for examples of limited POV in stories they read. They should pay close attention to the author's use of POV.

# Example of Limited Point of View: Final Batter

The following story is written in the third-person, limited point of view.

From the on-deck circle Jessie looked out across the field to the filled stands. The home crowd was roaring. She glanced up at the scoreboard: seven to six with one out, a runner on first in the bottom of the ninth. Already her team, the Stars, had scored three runs this inning.

"Come on, Maria!" Jessie called. She prayed that Maria would hit a homer and end the game. Jessie did not want to bat with the game on the line. Her stomach was knotted with tension. "You can do it, Maria!"

Jessie watched anxiously as the count went to three balls and two strikes. Maria waited at the plate. The pitch came and the crowd groaned—strike three.

"Okay, Jessie," called Lisa, the Stars' coach. "Just meet the ball . . . a hit keeps the rally going."

Jessie looked back at Lisa and nodded, then walked to the plate, the pressure nearly choking her. She passed Maria, who was slowly returning to the dugout.

"Wait for her curve, Jess," Maria said. "Nobody can hit that fastball."

Jessie forced a small smile, thankful for the tip. Stepping into the batter's box, she tapped the plate and lifted her bat. She took a deep breath to steady her nerves.

"Wait for the curve," she said to herself. "Wait for the curve . . . "

The first two pitches were fastballs that Jessie let go. They were so fast that Jessie knew she could never hit them. Another fastball, and the count went to one ball and two strikes. Jessie's hands tightened on the bat as the pitcher began her wind-up.

The pitch was a curve. It hung just a little over the plate. Recognizing her chance, Jessie swung and the ball shot off the bat, sailing far over the left-field fence.

# Mini-Lesson 43: **Multiple Point of View**

Multiple point of view allows authors great latitude in telling their stories, because the authors can use several viewpoint characters. These viewpoint characters may be both major and minor characters in the story.

## Procedure

1. Explain that unlike the limited POV, in which the author limits the point of view to a lead character, choosing multiple POVs permits the author to use several characters to tell the story. The author has the freedom to move from character to character as necessary to tell the story effectively.

2. Mention that many novelists use multiple POVs to tell their stories. The authors switch smoothly among several viewpoint characters, usually at the end of chapters or scenes. Sometimes they switch viewpoint characters within a scene if the action demands it. (Emphasize that switching POV at the end of chapters or scenes is far more common than switching within scenes.)

3. Note that authors must be careful not to switch viewpoint characters abruptly, or they might confuse their readers.

4. Distribute copies of the accompanying "Example of Multiple Points of View: Final Batter." Ask your students to read the story and discuss how the author used multiple POVs. (Note that this story was also used for "Example of Limited Point of View: Final Batter"; however, it is rewritten using multiple POV.) Emphasize how the author included Lisa's thought in a POV switch. The blank lines clue the reader to the shift.

5. Emphasize that the major advantage of the multiple POVs is that it allows authors to tell complicated stories, using the perspectives of various characters.

# Example of Multiple Points of View: Final Batter

The following story is written in the third-person, omniscient point of view (POV):

From the on-deck circle Jessie looked out across the field to the filled stands. The home crowd was roaring. She glanced up at the scoreboard: seven to six with one out, a runner on first in the bottom of the ninth. Already her team, the Stars, had scored three runs this inning.

"Come on, Maria!" Jessie called. She prayed that Maria would hit a homer and end the game. Jessie did not want to bat with the game on the line. Her stomach was knotted with tension. "You can do it, Maria!"

Jessie watched anxiously as the count went to three balls and two strikes. Maria waited at the plate. The pitch came and the crowd groaned—strike three.

"Okay, Jessie," called Lisa, the Stars' coach. Lisa was worried. She knew that Jessie was no match for the girl who was pitching. "Just meet the ball . . . a hit keeps the rally going. Wait for your pitch. Be patient, Jessie." Patience was the key to getting a hit.

Jessie looked back at Lisa and nodded, then walked to the plate, the pressure nearly choking her. She passed Maria, who was slowly returning to the dugout.

"Wait for her curve, Jess," Maria said. "Nobody can hit that fastball."

Jessie forced a small smile, thankful for the tip. Stepping into the batter's box, she tapped the plate and lifted her bat. She took a deep breath to steady her nerves.

"Wait for the curve," she said to herself. "Wait for the curve . . . "

The first two pitches were fastballs that Jessie let go. They were so fast that Jessie knew she could never hit them. Another fastball, and the count went to one ball and two strikes. Jessie's hands tightened on the bat as the pitcher began her wind-up.

The pitch was a curve. It hung just a little over the plate. Recognizing her chance, Jessie swung and the ball shot off the bat, sailing far over the left-field fence.

# Mini-Lesson 44: **Avoiding Plagiarism**

*Plagiarism* occurs when a writer takes the words or expressions of another author and, through failure to use proper credit, claims them as his or her own. Plagiarism is stealing and is a violation of copyright laws.

**Procedure**

1. Explain that plagiarism violates copyright laws. Copyright laws ensure that an author's work remains hers and prevents others from copying it without receiving permission.

2. Emphasize that plagiarism is unethical. It is not only stealing but cheating. Students can make "fair use" of published material, but they must credit the author properly. *Fair use* is a provision of the copyright law that permits short passages from copyrighted material to be used without infringing on the rights of the owner. Generally, fair use is limited to no more than a few lines. Credit still must be given.

3. Distribute copies of (or project) the accompanying "Citing Sources" and review the information with your students.

# Citing Sources

To avoid plagiarism, you must give proper credit to the authors from whom you borrow material. You provide credit with footnotes. You should credit direct quotations, specific ideas used by another writer, an opinion of another, and any displays such as tables, charts, or diagrams that have been used in other work.

To credit information, authors identify the source. Quoted material can be linked to its source through an asterisk or numbers. Footnotes often appear at the bottom, or "foot," of the page. When they appear at the end of a chapter, or at the end of a report or book, they are called *endnotes*.

There are many formats for notes. Following are some examples:

**A book by one author**

Hayes B. Jacobs, *Writing and Selling and Nonfiction,* p. 8.

**A book by two or three authors**

Gerard I. Nierenberg and Henry H. Calero, *How to Read a Person Like a Book,* p. 65.

**A book by more than three authors**

Robert E. Eicholz et al., *Addison-Wesley Mathematics,* Book 6, p. 222.

**A magazine or newspaper article**

David LaGesse, "Our Wireless World," *U.S. News and World Report* (September 27, 2004), p. 48.

## Citing an Electronic Source

Although methods of citation for electronic sources vary, the following is acceptable for most papers:

Author's Name (if listed), "Title of Work." Article's original source, publication date, and page number. Publisher. Date researcher visited site. Electronic address or URL of the source.

# Mini-Lesson 45: **Choosing Titles**

Few students spend much time selecting titles for their pieces. The title, however, is the initial hook that catches a reader's attention. Moreover, a good title can lead smoothly into the piece.

## Procedure

1. Explain that titles are important to every piece. Good titles capture the attention of readers and lead them into the opening of the piece.

2. Distribute copies of the accompanying "Titles" and review the information with your students.

3. Emphasize that titles should always fit the piece that follows.

## Extension

- Suggest that students work with a partner and brainstorm titles. The first student gives one of her stories, articles, or poems to her partner. After the partner reads the piece, together the students brainstorm possible titles. They should write down every title that comes to mind. (Give students a minimum number they must decide on, or very few may come to mind!) After brainstorming, the author selects the title for the piece. The second student now gives one of her stories, articles, or poems to her partner to read. They then brainstorm possible titles for this piece. After brainstorming, the author selects the title. This activity permits students to see a variety of potential titles for their work.

# Titles

For *nonfiction,* titles should be appealing and informative. Examples of possible titles for common types of nonfiction follow:

- General nonfiction titles usually refer to the focus of the piece, taking into account the slant. Here are some examples for a piece about homework:

  "Homework Blues"

  "A Waste of Time"

  "The Burden of Youth"

  "How Much Homework Is Too Much?"

- Titles for how-to pieces tell the reader exactly what the article is about. Here are some examples:

  "How to Build a Backyard Bird Feeder"

  "10 Easy Steps to Financial Success"

  "Homework Without Tears"

  "How to Get Straight A's Without Trying"

- Articles for essays or persuasive pieces usually focus on the topic. Some examples include:

  "Should Girls Play Sports on Boys' Teams?"

  "It's Time for an Open Lunch for Seniors"

  "The Case Against the Incinerator"

For *fiction,* titles may describe the story or may highlight a key part of the plot. Sometimes the title may refer to an idea central to the story's theme. Here are some examples:

- A story in which everything goes wrong for the lead character: "Harry's Tough Night"

- A story about an unusual family that comes to live in a small town: "The Family"

- A story about a girl who suffers from depression: "Zero"

# SECTION 10

# MINI-LESSONS FOR THE MECHANICS OF WRITING

# Mini-Lesson 46: **Types of Sentences**

Complete sentences are the foundation of written English. A complete sentence requires a subject and predicate.

**Procedure**

1.  Explain that written material is based on complete sentences.

2.  Note that for a sentence to be complete, it must have a subject (noun or pronoun), which is the performer of the action, and a predicate (verb or verb phrase), which demonstrates the action or a state of being. You might wish to note that for some imperative and exclamatory sentences, the subject is understood to be "you," though "you" is not stated. *Example:* Close the door.

3.  Distribute copies of (or project) the accompanying "Sentences" and review the examples with your students.

4.  Mention that sometimes writers use an incomplete sentence of one word or a phrase for emphasis, but this is rare. Offer this example:

    Cold. That is all Jason remembered when he woke up in the ambulance. He was cold and shaking. Slowly he began to recall walking across the ice-covered pond, hearing the crack, and falling through into the numbing water.

    Explain that the use of the word *Cold* to start the paragraph immediately catches the reader's attention. Although this technique works here, note that using it too often becomes distracting, makes writing choppy, and disrupts the flow of ideas.

# Sentences

Written English is founded on sentences. Examples of the most commonly used types of sentences follow:

- A **simple sentence** may be one of four kinds:

  *Declarative (statement):* Tara enjoys in-line skating.

  *Interrogative (question):* Where did I leave my coat?

  *Imperative (order or command):* Please close the window.

  *Exclamatory (expresses great emotion):* Look out!

- A **compound sentence** contains two sentences joined by a comma and the conjunctions *and, but, or,* or *nor:*

  The Smiths went on vacation to the mountains, and they took dozens of photos.

  Sylvia likes to listen to jazz, but her sister prefers rock.

  They could play outside in the snow, or they could stay inside and watch a movie.

- A **complex sentence** contains a main clause and one or more subordinate clauses:

  Because of the blizzard, all flights to Denver were delayed indefinitely.

  If it snows all night, there will not be any school tomorrow.

  She could not remember where she left her keys.

# Mini-Lesson 47: **Sentence Patterns**

Most sentences in English are constructed in specific patterns that ensure a logical flow of ideas. Even long, seemingly complicated sentences can be broken down into basic patterns.

**Procedure**

1.  Explain that sentences in English follow basic patterns.

2.  Distribute copies of (or project) the accompanying "Examples of Sentence Patterns." Review the information with your students, noting that understanding these patterns can help them write more smoothly and with greater clarity.

3.  Suggest that when students write or revise their work and find a sentence that seems unclear, they should identify its basic pattern. Identifying the pattern will help them to clarify the sentence.

# Examples of Sentence Patterns

English sentences are constructed in specific patterns. Five common patterns and examples are shown below.

1. S – V (Subject – Verb)
   *Example:* Kittens played.
               S     V

2. S – LV – PN (Subject – Linking Verb – Predicate Nominative)
   *Example:* Ann is the secretary.
             S  LV     PN

3. S – LV – PA (Subject – Linking Verb – Predicate Adjective)
   *Example:* Steve was happy.
             S  LV  PA

4. S – V – DO (Subject – Verb – Direct Object)
   *Example:* Lee plays the trombone.
             S   V       DO

5. S – V – IO – DO (Subject – Verb – Indirect Object – Direct Object)
   *Example:* Luis gave the puppy a biscuit.
             S   V     IO    DO

**Note:** Sentences may be expanded without changing the basic pattern. Examples:
The kitten played in the afternoon.
        S     V

Ann is the secretary of the hiking club.
 S LV      PN

Having won the election, Steve was happy.
                S   LV  PA

Lee plays the trombone in the school band.
 S  V       DO

Yesterday, after the training session, Luis gave the puppy a biscuit.
                              S   V     IO    DO

# Mini-Lesson 48: Subject and Verb Agreement

The *subjects* of sentences must always agree with their *verbs*. Although this is not usually a problem for good writers, many students benefit from a review on this topic.

**Procedure**

1. Explain that singular subjects require the singular form of verbs and that plural subjects require the plural form of verbs. Subjects and verbs must always agree in number.

2. Using the board or an overhead projector, offer these examples of singular subjects and the singular form of verbs in the present tense:

   Juan works at the supermarket after school.
   He rides his bike to school.

3. Offer these examples of plural subjects and the plural form of verbs in the present tense:

   The boys work at the supermarket after school.
   They ride their bikes to school.

4. Mention that *I* and *you* require the plural form of verbs in the present tense. Offer these examples:

   I work at the supermarket after school.
   You ride your bike to school.

5. Note that the past tenses of verbs, except the verb "to be," are the same for singular and plural subjects. Offer these examples:

   Juan worked at the supermarket after school.
   The boys worked at the supermarket after school.

   The boy rode his bike to school.
   The boys rode their bikes to school.

# Mini-Lesson 49: **Compound Subject and Verb Agreement**

A *compound subject* is formed when two or more words or groups of words are connected to form the subject of a verb. This causes agreement confusion for some students.

**Procedure**

1. Explain that a verb may have a *compound subject:* two or more words or groups of words that form the subject. Depending on how they are connected, compound subjects may require either the singular or plural form of verbs.

2. Explain that when subjects are joined by *and,* they require a plural form of a verb. Offer these examples on the board or an overhead projector:

   Victor and Serge look like brothers.

   The puppy and kitten play together constantly.

3. Explain that when subjects are joined by *or* or *nor,* the subject closest to the verb determines its form. Offer these examples:

   Either Ali or Bert collects tickets at the front door.

   Neither Reg nor Maria has the directions to the party.

   Neither Jamal nor his brothers have homework.

   Peter, Sara, or Patrice is the leader of Group One.

# Mini-Lesson 50: **Subject and Verb Agreement with Intervening Phrases**

While most students have little trouble with the agreement between subjects and verbs when the verb directly follows the subject, sentences where phrases come between the subject and verb can pose problems.

### Procedure

1. Remind students that subjects and verbs must always agree in number. While in most cases this is relatively easy to do, some sentences require the careful attention of the writer to make sure that her subjects and verbs agree.

2. Write this sentence on the board or an overhead projector:

   The number of compulsory figures was the same for all contestants.

   Ask students if the sentence, as it is written, is correct. Some may say it is not, because they believe that the verb *was* should be *were* to agree with *figures*. Of course, the sentence is correct as it is. Explain that *number* is the subject and that it agrees with *was*. In its simplest form the sentence is:

   The number was the same for all contestants.

   Emphasize that this type of construction often leads to agreement mistakes. When a person writes a sentence in which the subject and verb are separated, the mind often links the verb with the nearest noun. Even professional authors make this mistake.

3. Offer these additional examples and point out the subjects and verbs:

   The manager, as well as the fans, was angry at the umpire's call.
   The students of Ms. Harper's class organize a charity drive each year.
   The flowers beneath the tree grow despite the shade of the leaves.
   Tamara, with three other students, writes the school announcements each morning.

# Mini-Lesson 51: Subject and Verb Agreement: Doesn't or Don't

A common agreement mistake students make is using *don't* with a singular subject, as in, "He don't go any more." The following mini-lesson can help students understand the correct use and avoid such agreement errors.

**Procedure**

1. Explain that the contractions *doesn't* and *don't* often lead to mistakes in agreement.

2. Note that *not* is not a part of the verb in either word. To ensure correct agreement of subjects with *doesn't* and *don't,* authors must match the subject of the sentence with *does* or *do.* Offer these examples on the board or an overhead projector:

   **Singular Subject**

   He doesn't finish his homework at night.

   He does not finish his homework at night.

   **Plural Subject**

   They don't finish their homework at night.

   They do not finish their homework at night.

3. Write these incorrect sentences on the board or an overhead projector:

   He don't like history.

   She don't believe in magic.

   Ask how to correct these sentences. Obvious suggestions would be the following:

   He doesn't like history.

   (He does not like history.)

   She doesn't believe in magic.

   (She does not believe in magic.)

4. Suggest that to be sure they are using the correct forms, students should break the contraction into two words and see if the subjects and verbs agree. Offer this example:

   She don't want to go skating.

   She do not want to go skating.

   Clearly this is incorrect. It should be, "She does not want to go skating." Breaking the contractions often helps students to see problems with agreement.

# Mini-Lesson 52: Subject and Verb Agreement: There's, Here's, and Where's

In conversation, we may say something like, "There's two ways you can go." Because students often write the way they speak, those types of constructions may slip into their writing. Although such constructions may be acceptable in conversation, they highlight an agreement problem in written language.

## Procedure

1. Emphasize that subject and verb agreement is important to written English. Offer these two sentences on the board or an overhead projector:

   There's your keys.
   There're your keys.

   Ask how many of your students think the first sentence is correct. Then ask how many believe the second is right.

2. Explain that the second is correct because *keys* is a plural subject of the sentence and requires the plural form verb *are*. Without the contraction, the sentence would read:

   There are your keys.

3. Suggest that students break down contractions to make sure that they do not use constructions with faulty agreement. Offer these examples:

   Where's your sisters?
   Where is your sisters?

   This should be, "Where are your sisters?"

   Here's your boots, scarf, and gloves.
   Here is your boots, scarf, and gloves.

   This should be, "Here are your boots, scarf, and gloves."

# Mini-Lesson 53: **Subject and Verb Agreement: Indefinite Pronouns**

Indefinite pronouns are words that do not refer to a specific noun. Because they lack specificity, they often cause agreement problems.

**Procedure**

1. Explain that indefinite pronouns do not refer to a specific person, place, or thing. When used as subjects, they must agree with verbs.

2. Explain that some indefinite pronouns are always singular and require the singular form of verbs. Offer these examples on the board or an overhead projector:

   each, either, neither, anyone, anybody, anything, something, someone, somebody, everyone, one, everything, everybody, nothing, no one

   Offer these sentences:

   Everybody wants to be successful.

   Each of the girls has her ticket.

   Emphasize that in both sentences, the indefinite pronouns are the subject and require the singular form of the verb.

3. Explain that some indefinite pronouns are always plural and require the plural form of a verb. Offer these examples:

   few, many, several, both, others

   Now offer these sentences:

   Both of the schedules have mistakes.

   Few were correct.

   Point out that the indefinite pronouns require a plural form of the verb.

4. Note that some indefinite pronouns can be singular or plural, depending on how they are used in a sentence. Offer these examples:

   all, any, some, most, none

   Now offer these sentences. The phrases in brackets show the context:

   Some [of the problems] were correct.

   Some were correct.

   Some [a part of a problem] was correct.

   Some was correct.

# Mini-Lesson 54: **Subject (Pronoun) and Verb Agreement**

Most of the pronoun forms present few problems for students, because the pronouns are used in written language the same way they are used in conversation. A few, however, are often used incorrectly in conversation, especially when used as the subjects of sentences. It is little wonder these pronouns are often used incorrectly in writing as well.

## Procedure

1. On the board or an overhead projector, list the following subject pronouns:

   I, you, he, she, it, we, you, they, who, whoever

2. Mention that some pronouns are frequently used incorrectly as subjects. Offer these examples:

   Her and I play tennis together. (incorrect)

   She and I play tennis together. (correct)

   Tom and me are going swimming after school. (incorrect)

   Tom and I are going swimming after school. (correct)

   Teresa and them go to the movies each Friday. (incorrect)

   Teresa and they go to the movies each Friday. (correct)

3. Explain that a good test to be certain that subject pronouns are used correctly in sentences like the examples above is to separate the pronouns and read each with the verb. Offer the following:

   I play tennis. (correct)

   Her play tennis. (incorrect)

   She plays tennis. (correct)

   Tom is going swimming. (correct)

   Me is going swimming. (incorrect)

   I am going swimming. (correct)

   Teresa goes to the movies each Friday. (correct)

   Them go to the movies each Friday. (incorrect)

   They go to the movies each Friday. (correct)

# Mini-Lesson 55: Agreement of Pronouns and Antecedents

Many of the agreement problems your students will have are likely to center on subjects and verbs. Some students, however, have problems with the agreement between pronouns and antecedents and will benefit from a mini-lesson on the topic.

**Procedure**

1. Explain that the *antecedent* of a pronoun is the word in a sentence to which the pronoun refers. If the antecedent is singular, the pronoun must be singular. If the antecedent is plural, the pronoun must be plural. If the antecedent is masculine, the pronoun must be masculine, and if the antecedent is feminine, the pronoun must be feminine. Offer these examples on the board or an overhead projector:

   *Manuel* twisted *his* ankle at basketball practice.

   *Marissa* twisted *her* ankle at basketball practice.

   Note that *Manuel* is singular and masculine and agrees with *his,* and that *Marissa* is singular and feminine and agrees with *her.*

   *Debbie* and *Rose* argued *their* points well.

   Note that *Debbie and Rose* is plural and agrees with *their.*

2. Explain that singular indefinite pronouns should be linked with singular pronouns. Offer this example of a common mistake:

   *Everyone* put *their* coats on.

   Explain that although this construction is commonly used in conversation, it is incorrect. *Everyone* is singular and requires singular pronouns. *Their* is plural. Offer ways this sentence can be corrected:

   *Everyone* put *his* or *her* coat on.

   *Everyone* put *his* coat on.

   *Everyone* put *her* coat on.

   *They* all put *their* coats on.

   Mention that the trend today in writing is to be nonsexist. If using the phrase "his or her" proves to be awkward, authors often alternate the use of "his" and "her." Whenever possible, many authors use a plural construction.

# Mini-Lesson 56: **Possessive Nouns**

The possessive case of nouns gives many students (and their teachers) severe headaches. While most students readily grasp the concept of ownership, using apostrophes correctly to denote that ownership in their writing often turns out to be guesswork. Even when they get the apostrophe right, some students do not know why.

**Procedure**

1.  Explain that when a noun is used to show that a thing belongs to someone or something, an apostrophe is needed.

2.  Emphasize that the possessive case of nouns is determined by three rules. Explain the rules, and offer examples on the board or an overhead projector.

    -   The possessive case of singular nouns is formed by adding an apostrophe and an *s*.

        the dog's leash

        the boss's briefcase

        New York's skyline

        Janice's car

    Note that for words that have more than one syllable and end in an *s*-sound, the singular possessive case may be formed by adding only the apostrophe. This avoids the awkward repetition of *s*-sounds:

        Moses' Commandments

        the princess' ring

    -   The possessive case of plural nouns that end in *s* is formed by adding an apostrophe after the *s*.

        the two boys' camping equipment

        the puppies' pillow

    -   The possessive case of plural nouns that do not end in *s* is formed by adding an apostrophe and an *s*.

        the women's basketball team

        the children's playhouse

3.  Suggest that a helpful way to remember these rules is to try to remember them with an example:

    *Singular possessive:* the kitten's toy

    *Plural possessive:* the three puppies' bed

    *Plural possessive:* children's bikes

# Mini-Lesson 57: **Paragraphing**

Although most of your students know that a paragraph is a group of related sentences about a main idea, many still have trouble developing solid paragraphs. A review of paragraphing is helpful, or even necessary, for many students.

## Procedure

1. Explain that a paragraph is a group of sentences that describes a main idea. A paragraph is usually a part of a larger work, but it can be an article in itself. This is especially true of short pieces.

2. Explain that in nonfiction, paragraphs usually have three parts:

   A *topic sentence,* which states the main idea

   *Supporting sentences,* which provide details about the main idea

   A *concluding sentence,* which summarizes or emphasizes the main idea and acts as a transition to the next paragraph

3. Explain that in fiction, paragraphs are dependent on various factors, including characters, action, dialogue, and suspense.

4. Mention that paragraphs are usually indented five spaces.

5. Explain that paragraphs vary in length. The length of a paragraph should be based on the amount of material necessary to explain its main idea fully.

6. Note the two most common weaknesses of paragraphs:

   • The topic sentence is unclear. To correct this, the topic sentence should focus on the main idea.

   • Too few details support the main idea. To correct this, general statements should be replaced with specific ones that clearly support the main idea.

## Extensions

• Distribute copies of the accompanying "Developing Paragraphs, Sample 1." Instruct your students to read the selection about alligators. Point out that it lacks paragraphs and instruct them to mark where they feel new paragraphs should begin. When they are done, discuss where the paragraphs should be. You may distribute copies of (or project) the accompanying "Developing Paragraphs, Sample 2," which shows where new paragraphs should begin.

• Suggest that students reread a work in progress and look for examples of weak paragraphs. They should revise the paragraphs.

# Developing Paragraphs, Sample 1

**Directions:** Read the following selection and mark where you think new paragraphs should start.

## Return of the Alligator

A few hundred years ago, alligators thrived in the southeastern part of the United States. It is estimated that Florida alone had more than a million of these reptiles. With the coming of great numbers of people during the colonial period, the days of alligator supremacy were about to end. Alligators were hunted for sport and killed for their hide, which was made into prized leather. As farms, towns, and cities spread across the land, alligator habitats were destroyed. By the mid-1960s alligators were in danger of becoming extinct, and in 1967 they were declared an endangered species. Hunting was prohibited, and habitats were protected. It was hoped that such measures would enable the alligator population to increase. Alligators have taken advantage of this protection. They have made a remarkable comeback. Their numbers have grown so rapidly that in many places hunting is allowed again. In fact, there are so many alligators in parts of Florida that they wander onto lawns and find their way into residential swimming pools!

# Developing Paragraphs, Sample 2

## Return of the Alligator

A few hundred years ago, alligators thrived in the southeastern part of the United States. It is estimated that Florida alone had more than a million of these reptiles.

With the coming of great numbers of people during the colonial period, the days of alligator supremacy were about to end. Alligators were hunted for sport and killed for their hide, which was made into prized leather. As farms, towns, and cities spread across the land, alligator habitats were destroyed.

By the mid-1960s alligators were in danger of becoming extinct, and in 1967 they were declared an endangered species. Hunting was prohibited, and habitats were protected. It was hoped that such measures would enable the alligator population to increase.

Alligators have taken advantage of this protection. They have made a remarkable comeback. Their numbers have grown so rapidly that in many places hunting is allowed again. In fact, there are so many alligators in parts of Florida that they wander onto lawns and find their way into residential swimming pools!

# Mini-Lesson 58: Varying Sentences to Make Writing Interesting

I often remind my students that a piece can be technically sound yet not be an example of good, interesting writing. Such writing is often bland or monotonous, adding up to boring. In many cases, such pieces lack a variety of sentence constructions.

**Procedure**

1. Explain that writing flows when the author uses a variety of sentence constructions and sentence lengths.

2. On the board or an overhead projector, offer these sentences with their revisions that demonstrate how sentence structure can be varied. Note how easily sentences can be changed by repositioning phrases and making minor changes to clauses:

> The storm clouds appeared without warning.
>
> Without warning, the storm clouds appeared.

> He soon became exhausted and had to drop out of the marathon.
>
> Soon becoming exhausted, he had to drop out of the marathon.

> Susan realized that she would not finish the report on time, because she could not obtain the information she needed.
>
> Because she could not obtain the information she needed, Susan realized that she would not finish the report on time.

> It was late, and Tom decided to leave.
>
> Since it was late, Tom decided to leave.

> Sara got caught in the rain and arrived home wet and cold.
>
> Having gotten caught in the rain, Sara arrived home wet and cold.

**Extension**

- Suggest that students reread one of their pieces in progress and pay close attention to sentence construction. They should revise where necessary to achieve variety in their constructions.

# Mini-Lesson 59: **Combining Sentences for Variation**

A major reason many students rely on simple sentences throughout entire pieces is that they are unsure how to construct longer sentences. To be safe, these students use several simple sentences in succession, which makes writing choppy and awkward.

**Procedure**

1. Remind students that varying sentences is necessary to help make writing flow smoothly.

2. Distribute copies of (or project) the accompanying "Example of Combining Sentences." Instruct your students to read the two paragraphs and then discuss why the second one flows more smoothly than the first. Point out how combining some of the sentences enhanced the flow.

3. Emphasize that combining short sentences can vary sentence construction. Offer the following examples on the board or an overhead projector. Point out how the sentences were combined:

> The human heart is a marvelous biological machine. It is the size of a person's closed fist.
>
> The human heart, which is the size of a person's closed fist, is a marvelous biological machine.

> Tanya had to do her homework. Then she went to work.
>
> After Tanya did her homework, she went to work.

> Jermaine came home at midnight. He was exhausted. He went right to sleep.
>
> Exhausted, Jermaine came home at midnight and went right to sleep.

> Ruby was sure that Tate had stolen Mrs. Wilson's purse. She did not know what to do.
>
> Ruby was sure that Tate had stolen Mrs. Wilson's purse, but she did not know what to do.

# Example of Combining Sentences

Read the following two paragraphs. Note how they are alike and how they are different. Which one flows more smoothly? Why?

Randall looked in the mirror. He squirmed. He felt uncomfortable in the tux. He did not like the way the jacket fit his shoulders. The collar was too tight. The bow tie seemed to be strangling him. He turned to see himself from different angles. He began to think that maybe it was not so bad. He was going to his sister's wedding. Plenty of her friends would be there. He should look his best.

Randall looked in the mirror and squirmed. He felt uncomfortable in the tux. He did not like the way the jacket fit his shoulders, the collar was too tight, and the bow tie seemed to be strangling him. Turning to see himself from different angles, he began to think that maybe it was not so bad after all. He was going to his sister's wedding, and plenty of her friends would be there. He should look his best.

# Mini-Lesson 60: **Sentence Fragments**

*Fragments* are incomplete sentences. Occasionally authors use a fragment for emphasis or to enhance a mood, but in most cases, fragments distract readers and should be avoided.

## Procedure

1. Explain that *fragments* are parts of sentences. They lack a subject or predicate (or both) and fail to express a complete thought. Offer these examples on the board or an overhead projector:

   The stars twinkled like diamonds. In the night sky.

   Point out that although "In the night sky" begins with a capital letter and ends with a period, it does not express a complete thought. It lacks a subject and predicate. Read by itself, it means nothing.

   Since he could not find his homework. Tom did it over.

   In this example, the opening clause is not a complete thought.

   Pam enjoys various activities. Such as skiing, horseback riding, and reading.

   In this example, the second statement lacks a subject and predicate.

2. Explain that sometimes authors write fragments because they are writing as they are thinking. Since thoughts often come in short bursts, they may find their way into writing as sentence fragments.

3. Emphasize that the best way to avoid writing fragments is to make sure every sentence has a subject and predicate and expresses a complete thought.

4. Suggest that a good way to find fragments is to read each sentence out loud and see if it can stand alone. If it cannot, it is a fragment.

5. Explain that a good way to correct fragments is to combine the fragment with another idea, making a new sentence. Fragments can also be corrected by adding the missing subject or verb.

## Extensions

- Students work with a partner and read a recent piece written by their partner. Each is to circle any fragments he or she finds in the partner's work. After discussing the fragments, authors should revise their work.

- Distribute copies of the accompanying "Find the Fragments." Instruct your students to read the article, circle all the fragments, and revise them. Read the article and go over the revisions as a class.

  *These are the fragments:* Because of fragments; Parts of sentences that do not carry a complete thought; By reading your sentences out loud; To share your ideas.

  Accept any reasonable revisions.

# Find the Fragments

**Directions:** Read the following article and circle all the sentence fragments you find. Revise the article, correcting the fragments.

This article is an example of poor writing. Because of fragments. Fragments are incomplete sentences. Parts of sentences that do not carry a complete thought. Fragments make your writing rough and choppy. They call attention to themselves and steal the clarity of your ideas.

You can find fragments in your writing. By reading your sentences out loud. If a sentence cannot stand alone, it is a fragment. You should revise it.

It is easy to revise fragments. You can combine the fragment with another idea and make a new sentence. Or you can add the missing subject or verb. Revising sentence fragments in your writing will make your writing smoother and helps you. To share your ideas.

_____

_____

_____

_____

_____

_____

_____

_____

_____

_____

_____

_____

_____

# Mini-Lesson 61: **Run-On Sentences**

A *run-on sentence* is a sentence that should be rewritten as two or more individual sentences, or the individual ideas should be combined with a conjunction. Instead of expressing one complete thought or using a conjunction or semicolon to link two related thoughts, a run-on "runs" together more than one complete thought in a way that confuses or distracts most readers.

## Procedure

1.  Explain that a run-on sentence is precisely what its name implies: a sentence that keeps going long after it should stop. A run-on sentence must be revised. Offer these examples on the board or an overhead projector:

    Peter is an excellent athlete, he lettered in three sports.

    They went to the park they had a picnic.

    In both examples, point out the two separate thoughts in the run-on sentence.

2.  Explain that most run-on sentences can be corrected easily in either of two ways: (1) divide the sentence into two separate sentences or (2) revise the sentence with a conjunction. (In some cases, a semicolon can be used instead of a conjunction, but this is less common.) Offer these examples:

    Peter is an excellent athlete. He lettered in three sports.

    Peter is an excellent athlete, and he lettered in three sports.

    They went to the park and had a picnic.

3.  Suggest that reading sentences out loud to see if each part of the sentence can stand alone is a good way to find run-on sentences. If the parts of a sentence can stand alone, it is likely to be a run-on. Also, suggest that students listen for pauses as they read aloud. A pause often indicates the need for a period.

## Extensions

*   Distribute copies of the accompanying "Finding and Fixing Run-Ons." Ask your students to read the sentences. They are to identify and correct the run-ons. Caution them that some sentences are correct. *Answers:* Numbers 2, 3, 4, 6, 7, 8 are run-ons. Accept any reasonable revisions.

*   Suggest that students reread a work in progress and correct any run-on sentences they find.

# Finding and Fixing Run-Ons

**Directions:** Read each sentence. Find those that are run-ons, and correct them. If a sentence is correct, write "correct."

1.  Once the rain started, Josh was certain the baseball game would be rained out.

   _____

   _____

2.  After school Tyrone went to soccer practice he stopped at the library before going home.

   _____

   _____

3.  Jennifer is a fine dancer, she hopes to be a dance instructor someday.

   _____

   _____

4.  Lori finished her homework, she went online to check her e-mail.

   _____

   _____

5.  On Saturday, Ashley had to work at her part-time job, finish her science report, and baby-sit for her neighbor.

   _____

   _____

6.  While on vacation, the Smiths went swimming, boating, and hiking they also went sightseeing and visited museums.

   _____

   _____

7.  Theo enjoys school he doesn't enjoy homework.

   _____

   _____

8.  Susan and Tara shopped at the mall, they went to the movies.

   _____

   _____

# Mini-Lesson 62: **Avoiding Misplaced Modifiers**

Modifying clauses and phrases can add details and variety to writing. Generally, modifiers should be positioned close enough to the word they modify so that there is a clear relationship. When writers allow modifiers to slip away from the word they want to describe or provide no word for the modifier to describe, expression becomes confused (and sometimes unintentionally amusing). Such modifiers are called *misplaced*, or, sometimes, *dangling, modifiers*.

**Procedure**

1. Explain that modifying clauses and phrases describe a word or words in a sentence. When it is unclear what a modifier describes, it is called a *misplaced modifier*. This weakens writing by muddying the meaning of a sentence.

2. On the board or an overhead projector, offer these examples of misplaced modifiers:

   > Driving alone for the first time, the sputtering motor frightened her.

   Note that the modifying phrase, "Driving alone for the first time," seems to imply that the motor was doing the driving.

   > While in the final mile of the race, her ankle twisted.

   The modifying phrase, "While in the final mile of the race," seems to modify *ankle*. It sounds as if the ankle was in the final mile of the race. Although technically it was, that is not what the author intended to say.

   > Magnificent and awe inspiring, he wanted to reach the peak of the mountain.

   This construction sounds as if the mountain climber was "magnificent and awe inspiring" when the phrase is supposed to describe the peak.

3. Explain that to avoid misplaced modifiers, writers must make sure that modifying phrases and clauses clearly are linked to the words they are supposed to describe. Show students the ways to correct the above examples:

   > Driving alone for the first time, she was frightened by the sputtering engine.

   The opening phrase clearly modifies *she* in this construction.

   > While in the final mile of the race, Kelly twisted her ankle.

   The opening clause modifies *Kelly*.

   > Because the peak of the mountain was magnificent and awe inspiring, he wanted to reach it.

   > He wanted to reach the magnificent and awe-inspiring peak.

   In either revision for this sentence, it becomes obvious that "magnificent and awe-inspiring" modifies the mountain peak.

4. Mention that modifying clauses usually modify the word right next to them.

**Extension**

- Suggest that students reread a piece in progress and look for examples of misplaced modifiers. Encourage them to revise any they find.

# Mini-Lesson 63: **Tenses: Choosing the Present or the Past**

Before writing a piece, the author must decide whether to use the present or past tense. Although use of the past tense is far more common, there are times when students find the present tense helpful in communicating their ideas.

**Procedure**

1. Explain that articles or stories can be written in the present or past tense.

2. Note that the past tense is the most commonly used tense in stories and articles, because most pieces are written about events that have already happened. Using the past tense therefore is logical. Offer these examples of simple past tense on the board or an overhead projector:

   Sammy applied for the job.

   She was elected class president.

3. Discuss that the present tense, although rarely used in stories, is commonly used in essays, editorials, and how-to articles. Authors use it when they want to communicate a feeling that something is occurring right now. Use of the present tense can evoke a sense of immediacy, as if the reader, along with the author, is experiencing the events as they happen. Offer these examples:

   She plays clarinet in the state orchestra.

   First, attach the hinges to the door, and then set the door in the frame.

4. Emphasize that whatever tense an author selects, he or she should be consistent with it. Switching from past to present and then back to past is disruptive and confusing to readers.

**Extension**

• Explain that writers sometimes use future tense. Future tense verbs show action that has not happened yet. Offer this example:

   Ben will drive his sister to school tomorrow.

# Mini-Lesson 64: The Past Perfect Tense: Showing Previous Past Action

Most students handle simple past tense adequately. They are familiar with it because they use it in speaking. Showing previous past action, however, can be troublesome.

## Procedure

1. Explain that action that happens before some other past action needs to be designated in writing. The most effective way of doing this is to use the past perfect tense. This verb form uses *had* and the past participle of the main verb. Offer these examples on the board or an overhead projector:

> After she had gone to evening school, she applied for the position of manager.

Note that the action of going to school came before applying for the manager's position, and it is shown by the past perfect verb phrase "had gone."

> He had had good seasons, but this one was the best.

Point out that "had had" is correct. Many students assume this form is wrong because of the repetition of *had*. The sentence, however, shows that he "had" good seasons in the past, before the one that "was the best."

> After she had made the plans, the vacation was canceled.

Note that "had made" shows that the plans were made before the vacation was canceled.

2. Emphasize that past perfect tense is often used to introduce flashbacks for stories. (See Mini-Lesson 37 in Section Nine.) Note that once the flashback is established, the past perfect is dropped in favor of the simple past. Overusing the past perfect can result in cumbersome, awkward writing.

## Extension

- Explain that along with past perfect tense, there are times when writers need to use present perfect tense or future perfect tense. Explain that present perfect tense shows an action that started in the past and continues in the present. This form requires the helping verb *has* or *have* with the past participle. Offer this example:

> Sasha's mother has driven her to school all year so far.

Explain that future perfect tense shows a future action that will have ended before another action starts. This form requires *will* (or *shall*) *have* and the past participle. Offer this example:

> Sasha's mother will have taken her to school this morning before going to work.

# Mini-Lesson 65: **Using Did or Done Correctly**

Some students make the mistake of using *done* for the past tense of *do*. This mini-lesson can reduce the confusion.

**Procedure**

1. Explain that the past tense of *do* is *did*. Some students mistakenly write *done* instead. Although *done* is used as the past tense in some places in spoken language, it is not used in that manner in correct English. Offer this example on the board or an overhead projector:

   They done the project at home. (incorrect)
   They did the project at home. (correct)

2. Note that *done* always requires a helping verb; for example, *was done, has done, had done, will have done,* and so on. Offer these examples:

   The firefighters could not have done anything more.
   The job will be done on time.

3. Caution students to avoid using *done* as the past tense with singular nouns and pronouns. Offer this example:

   Dan done all he could to find the missing ring. (incorrect)
   Dan did all he could to find the missing ring. (correct)

# Mini-Lesson 66: **Writing with Sounds That Are Not Words**

Many authors, particularly students, use sound effects in their writing. To help ensure that they use such words correctly, consider offering this mini-lesson.

**Procedure**

1. Explain that authors sometimes use sound effects in their writing. Sound effects can heighten drama, add emphasis, or make dialogue seem more realistic.

2. Caution students not to overuse sound effect words, because they can become distracting and undermine ideas. Moreover, used too often, they may make writing sound juvenile.

3. On the board or an overhead projector, offer these examples of sound effect words with their meanings:

   *aah*—a pause, or an interjection that shows emotion

   *arghhh*—agony or pain

   *gasp*—a short, sharp intake of breath, usually during great emotion

   *hmm*—a thoughtful pause

   *mmm*—a sound of noncommitment

   *oh*—an interjection that usually shows surprise or great emotion

   *shh*—an urge to silence

   *sigh*—a long exhalation of breath

   *uhh*—hesitation

   *uh-huh*—yes

   *uh-oh*—oh no

   *uh-uh*—no

   *yeah* or *yeh*—yes

   *yah*—a cheer

4. Note a caution on the use of *gasp* and *sigh*. Occasionally these words are used with dialogue: "Look out!" gasped John, or "It's finally over," she sighed. In a technical sense, neither construction is correct. A person cannot gasp or sigh words. A gasp is a short intake of breath. When one takes breath in, he or she cannot speak. Speech is formulated by the exhalation of air over the vocal cords. When one sighs, he or she releases air but does not speak. A person who is speaking is not sighing.

# Mini-Lesson 67: **Avoiding Double Negatives**

*Double negatives* are considered to be poor usage because they use two negative words when only one is needed. There are several word combinations that result in double negatives.

## Procedure

1.  Explain that double negatives are instances in which two negative words are used when one is necessary. Negative words imply *no*. Offer this example of a glaring double negative on the board or an overhead projector:

    We don't have no gym class today because of the assembly.

    Point out that the *no* and *not* in *don't* are two negatives. In a strict reading, if you *don't* have *no* gym, you *have* gym. Thus, in many cases, double negatives cancel each other out and result in the opposite meaning. Offer the corrected sentence:

    We don't have any gym class today because of the assembly.
    We have no gym class today because of the assembly.

2.  Explain that several common uses result in double negatives. Words like *hardly, scarcely,* and *but* when combined with *not* often result in double negatives. Offer this example with its following correction:

    You can't hardly tell the differences among the varieties of tomatoes. (incorrect)
    You can hardly tell the differences among the varieties of tomatoes. (correct)

3.  Emphasize that the best way to eliminate double negatives is to drop one of the negative words.

4.  Note that, for fiction, having a character speak with double negatives can be an excellent means of showing an uneducated character.

# Mini-Lesson 68: **Using Italics for Titles and Names**

*Italics* are used to identify or designate certain titles and names. *In print, italicized words lean to the right, as this sentence shows.* When writing in longhand or using a typewriter or word processor that does not have italicizing capabilities, writers indicate italics by underlining. Students often confuse italics with quotation marks, especially for titles.

**Procedure**

1. Explain that italics is a print style in which words lean to the right. Show students an example (if possible from one of their texts) or copy or project the top part of this page.

2. Write the following examples of the uses of italics on the board or an overhead projector:
   - Titles of books
   - Titles of magazines and newspapers
   - Titles of movies
   - Titles of plays
   - Titles of operas and long musical compositions
   - Titles of paintings and statues
   - Names of planes
   - Names of trains
   - Names of ships
   - Names of spacecraft

3. Note that if they cannot show italic type in their writing when it is needed, students should use underlining.

# Mini-Lesson 69: **Using Italics for Emphasis**

*Italics* are often used for emphasis. Since many students misunderstand the use of italics in general, a mini-lesson showing how italics can highlight words and ideas can be helpful.

**Procedure**

1.  Remind students that italics are indicated by words that are slanted to the right.

2.  Explain that italics have two important uses: to (1) designate titles (see Mini-Lesson 68) and (2) provide emphasis for words and ideas. Mention that quotation marks can also be used for emphasis and that writers choose how they highlight their work. Offer these examples on the board or an overhead projector:

    "Did you see *that*?" Carol said.

    Note how the use of italics for *that* indicates the word is to be emphasized.

    She read the final clue on the treasure map: "*Look below the hollow oak.*"

    Note that the clue is italicized, which adds emphasis.

3.  Caution students not to overuse italics for emphasis. Too much italicized text, for example, calls attention to itself and undermines the words and ideas it is supposed to be highlighting.

# Mini-Lesson 70: **Using Quotation Marks for Titles**

*Quotation marks* have many uses in writing. One of these uses is to designate titles. (For the use of quotation marks with dialogue, see Mini-Lesson 35 in Section Nine, and for the use of quotation marks for emphasis, see Mini-Lesson 71.)

**Procedure**

1. Show an example of quotation marks " " on the board or an overhead projector.

2. Explain that one of the uses of quotation marks is to identify the titles of stories, magazine articles, short poems, chapters in books, and episodes of TV shows. Offer these examples:

   "The Open Window" by Saki (H. H. Munro) is an amusing short story.

   "Ozymandias" is a poem written by Percy B. Shelley.

   "How to Travel with Your Pet" is an article that all pet owners who travel with their pets should read.

   Chapter 6, "Acing Your Tests," was the best part of the book *Study for Success*.

   The TV show "I Love Lucy" remains popular today.

3. Emphasize the distinction between quotation marks and italics for titles. Offer these examples:

   *Gone with the Wind* is a novel about the Civil War.

   *The Matrix* was an excellent movie.

   Many consider *Death of a Salesman* to be a classic American play.

# Mini-Lesson 71: **Using Quotation Marks for Emphasis**

Along with other uses (such as setting off dialogue, quoting sources, and identifying titles), quotation marks can be used for emphasis. (For the use of quotation marks with dialogue, see Mini-Lesson 35 in Section Nine, and for the use of quotation marks for titles, see Mini-Lesson 70.)

**Procedure**

1. Explain that quotation marks can be used to emphasize words that an author uses in special ways. Offer this example on the board or an overhead projector:

   Tom is "energetic." He has trouble sitting still in one place very long.

   In this case, "energetic" was used to suggest politely that Tom is hyperactive. The author is drawing attention to a case of deliberate understating.

2. Point out that quotation marks can be used to emphasize the introduction of new or unfamiliar words. Offer this example:

   E-mail, "electronic mail," has become a popular means of communication.

   In this case, the quotation marks are used to highlight the full term of e-mail.

3. Mention that in most cases, quotation marks for emphasis can be replaced with italics or underlining (in lieu of italics).

# Mini-Lesson 72: **Using Parentheses**

*Parentheses* are used for including additional, but not essential, information to a sentence. Separating this information from the rest of the sentence makes the sentence easier to understand.

**Procedure**

1.  Show the parentheses sign ( ) on the board or an overhead projector.

2.  Explain that parentheses are used to provide additional or incidental information to a sentence. Since this information is not as important as the rest of the material, it is separated from the rest of the sentence with parentheses. Offer these examples:

    Ernest Hemingway (1899–1961) is one of the best-known American authors.

    Note that since the years of his life are not essential information, they are put in parentheses.

    The inside of a computer (see Figure 3) has few moving parts.

    The reference to Figure 3 directs readers to a picture that supports the text. This information would disrupt the sentence if it were not in parentheses.

3.  To check if they have used parentheses correctly, suggest that students ask themselves if the material they placed inside parentheses is necessary to the sentence. If the answer is yes, parentheses should not be used. The exception might be in informal writing, as in the case of an authorial aside.

4.  Explain that punctuation marks fall outside parentheses unless they apply to the information inside. Offer these two examples:

    He could not go (not that he wanted to).

    John said (surprise!) that he did not want to go.

# Mini-Lesson 73: **Using the Dash**

*Dashes* should be used conservatively in writing. Too many make an author's style choppy. However, the dash can be used effectively as a dramatic pause or to set off information to come.

## Procedure

1. Show students the dash — on the board or an overhead projector. Mention that most word processing software contains the dash, but on typewriters, the dash is made by typing two hyphens, with one space on either side.

2. Explain that the dash can be used for a dramatic pause or to set off information. It may set off information at the end of a sentence, or it may interrupt a sentence. Offer these examples:

   There was no way out of this—Lisa had to tell her parents the truth.

   She was convinced that she had been here before—she knew every detail of the ruins—but that was impossible.

3. Mention that dashes should be used only when necessary. Too many disrupt the flow of an author's style and make writing rough.

# Mini-Lesson 74: Using Hyphens with Compound Words and Numbers

*Hyphens* are used to form some compound words and compound numbers from 21 to 99, or numbers that end with 21 through 99. Students often have trouble with, or ignore, the use of hyphens in such instances.

**Procedure**

1. Explain that hyphens are used to form some compound words. Compound words may also be closed (homeroom) or open (home run). Offer these examples on the board or an overhead projector of hyphenated compound words:

    brother-in-law     all-around     good-looking
    able-bodied        well-to-do     life-size

2. Note that compound words can be tricky. Even dictionaries do not always agree as to which ones need hyphens. Students should consult a dictionary whenever they are uncertain whether to use a hyphen for compound words.

3. Many word processing software spell checkers correct compound words.

4. Point out that hyphens should always be used to join two or more words that form a single adjective before a noun. Offer these examples:

    fifteen-year-old girl        well-known author

5. Explain that hyphens are used with compound numbers from 21 to 99. Offer these examples:

    twenty-one               ninety-nine

6. Mention that as a compound construction becomes part of the language, the hyphens usually disappear. The exceptions are when the result would be unwieldy, for example, "brotherinlaw" or "welltodo."

# Mini-Lesson 75: **Writing Lists with Colons and Commas**

Most students know that commas are used with lists such as "apples, pears, and oranges" (or, depending on the style used, "apples, pears and oranges"). Some, however, are not familiar with the use of colons to set off lists.

**Procedure**

1. Explain that commas are used to separate items in a list. Colons are sometimes used to signal that a list is to follow. Offer these examples on the board or an overhead projector:

   *With commas only:* They packed sandwiches, lemonade, and cookies for the picnic.

   *With colon and commas:* The following students earned awards: Renée, Sheila, and Paulo.

2. Note that a colon should not be used after a verb or a preposition.

   The afternoon's major events are: tug-of-war, relay races, and softball. (incorrect)

   Point out that the list follows the verb *are*.

   Here are the afternoon's major events: tug-of-war, relay races, and softball. (correct)

   There were several sports he excelled in: football, basketball, and soccer. (incorrect)

   Point out that the list follows the preposition *in*.

   He excelled in several sports: football, basketball, and soccer. (correct)

# Mini-Lesson 76: **Spelling Strategy 1: Dictionaries and Spell Checkers**

Spelling is a weakness for many students. Although no spelling strategy and no amount of memorization will turn poor spellers into champions, the use of sound spelling strategies can reduce mistakes.

**Procedure**

1. Explain to your students that correct spelling is important to their final copies. Pieces that are marred with spelling errors make a poor impression on readers. The errors stick out and detract from the writer's ideas.

2. Mention that any piece that is submitted to a publication should be free of errors in spelling and mechanics. Pieces marred by spelling errors fail to make good impressions on editors.

3. Point out that every time a person misspells a word, she reinforces that incorrect spelling in her mind. Thus, she is likely to misspell the word again. This is why some people keep misspelling the same words over and over. Likewise, every time a word is spelled correctly, the correct spelling is reinforced.

4. Explain that students should consult a dictionary whenever they are unsure of the correct spelling of a word. Even professional authors rely on dictionaries for the proper spelling, pronunciation, meaning, and usage of words.

5. Encourage students to use spell checkers when they write on computers. Virtually all word processing software includes spell checkers these days. Explain that the spell checker will give them alternatives to incorrectly spelled words, but that they must be sure that the alternative they select is correct. Note that sometimes they will still need to refer to a dictionary.

6. Be ready for the standard complaint of students. Inevitably, some will argue that they cannot hope to find words in the dictionary that they do not know how to spell in the first place. Explain that usually only a few letters in a misspelled word are wrong, often in the middle or near the end of the word. By looking up the first syllable or first few letters, they can find most words. (There are some exceptions, for example, *psychology*, but these are rare.)

# Mini-Lesson 77: **Spelling Strategy 2: Proper Pronunciation**

Many students (and adults!) spell words incorrectly because they mispronounce them. They spell the word the way it sounds to them.

## Procedure

1. Explain that proper pronunciation is one of the keys to good spelling. People who do not say words correctly often have trouble spelling them. On the board or an overhead projector, offer these commonly mispronounced and misspelled words with their correct forms:

   idear—idea

   childern—children

   probly—probably

   tempature—temperature

   temperment—temperament

   disasterous—disastrous

   enviroment—environment

   stold—stole

2. Emphasize that students should listen carefully to the way words are spoken. If they are unsure of a pronunciation, they should consult a dictionary.

3. Suggest that students record words they find hard to spell on a page of their journals. Once a week they might share the words with a partner.

# Mini-Lesson 78: **Spelling Strategy 3: Spelling Confusions**

Students often confuse words that have similar spellings. They may spell a word correctly, but it is not the word they intended. Homophones are a major source of such confusion, but they are not the only culprits.

## Procedure

1. Explain that *homophones* are words that have identical pronunciations but different meanings and spellings. Because of this, they are easy to misuse.

2. Note that in addition to homophones, other words close in pronunciation or spelling are also easily confused.

3. Distribute copies of (or project) the accompanying "Spelling Confusions" and review the pairs of words with your students. Note that these are only some examples; ask students to supply additional words for the list.

4. Emphasize that the best way to avoid misusing homophones and other easily confused words is to become familiar with the different forms or consult a dictionary.

## Extension

- Suggest that students keep a copy of "Spelling Confusions" for future reference.

# Spelling Confusions

Sometimes authors simply spell the wrong word. The following words are *homophones*: words that sound alike but have different meanings and spellings. Guard against misusing them, and others like these examples, in your writing.

| | |
|---|---|
| allowed, aloud | ate, eight |
| brake, break | capital, capitol |
| chord, cord | coarse, course |
| dual, duel | flea, flee |
| foul, fowl | know, no |
| lead, led | lessen, lesson |
| made, maid | not, knot |
| one, won | patience, patients |
| peace, piece | pray, prey |
| principal, principle | rain, reign, rein |
| right, rite, write | sew, so |
| soar, sore | some, sum |
| stake, steak | tail, tale |
| who's, whose | your, you're |

Homophones are not the only words that authors may confuse. Some words sound so much alike or are spelled so similarly that they are often used in place of each other:

| | |
|---|---|
| advice, advise | bazaar, bizarre |
| breath, breathe | clothes, close |
| confidant, confident | country, county |
| device, devise | emigrate, immigrate |
| envelop, envelope | farther, further |
| later, latter | lightening, lightning |
| medal, metal | moral, morale |
| picture, pitcher | than, then |
| veracious, voracious | were, where |

Note that there are many more words in both groups. Add more on the lines below:

_____

_____

# Mini-Lesson 79: **Spelling Strategy 4: Personal Spelling Lists**

Maintaining personal lists of difficult words is an easy way for students to improve their spelling. Students may maintain lists in notebooks or as computer files.

**Procedure**

1. Explain that keeping a personal list of hard-to-spell words is a helpful spelling strategy for many people. Every time the person misspells a word, he or she records its correct spelling for future reference.

2. For students who prefer to keep their lists on paper, suggest that they use notebooks with loose-leaf pages. They should enter the words alphabetically, skipping a few spaces between entries so that they can add more words later. (For students who have only a few troublesome words, suggest that they write them on a file card, which they can keep close by while writing.)

3. For students who wish to maintain their lists as computer files, caution them to make backup copies of their lists on disks. This not only maintains a second copy in case their computer crashes, but it also enables students to access their lists on other computers. Remind them that they should periodically update their backup files. Maintaining lists as computer files offers the added advantages of easy updating and printing as needed.

4. Emphasize that students should check their lists when they must spell a word that gives them trouble. Using the word correctly will reinforce the right spelling. In time, they will be using their lists less frequently.

# Mini-Lesson 80: **Overusing So and Then**

*So* and *then* are two of the most overused words in student writing. I have found that the major reason students rely on these words *so* much is that they are not aware of the alternatives.

## Procedure

1. Explain that *so* and *then* are often overused. They frequently result in awkward constructions. On the board or an overhead projector, offer these examples:

   We didn't have our badges, so we couldn't get onto the beach.

   Angelo finished work, then he decided to call Ralph.

   Teresa saw the dark clouds gathering, so she knew it was going to rain.

2. Mention that the words *when* and *since* can often be used to revise sentences using *so* and *then*. Offer these revisions of the previous examples:

   Since we didn't have our badges, we couldn't get onto the beach.

   When Angelo finished work, he called Ralph.

   When Teresa saw the dark clouds gathering, she knew it was going to rain.

3. Note that sometimes *so* and *then* can be replaced with a conjunction such as *and, but,* or *or.* Offer this example:

   Teresa saw the dark clouds gathering, and she knew it was going to rain.

4. Caution students to avoid using *so* and *then* to start sentences. Offer these examples:

   So I went to work late.

   Then we got a ton of homework.

   Note that *so* is unnecessary to the beginning of almost any sentence. Although *then* can start a sentence, particularly when a time change is needed, it should be used with care.

# Mini-Lesson 81: **Using Affect and Effect Correctly**

The use of *affect* and *effect* regularly confuses students and adults. A mini-lesson can clarify their meanings and use.

**Procedure**

1. Explain that *affect* and *effect* are not synonyms, as many people believe they are. They cannot be used in place of each other.

2. Note that *affect* is most commonly used as a verb to mean influence, sway, or impress. Offer these examples on the board or an overhead projector:

   The loss of the tennis match will affect Kelli's confidence.

   The failure affected his mood for weeks.

   You might mention that *affect* is used as a noun in psychology, meaning emotion or feeling; however, few students will see the word used in this manner.

3. Explain that *effect* is used as a noun or a verb. As a noun, *effect* means the result of some action. Offer these examples:

   The effect of cooperation was an increase in production.

   What was the effect of the boycott?

   As a verb, *effect* means to accomplish something. Offer these examples:

   The new class president effected several important changes in school.

   The school administration will effect a new graduation policy by the spring.

4. Suggest that since these words are easily confused, students should consult dictionaries whenever they use them until they become certain they are using *affect* and *effect* correctly.

# Mini-Lesson 82: **Using All Right and (Not) Alright**

*All right* and *alright* are often found in print. I recall one article where the author used both forms within the space of a few paragraphs. Although many people use these words interchangeably, *all right* is the preferred usage.

**Procedure**

1. Write the following two sentences on the board or an overhead projector and ask students which one is correct:

   Everything is all right now.
   Everything is alright now.

2. Explain that although they likely will see *alright* in some of the material they read, the word is not the preferred form in written English. It may be one day, as language is constantly evolving, but not yet.

3. Point out that the preferred form is *all right*. Offer these examples:

   The thunderstorm is done, and it is all right to go outside.
   "All right," said Les. "I'll see you at six."
   Is it all right to continue?

4. Suggest that students will find the correct form easier to remember by thinking of *all right* as two words. When they do they will most likely write *all right* and not *alright*.

# Mini-Lesson 83: **Using Among and Between Correctly**

In standard English, *among* and *between* have distinct uses. You should share the distinction with your students.

**Procedure**

1.  Explain that although many people casually use the prepositions *among* and *between* in the same constructions, the words have distinct uses.

2.  Point out that *among* is used with more than two people, ideas, or things. Offer these examples on the board or an overhead projector:

    The position of group leaders alternates among five people.

    Ellen was uncomfortable among the other applicants.

3.  Note that *between* is used when speaking of two people, ideas, or things. Offer these examples:

    What is the difference between History I and History IA?

    The puppy ran between Chuck and Brian and streaked across the yard.

    There are many differences between mammals and reptiles.

# Mini-Lesson 84: **Using Bad and Badly Correctly**

*Bad* and *badly* are different parts of speech and have different roles in a sentence. Many students treat these words the same, however, which results in mistakes in use.

**Procedure**

1. Explain that *bad* and *badly* have different functions in a sentence.

2. Note that *bad* is an adjective and can only modify nouns or pronouns. It is often used after the verb "to be" and verbs that refer to the senses, such as *feel, look, seem, appear, smell, sound,* and *taste.* Offer these examples on the board or an overhead projector:

   He hated being called the bad apple.

   *Bad* modifies the noun, *apple.*

   After sweating all day, he smelled bad.

   *Bad* modifies the pronoun *he.*

3. Explain that *badly* is an adverb. Most often it modifies verbs. It does not modify nouns or pronouns. Offer these examples:

   He played badly and struck out three times.

   *Badly* modifies the verb *played.*

   Too many people drive badly in this town.

   *Badly* modifies *drive.*

# Mini-Lesson 85: **Avoiding Could Of and Similar Constructions**

How many times have you heard your students say something like, "I could of done that"? You probably see that phrase and others like it in their writing just as often.

**Procedure**

1. Explain that phrases like *could of* (which authors use to mean *could've*) easily slip into writing, because they are used in everyday speech. However, such phrases are careless expressions. Instead of *could of*, the author means *could have.* Offer these other examples of such phrases on the board or an overhead projector:

   | | | |
   |---|---|---|
   | might of | must of | couldn't of |
   | should of | shouldn't of | mustn't of |

2. Point out that in all the above phrases, *of* should be replaced with *have*. Offer these examples of sentences with their corrections:

   She could of asked him why. (incorrect)
   She could have asked him why. (correct)

   He shouldn't of done that. (incorrect)
   He shouldn't have done that. (correct)

   Rochelle must of spent $500 on school clothes. (incorrect)
   Rochelle must have spent $500 on school clothes. (correct)

3. Emphasize that phrases such as "could of" are examples of incorrect writing. They must always be revised, replacing the *of* with *have*.

# Mini-Lesson 86: **Using Farther and Further Correctly**

Few students are aware of the different uses of *farther* and *further*. Teaching them such subtle points of writing will help them gain an appreciation for the depth and richness of English.

**Procedure**

1. Explain that *farther* and *further* have different meanings.

2. Note that *farther* is concerned with physical distance. Offer these examples on the board or an overhead projector:

   Randy hiked farther than he ever had before.

   How much farther is the next rest area?

   The sun is much farther from the earth than the moon is.

3. Point out that *further* is concerned with degree or quantity. It is often used to mean "more" or "in addition." Offer these examples:

   A further reason to leave early was to avoid rush-hour traffic.

   "Further," said Professor Stone, "economics was a major factor of the Civil War."

   Further investigation revealed that she had driven farther than she had claimed.

4. Suggest this easy way to remember when to use *farther* or *further*:
   - Distance requires *farther*; an example is "a mile farther."
   - Quantity, degree, or reasons require *further*.

# Mini-Lesson 87: **Using Fewer and Less Correctly**

Many writers overlook the correct use of *fewer* and *less*. These two words represent one of the finer points of written language that your students should recognize.

**Procedure**

1. Explain that *fewer* and *less* have different uses in the sentence.

2. Point out that *fewer* refers to the number of things you can count and is used before plural nouns. Offer these examples on the board or an overhead projector:

   Fewer spectators watched the game yesterday.

   Note that *spectators* is a plural noun and that *fewer* refers to the number of spectators.

   This monorail seats fewer people than the last one did.

   Note that *fewer* refers to the number of people.

3. Explain that *less* refers to degree or size or the amount of something that cannot be counted, such as hair or sand, and is used with singular nouns. Offer these examples:

   With the camping equipment loaded, the car has less space for passengers.

   Note that *less* refers to the amount of space in the car. Also note that *space* is a singular noun.

   They had less trouble at last night's dance.

   Note that *less* refers to the degree of trouble. *Trouble* is a singular noun.

   There is less sand at this end of the beach.

   Note that *less* refers to the amount of sand, which cannot be counted.

# Mini-Lesson 88: **Using Good and Well Correctly**

*Good* and *well* are often misused. Understanding their functions in the sentence can help students avoid mistakes with these two words.

## Procedure

1. Ask your students to raise their hands if they are sure how *good* and *well* are used in sentences. It is unlikely that you will see many hands up.

2. Explain that *good* is always an adjective. It modifies nouns or pronouns. It follows linking verbs such as *be, feel, look, seem, appear, smell, sound,* and *taste*. Offer these examples on the board or an overhead projector:

   It had been a good day.

   Note that *good* modifies *day*.

   He felt good after his workout.

   Note that *good* modifies *he*.

3. Point out that *well* may be used as either an adjective or an adverb. Explain that as an adjective, *well* is often used to refer to health. Offer this example:

   Lance had a cold, but now he feels well.

   Mention that as an adjective, *well* may also refer to a satisfactory condition. Offer this example:

   After the initial problem was corrected, everything was well.

   Note that as an adverb, *well* means to do something capably. Offer this example:

   Mira performed well in the play.

4. Caution students to consult author's stylebooks or their language texts regularly until they gain a thorough understanding of *good* and *well*.

# Mini-Lesson 89: **Using In and Into Correctly**

Few students have any inkling of the different uses of *in* and *into*. Still, the distinction is an example of one of the finer points of writing that you should share with them.

## Procedure

1. Explain that *in* and *into* have slightly different uses.

2. Explain that *in* means within or being inside. Offer these examples on the board or an overhead projector:

   They waited in the hospital's lounge.

   Note that they were already inside; thus, *in* is used.

   The old furniture is stored in the garage.

   Note that the furniture is already within the garage, and the construction requires *in*.

3. Explain that *into* implies movement to the inside. Offer these examples:

   They walked into the house.

   Point out that the movement is from outside to inside.

   After making her wish, Vera tossed the coin into the wishing well.

   Note that the coin moves from outside the well to inside the well.

4. Suggest this easy way to remember the difference between *in* and *into:*
   - *In* means *already* inside.
   - *Into* means moving to the inside.

# Mini-Lesson 90: **Using It's and Its Correctly**

*It's* and *its* are two of the most commonly confused pronouns. Mistakes in their use even slip into printed material, and *it's* not surprising that students mix up the two forms.

**Procedure**

1. Explain that to use the pronouns *it's* and *its* correctly, authors must understand the meanings of the two words.

2. Point out that *it's* is a contraction for *it is*. On the board or an overhead projector, offer this example:

   It's going to rain.
   *It is* going to rain.

   Note that the contraction takes the place of *it is* and requires the apostrophe.

3. Emphasize that *its* is the possessive form of the pronoun *it*. An apostrophe is *not* used, which is an exception to the customary rules of possession. Offer this example:

   The valley was a lonely place, but its beauty was breathtaking.

   Note that *its* refers to the valley. The valley's beauty was breathtaking.

4. Tell students that by breaking apart the contraction for *it's*, they will be able to see if they are using the correct form. Offer this correct example:

   It's a nice day for a picnic.
   *It is* a nice day for a picnic.

   Now offer this example, which highlights a mistake:

   It's fur is brown and tan.
   *It is* fur is brown and tan.

   Emphasize that in this example, *its* is the correct form.

   Its fur is brown and tan.

# Mini-Lesson 91: Using There, Their, and They're Correctly

These three words are bewildering for some students, as well as for some adults. Even after offering a mini-lesson about them, you will still need to review their use during writing conferences.

**Procedure**

1. Explain that writers must understand the differences among *there*, *their*, and *they're*.

2. Point out the various meanings of *there*, and offer these examples on the board or an overhead projector:

   - *There* means in that place.

     The coat rack is over there.

   - *There* can start sentences when linked with the verb "to be."

     There is a parking lot at the hotel.

   - *There* can be used as an interjection.

     There! I've finally finished.

3. Explain that *their* is a possessive pronoun. Offer this example:

   They left their bikes behind the school.

   Note that *their* is plural and must be linked to plural nouns or pronouns. Offer this example:

   Someone left their gloves on the table. (incorrect)
   Someone left his or her gloves on the table. (correct)

   Note that *Someone* is singular and requires a singular pronoun—either *his* or *her*. Changing *Someone* to *they* agrees with *their*.

4. Explain that *they're* is a contraction for *they are*. Offer this example:

   They're planning to leave by six.

   Note that to ensure they are using *they're* correctly, students should break the contraction and substitute *they are* in the construction:

   They are planning to leave by six.

# Mini-Lesson 92: **Using Who's and Whose Correctly**

*Who's* and *whose* are the culprits of plenty of mistakes. A good mini-lesson can help students see and remember the differences between these two words.

**Procedure**

1. Explain that *who's* and *whose* do not mean the same thing.

2. Note that *who's* is a contraction for *who is* or *who has*. Offer these examples on the board or an overhead projector:

   Who's the driver of that car?
   *Who is* the driver of that car?

   Who's left the milk on the table?
   *Who has* left the milk on the table?

3. Emphasize that *whose* is a possessive pronoun that shows ownership. Offer these examples:

   Whose car is that?
   Whose books are they?

   Note that in the examples, *whose* indicates ownership of the car or the books.

4. Suggest that breaking the contraction *who's* can help with usage. Offer these examples:

   Who's hat is on the rack?
   *Who is* hat is on the rack?
   Whose hat is on the rack?

   Show your students that breaking the contraction makes it easy to see the correct form. Note that *whose* is correct in this sentence.

# Mini-Lesson 93: **Using Your and You're Correctly**

Like other pronouns and contractions that are homophones, *your* and *you're* are regularly substituted for each other. The following mini-lesson offers guidelines for proper usage.

**Procedure**

1. Explain that *your* and *you're* are homophones. Although they sound the same, they have different spellings and meanings.

2. Point out that *your* is a possessive pronoun. Offer these examples on the board or an overhead projector:

   Where is your jacket?

   Your books are on the table.

   Remember to lock your car doors.

3. Note that *you're* is a contraction for *you are*. Offer these examples:

   You're taking Flight 209.

   *You are* taking Flight 209.

   Be careful where you're going.

   Be careful where *you are* going.

4. Suggest that breaking the contraction can help ensure correct usage. Offer this example:

   Your an excellent typist.

   Ask how many students believe the sentence is correct. Substitute the contraction *you're;* then break it.

   You're an excellent typist.

   *You are* an excellent typist.

   Emphasize the correct form.

# Mini-Lesson 94: **Using Lay and Lie Correctly**

It is the rare person who does not, at least on occasion, confuse *lay* and *lie*. This mini-lesson will help to reduce the confusion.

**Procedure**

1. Explain that *lay* and *lie* are two verbs that are constantly being confused.

2. Note that *lay* means to put something down or to place something. Its principal parts are *lay, laid, (have) laid,* and *laying.* Offer these examples on the board or an overhead projector:

   Reece laid the tools down on the table.

   "Lay the seat covers there," said Martin.

   Where did I lay my books?

   Note that in each case, *put* can replace *lay.*

3. Point out that *lie* means to rest or recline. Its principal parts are *lie, lay,* (have) *lain,* and *lying.* (Note that it is not *lying* as in speaking an untruth.) Emphasize that its past tense, *lay,* should not be confused with the verb *lay* (meaning to put). Offer these examples:

   She likes to lie down after work.

   He lay on the couch and napped for an hour.

   Jules is lying in the hammock.

   Alisha is not feeling well; she has lain in bed all afternoon.

4. Suggest that the best way to use these verbs correctly is to memorize their parts. Offer these two tips as well:

   • When a verb is needed to express the action of reclining, *lie* should be used.

   • When a verb is needed to express the action of putting something down, *lay* should be used.

# Mini-Lesson 95: **Using Lose and Loose Correctly**

While most of your students will know the meanings of these two words, some will be unsure of the spellings and will use them incorrectly. A mini-lesson can be helpful.

**Procedure**

1.  Explain that *lose* and *loose* have different pronunciations and meanings.

2.  Explain that *lose* means to experience a loss. Offer these examples on the board or an overhead projector:

    When did you lose your keys?
    Brad will lose the game if he does not concentrate.

3.  Note that the past tense of *lose* is *lost*. Offer this example:

    Brianne lost her purse.

4.  Explain that *loose* means unconnected or not close together. Offer these examples:

    The animals ran loose in the park.
    The hinge of the door was loose.

5.  Suggest that students remember when to use *lose* by recalling this example:

    I hate to *lose* money.

    *Lose* implies a loss of some kind. Note that understanding when to use *lose* will help students to know when to use *loose*.

# Mini-Lesson 96: **Using Off Rather Than Off Of**

*Off of* is frequently used when *off* is sufficient. This is an example of overwriting.

**Procedure**

1.  Explain that many people use the phrase *off of* when they should simply use *off*. Offer these examples on the board or an overhead projector:

    William moved the box off of the table.
    William moved the box off the table.

    The squirrel jumped off of the tree branch.
    The squirrel jumped off the tree branch.

    Note that in each case, *of* is not needed.

2.  Note that sometimes the phrase *off from* is used. This, too, should be avoided because *off* is sufficient. Offer this example:

    Shel climbed off from the ledge.
    Shel climbed off the ledge.

# Mini-Lesson 97: **Using Sit and Set Correctly**

Since *sit* and *set* are commonly misused in speaking, it is easy to understand why they are regularly interchanged in writing. Even some professional authors have trouble with these two words.

**Procedure**

1. Explain that *sit* and *set* are two commonly misused words. Offer these definitions on the board or an overhead projector:

   - *Sit* means to be in an upright position; sitting in a chair.
   - *Set* means to place or put something somewhere.

2. Offer these examples:

   Julio is sitting in the third row.

   He sat through a two-hour lecture.

   Artie set the vase on the windowsill.

   Priya is setting the table now.

3. Suggest that students remember the differences between the two words in this way:

   After I *set* the table, I *sat* down and ate.

**Extension**

- To give students more help with *sit* and *set*, offer the forms of these verbs on the board or an overhead projector:

|      | Past | Present Participle | Past Participle |
|------|------|--------------------|-----------------|
| **sit** | sat | is sitting | (have) sat |
| **set** | set | is setting | (have) set |

# Mini-Lesson 98: **Using Than and Then Correctly**

*Than* and *then* are regularly confused. Only a clear understanding of their meanings and use can prevent mistakes.

## Procedure

1. Emphasize that in order to use *than* and *then* correctly, writers must understand their meanings.

2. Note that *than* is a conjunction, a word that joins parts of a sentence, especially before a comparison. Offer these examples on the board or an overhead projector:

   Mary is taller than Rose.

   Point out that *than* connects "Rose" with "Mary is taller."

   The science test was harder than the math test.

   Here *than* connects the first part of the sentence with the second.

3. Note that *then* is usually an adverb. It means "at that time." Its purpose in a sentence is to denote time, a relationship regarding time, or a sequence. Offer these examples:

   First they went skating. Then they built a snow sculpture.
   Kara finished the report on time and then relaxed by watching a movie.

4. Suggest that your students can remember the difference between *than* and *then* by recalling these sentences:

   AA is greater than A. [*A* is for *than*.]

   Remind them that *than* connects parts of a sentence, usually showing a comparison.

   Do E first; then go on. [*E* is for *then*.]

   Remind them that *then* denotes time or a sequence.

# Mini-Lesson 99: **Using To, Too, and Two Correctly**

At one time or another, most students misuse *to, too,* or *two.* A mini-lesson on the use of these words is necessary in most writing workshops.

**Procedure**

1. Explain that *to, too,* and *two* are often misused.

2. Point out that *to* is a preposition or part of an infinitive. Offer these examples on the board or an overhead projector:

   Carla went to Europe for three weeks.

   *To* is a preposition.

   After his car broke down, Tim had to wait three hours for a tow truck.

   *To* is part of the infinitive *to wait.*

3. Note that *too* is an adverb. It usually means an excessive amount or also. Offer these examples:

   It was raining too hard to walk home.

   *Too hard* means an excessive amount.

   Keeshon wanted to go, too.

   *Too* means also. Note that when used to mean also, *too* is usually set off with commas. However, using commas with *too* is becoming less common.

   We, too, missed our plane. (We, also, missed our plane.)

4. Emphasize that *two* is the numeral. Offer these examples:

   They arrived at two o'clock.
   Stan waited two hours for his train.

5. Emphasize that substituting *to, too,* or *two* for each other is easy. *Too* easy. To avoid misusing these words, authors must understand their meanings and proofread their work carefully.

# Mini-Lesson 100: **Using Who and Whom Correctly**

The correct uses of *who* and *whom* bedevil many writers. For many the confusion begins in elementary school and continues long afterward. By presenting a mini-lesson on the topic and reviewing the proper uses of these words during writer's conferences, you will help your students use them correctly in their writing.

**Procedure**

1.  Explain that authors must be careful to use *who* and *whom* correctly. These two words are often misused.

2.  Point out that *who* is a nominative case pronoun and *whom* is an objective case pronoun. The easiest way to remember the correct use is to substitute *he* or *she* for *who* and *him* or *her* for *whom*. Offer these examples on the board or an overhead projector:

    Who was at the door?

    He [or she] was at the door.

    Note that questions are rewritten as statements when *he* or *she* is substituted. Also point out that *He* fits the construction; therefore *who* is correct. Offer this next example:

    Whom lost his keys?

    Him lost his keys.

    Note that substituting *Him* for *Whom* in this sentence is not correct. Obviously the sentence does not sound right. Instead of *whom, who* is needed. Offer this example:

    Whom did Josie see?

    Josie saw him [or her].

    Note that in this case, substituting *he* for *whom* clearly is incorrect. Since *him* is the proper substitute, *whom* is correct.

3.  Explain that *whom* often follows prepositions such as *to, for, with,* or *from*. Offer these examples:

    To whom was the letter sent?

    With whom did you drive to Texas?

4.  Emphasize that memorizing the correct uses of *who* and *whom* is the best way to ensure using these words correctly.

5.  Remind students that substituting *he* or *she* for *who* and *him* or *her* for *whom* is a good way to self-test the correct use of these words.

# RESOURCES

Writing is one of the most difficult subjects to teach. Among the numerous books on the subject, the following are especially helpful.

Atwell, N. *In the Middle: New Understanding About Writing, Reading, and Learning.* Portsmouth, N.H.: Boynton/Cook, 1998.

Blacker, I. R. *The Elements of Screenwriting.* White Plains, N.Y.: Longman, 1996.

Brogan, K. S. (ed.). *Writer's Market.* Cincinnati, Ohio: Writer's Digest Books, updated yearly.

Calkins, L. *The Art of Teaching Writing.* Portsmouth, N.H.: Heinemann, 1986.

Elbow, P. *Writing with Power: Techniques for Mastering the Writing Process.* New York: Oxford University Press, 1981.

Graves, D. H. *Writing: Teachers and Children at Work.* Portsmouth, N.H.: Heinemann, 1983.

Graves, D. H. *A Fresh Look at Writing.* Portsmouth, N.H.: Heinemann, 1994.

Henderson, K. *The Young Writer's Guide to Getting Published.* Cincinnati, Ohio: Writer's Digest Books, 2001.

Hillerich, R. *Teaching Children to Write, K–8.* Upper Saddle River, N.J.: Prentice Hall, 1985.

Johnson, P. *Creative Bookbinding.* New York: Dover, 1990.

Koch, K. *Rose, Where Did You Get That Red?* New York: Vintage Books, 1989.

Muschla, G. R. *The Writing Teacher's Book of Lists.* (2nd ed.) San Francisco: Jossey-Bass, 2004.

National Writing Project, and Nagin, C. *Because Writing Matters: Improving Student Writing in Our Schools.* Hoboken, N.J.: Wiley, 2003.

O'Connor, Patricia T. *Woe Is I: The Grammarphobe's Guide to Better English in Plain English.* New York: Riverhead Books, 1996.

Padgett, R. (ed.). *The Teachers and Writers Handbook of Poetic Forms.* New York: Teachers and Writers Collaborative, 1987.

Perl, S., and Wilson, N. *Through Teacher's Eyes: Portraits of Writing Teachers at Work.* Portsmouth, N.H.: Heinemann, 1986.

Piazza, C. *Journeys: The Teaching of Writing in the Elementary Classroom.* Upper Saddle River, N.J.: Prentice Hall, 2002.

Reid, J. M. *Teaching ESL Writing.* Upper Saddle River, N.J.: Pearson, 1993.

Shepherd, R. *Hand-Made Books: An Introduction to Bookbinding.* Petaluma, Calif.: Search Press, 1995.

Soven, M. I. *Teaching Writing in Middle and Secondary Schools: Theory, Research, and Practice.* Needham Heights, Mass.: Allyn and Bacon, 1998.

Strunk, W., and White E. B. *The Elements of Style.* (4th ed.) White Plains, N.Y.: Longman, 2000.

Zemelman, S., and Daniels, H. *A Community of Writers: Teaching Writing in the Junior and Senior High School.* Portsmouth, N.H.: Heinemann, 1988.

Zinsser, W. *On Writing Well.* (4th ed.) New York: HarperCollins, 1990.

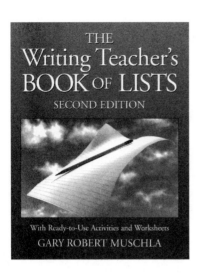

# The Writing Teacher's Book of Lists: With Ready-to-Use Activities and Worksheets, Second Edition

## By Gary Robert Muschla

Paper    ISBN: 0-7879-7080-8
www.josseybass.com

This is the second edition of the unique information source and timesaver for English and language arts teachers. *The Writing Teacher's Book of Lists: With Ready-to-Use Activities and Worksheets* includes 90 useful lists for developing instructional materials and planning lessons for elementary and secondary students. In addition, the book includes innovative activities and reproducible black line masters that help students to improve their writing skills, word usage, and vocabulary.

For quick access and easy use, all of these lists and activities are organized into seven sections and individually printed in a format that can be photocopied as many times as required for individual or group instruction. This handy resource is filled with helpful lists, activities, teaching suggestions, and reproducible worksheets.

**Lists and Activities for Special Words and Word Groups:** Contains the information students need on topics such as synonyms, antonyms, hard-to-spell words, easily confused words, and words associated with time.

**Lists and Activities for Nonfiction Writing:** Aids students in their understanding of nonfiction topics including advertising, ecology, education, government and politics, newspapers and magazines, sciences, and travel.

**Lists and Activities for Fiction Writing**

**Lists and Activities for Writing Style**

**Rules, 'Check' Lists, and Activities for Student Writers**

**Special Lists for Student Writers**

**Special Lists for Teachers**

**Gary Robert Muschla,** B.A., M.A.T., taught reading and writing for more than twenty-five years at Appleby School in Spotswood, New Jersey. He is the author of several practical resources for teachers, including *Writing Workshop Survival Kit, English Teacher's Great Books Activities Kit, Reading Workshop Survival Kit,* and three books of *Ready-to-Use Reading Proficiency Lessons and Activities,* 4th-, 8th-, and 10th-Grade Levels, all published by Jossey-Bass.

## Other Books of Interest

# Reading Workshop Survival Kit

### By Gary Robert Muschla

Paper     ISBN: 0-87628-592-2
www.josseybass.com

For reading and classroom teachers in grades 5–12, this is a complete, step-by-step guide to setting up and running successful reading workshops where reading is the priority. The *Survival Kit* is conveniently organized into two parts.

**Part I: Management of the Reading Workshop** shows how to create a reading workshop, offers specific tools and strategies for classroom management, and includes reproducible handouts. Divided into three chapters, it includes:

**An Overview:** Emphasizes that through reading and responding to what is read, students communicate and share ideas while they learn skills.

**Management:** Includes everything from beginning your day to building a positive atmosphere and organizing discussion groups.

**Evaluation:** Provides descriptions of various evaluation methods such as portfolios, daily logs of student performance, and conferencing.

**Part II: Using Mini-Lessons in the Reading Workshop** contains 100 different mini-lessons focusing on specific reading topics and skills. Each of the lessons stands alone, can be used in any order you wish, and is accompanied by one or two reproducibles. The lessons cover:

**Types of Reading and Related Topics:** Fifty mini-lessons feature topics such as Helping Students Select Books for Reading, The Publishing Process, Book Reviews, Mysteries, Mythology of Native Americans, and Poetry of African-Americans.

**Story Elements:** Twenty-five mini-lessons focus on story elements like What Makes a Good Lead, Motivation, Style and Tone, Symbolism, First-Person Point of View, and Foreshadowing.

**Specific Reading Skills:** Twenty-five mini-lessons cover a wide array of reading skills, such as Identifying Fact and Opinion, Strategies for Improving Reading Comprehension, Recalling Details, Cause and Effect, Test-Taking Strategies, and SQ3R.

In short, the *Reading Workshop Survival Kit* provides all the guidelines and tools a teacher needs to use the workshop approach effectively, plus 100 ready-to-use mini-lessons and over 120 reproducible worksheets and handouts for teaching and reinforcing specific reading skills and topics in any program.

# Rain, Steam, and Speed: Building Fluency in Adolescent Writers

## By Gerald Fleming and Meredith Pike-Baky

Paper    ISBN: 0-7879-7456-0
www.josseybass.com

"With enormous pleasure and pride, the students in *Rain, Steam, and Speed* are writing more, faster, and better than they have ever written before. How to make, or let, that happen with our own students in our own classrooms is what Gerald Fleming and Meredith Pike-Baky have to teach us."

—William Slaughter, professor and chair, Department of English, University of North Florida, Jacksonville

Many books focus on teaching the technical skills and processes of writing, but few works address issues of fluency—how to help students write with ease and facility on a variety of topics. Even when students understand the drafting and revision stages of the writing process, they often stall when confronted with a writing task, feeling they lack ideas or language, or that they have "nothing to say." This book offers a carefully structured approach for helping students overcome writing blocks so they can communicate quickly, confidently, and thoughtfully when the demand arises.

Featuring over 150 writing prompts on provocative topics, the book includes everything a teacher needs to know to inspire and engage students in systematic writing practice, including classroom protocols, grading, assessment, and feedback approaches. Easily implemented in any English/language arts classroom, the program involves about one hour of instruction per week (ideally in half hour segments), taking students through a series of timed writing exercises and enabling them to dramatically improve their thinking and writing facility over time. The book:

- Offers structured process for improving student writing.
- Features over 150 provocative writing exercises.
- Includes extensive examples of student work (along with testimonials).
- Benefits all types of students, including English learners.
- Strengthens literacy skills for cross-content academic learning.
- Adapts to all levels of English/language arts classrooms.

**Gerald Fleming** is an award-winning teacher who has taught in the San Francisco Public Schools for over thirty years. He teaches English, social studies, and journalism, and also teaches curriculum and instruction at the University of San Francisco.

**Meredith Pike-Baky** is a curriculum and assessment coordinator, a teacher educator, and a teacher consultant with the Bay Area Writing Project.

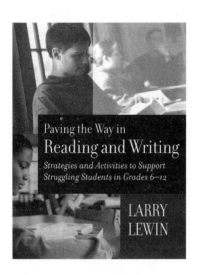

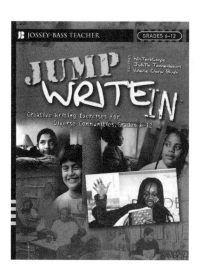

# Jump Write In: Creative Writing Exercises for Diverse Communities, Grades 6–12

## By WritersCorps, edited by Judith Tannenbaum and Valerie Chow Bush

Paper    ISBN: 0-7879-7777-2
www.josseybass.com

Teachers often feel they must choose between using standards-based lessons and offering activities that engage their students' creativity and encourage personal expression. In *Jump Write In*, however, the experienced teachers from WritersCorps offer numerous exercises that build key standards-based writing skills and also reach out in a meaningful way to all students, particularly at-risk youth.

Through poetry, personal narrative, and essays, students from diverse ethnic, educational, and economic backgrounds will improve their writing skills by accessing their personal voices. Perfect for a moment of improvisation or inspiration, these easy-to-use and field-tested activities can transform any lesson into an opportunity to involve a hard-to-reach student through creative writing.

Each chapter includes:

- Dozens of exercises accompanied by teacher notes and suggestions.
- Links to standards for each activity.
- Examples of student work.
- Suggestions for further reading.

**WritersCorps** is an independent program based in San Francisco whose mission is to help children and teens of all ethnic and economic backgrounds improve their literacy and communication skills through creative expression. Founded in 1994 with funding from the National Endowment of the Arts, WritersCorps has helped over 10,000 students. This important achievement was recognized recently when the White House named WritersCorps as one of the two most exemplary programs for at-risk youth. WritersCorps has ties to similar programs in New York City and Washington, D.C., and connections to influential education figures. The WritersCorps Web site is www.writerscorps.org.

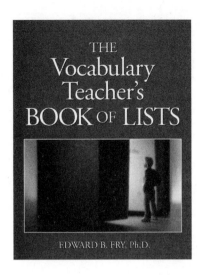

# The Vocabulary Teacher's Book of Lists

## By Edward B. Fry, Ph.D.

Paper   ISBN: 0-7879-7101-4
www.josseybass.com

"Edward Fry has the uncanny ability to take a complex concept—in this case vocabulary—and present it in a form useful to students and teachers."
—Allen Berger, Heckert Professor of Reading and Writing, Miami University

Replete with lists of words, books, teaching strategies, and many other useful tidbits of information related to language and literacy, this book picks up where Dr. Fry's best-selling *Reading Teacher's Book of Lists* leaves off. Its primary focus is on vocabulary improvement for reading and writing.

It contains a comprehensive section on roots and word origins; extensive lists of words used in science, psychology, and literature; and an entire chapter on vocabulary teaching methods and options for curriculum content. Other chapters include spelling, homophones, exonyms, affixes, and specialized subject area terms.

*The Vocabulary Teacher's Book of Lists* has a special focus on commonly misused words as well as those words that are homophones, homographs, and homonyms—words that are especially troublesome to students at multiple grade levels. This volume provides long lists of these difficult words and each is included in a sentence context.

With a wide variety of levels and lengths, some lists may be appropriate for individual students as extra credit, other lists will help ESL students to master English, and yet other students will use these lists to prepare for college entrance exams.

**Edward B. Fry,** Ph.D., is professor emeritus of education at Rutgers University, where for twenty-four years, he was director of the Reading Center. He is known internationally for his Readability Graph and is the author of many books, including *The Reading Teacher's Book of Lists,* now in its fourth edition from Jossey-Bass.

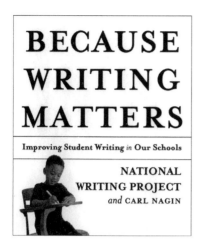

# Because Writing Matters: Improving Student Writing in Our Schools

## By National Writing Project and Carl Nagin

Cloth ISBN: 0-7879-6562-6
www.josseybass.com

"At last a book that is both comprehensive and up-to-date on the status and importance of writing in America. [This] carefully researched book shows how writing can be marginalized through ineffective assessments yet be a force in student lives. This book is must reading for teachers, school district leaders, and policy makers who wish to restore writing to its rightful place in student learning."

—Donald Graves, professor emeritus, Education, University of New Hampshire

## The definitive guide to teaching writing in our schools

This book looks at the myths and realities surrounding the teaching of writing in schools—examining how kids learn best and what schools need to do to teach them to write effectively. Sponsored by the National Writing Project, a nationally-recognized organization, *Because Writing Matters* offers recommendations based in solid research and practice, with action steps prioritized from the easily-achieved to the larger and longer-term. The best writing teachers address more than just content and skills—they use multiple teaching strategies that deal with both process and product, both form and content. With concrete suggestions about what and how to teach, *Because Writing Matters* will provide a blueprint for improving writing in schools.

"*Because Writing Matters* is a highly accessible, reader-friendly book that reviews what we know about written language and that explains clearly how that knowledge can be used to build effective programs for teaching writing. I predict that this book will become an indispensable guide for policy makers and legislators as well as for professional educators who strive to build research-based instructional programs."

—Sarah Warshauer Freedman, Professor of Education,
University of California, Berkeley

**The National Writing Project** (NWP) is a nationwide professional development program for teachers begun in 1974 at the University of California, Berkeley. Through its extensive network of teachers, the NWP seeks to promote exemplary instruction of writing in every classroom in America.

**Carl Nagin** (Berkeley, CA) is a journalist, editor, and teacher who has written for *The New York Times* and *The New Yorker.* He is a former staff reporter for the PBS series *Frontline.*